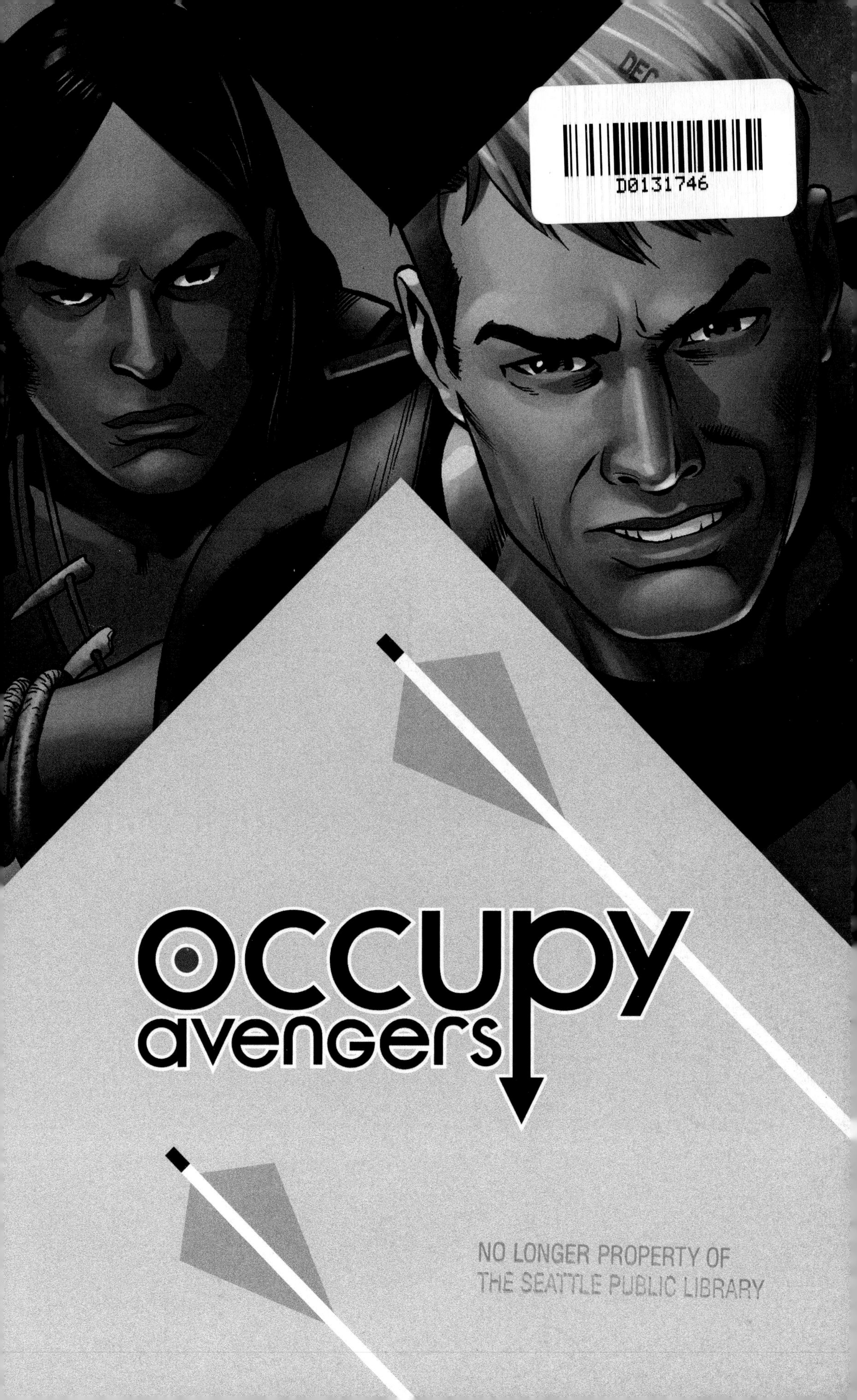
occupy
avengers

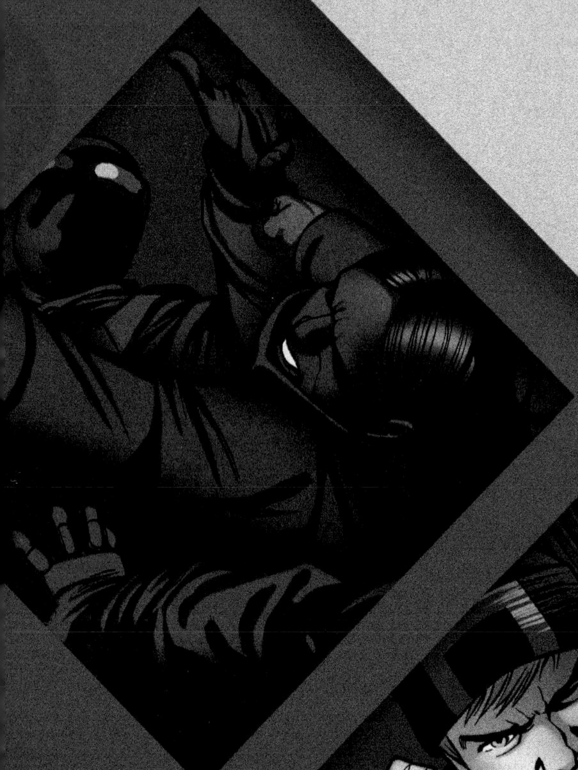

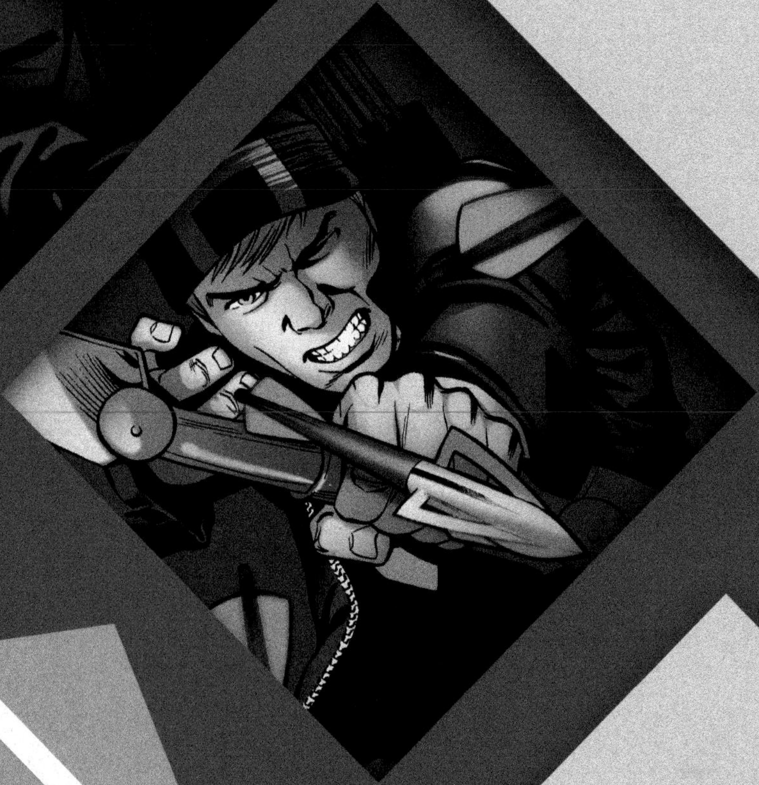

collection editor Jennifer Grünwald
assistant editor Caitlin O'Connell
associate managing editor Kateri Woody
editor, special projects Mark D. Beazley
vp production & special projects Jeff Youngquist
svp print, sales & marketing David Gabriel
book designer Jay Bowen

editor in chief Axel Alonso
chief creative officer Joe Quesada
president Dan Buckley
executive producer Alan Fine

OCCUPY AVENGERS VOL. 1: TAKING BACK JUSTICE. Contains material originally published in magazine form as OCCUPY AVENGERS #1-4 and AVENGERS #80-81. First printing 2017. ISBN# 978-1-302-90638-2. Published by MARVEL WORLDWIDE, INC., a subsidiary of MARVEL ENTERTAINMENT, LLC. OFFICE OF PUBLICATION: 135 West 50th Street, New York, NY 10020. Printed in the U.S.A. DAN BUCKLEY, President, Marvel Entertainment; JOE QUESADA, Chief Creative Officer; TOM BREVOORT, SVP of Publishing; DAVID BOGART, SVP of Business Affairs & Operations, Publishing & Partnership; C.B. CEBULSKI, VP of Brand Management & Development, Asia; DAVID GABRIEL, SVP of Sales & Marketing, Publishing; JEFF YOUNGQUIST, VP of Production & Special Projects; DAN CARR, Executive Director of Publishing Technology; ALEX MORALES, Director of Publishing Operations; SUSAN CRESPI, Production Manager; STAN LEE, Chairman Emeritus. For information regarding advertising in Marvel Comics or on Marvel.com, please contact Vit DeBellis, Integrated Sales Manager, at vdebellis@marvel.com. For Marvel subscription inquiries, please call 888-511-5480. Manufactured between 4/28/2017 and 5/30/2017 by QUAD/GRAPHICS WASECA, WASECA, MN, USA.

10 9 8 7 6 5 4 3 2 1

A vision of the future forced
Clint Barton, A.K.A. Hawkeye, to kill
his longtime friend and ally, the Hulk.

He went to trial and was acquitted of
all charges. The public sees him as
a savior. The super hero community
sees him as a pariah.

But how does he see himself?

OCCUPY AVENGERS

David F. Walker
writer

Carlos Pacheco
penciler

Rafael Fonteriz
inker

Sonia Oback (#1-3) & Wil Quintana (#3-4)
colorists

VC's Clayton Cowles (#1, #3-4) & Travis Lanham (#2)
letterers

Agustin Alessio (#1, #3); Carlos Pacheco, Raphael Fonteriz & Sonia Oback (#2); and Mike Deodato & Frank Martin (#4)
cover art

Alanna Smith
assistant editor

Tom Brevoort with Darren Shan
editors

Avengers created by **Stan Lee** & **Jack Kirby**

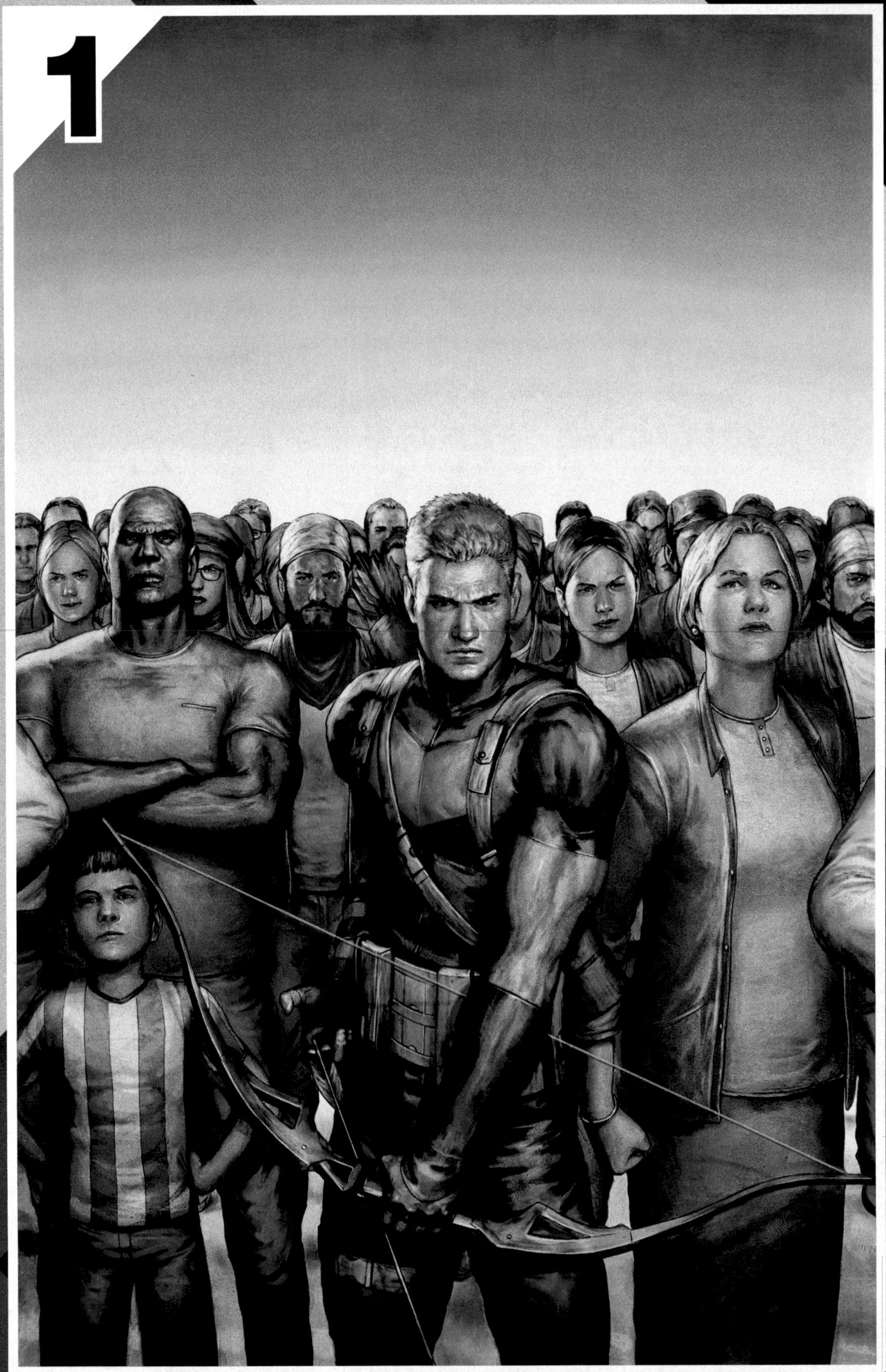
1

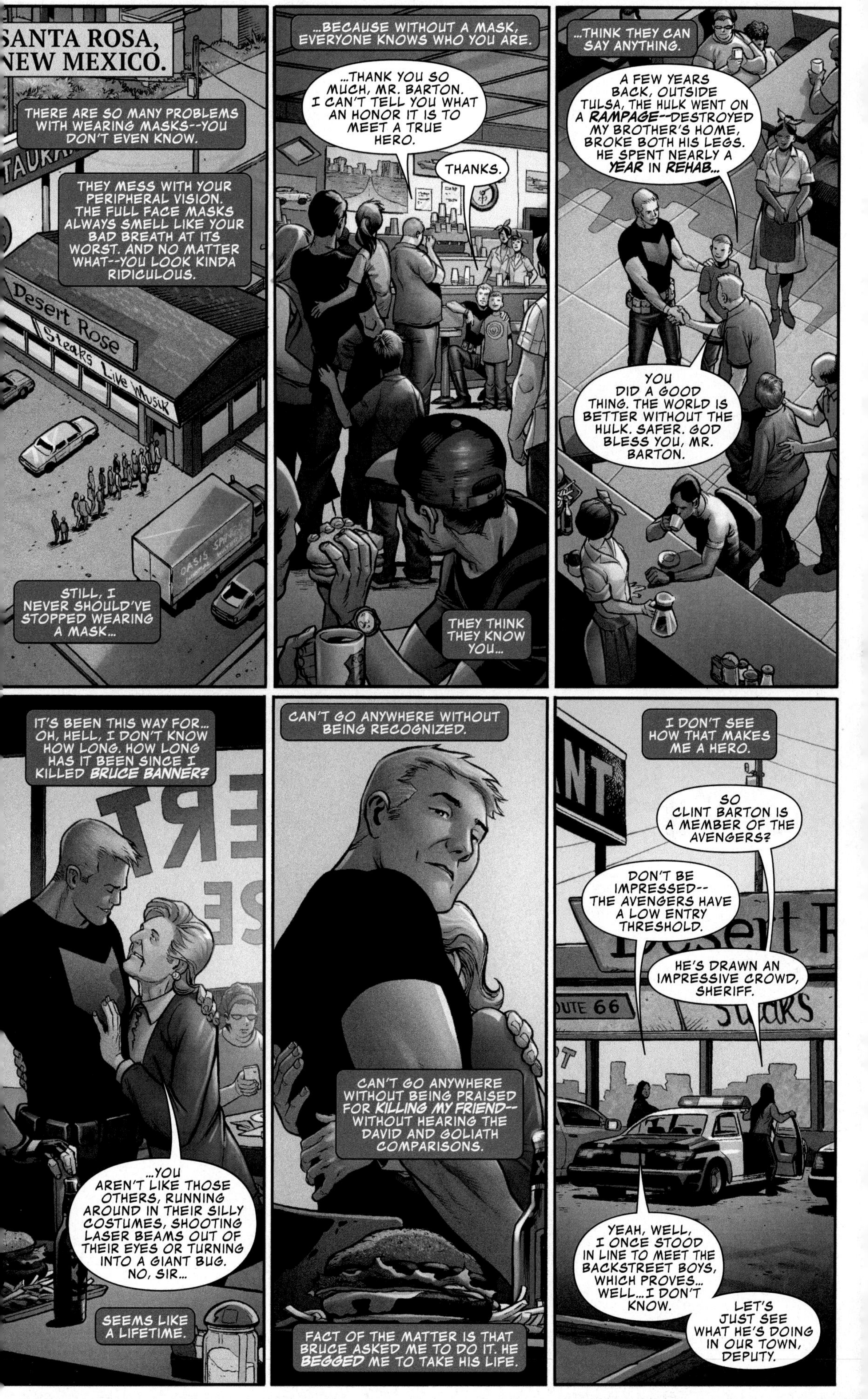
SANTA ROSA, NEW MEXICO.
THERE ARE SO MANY PROBLEMS WITH WEARING MASKS--YOU DON'T EVEN KNOW.
THEY MESS WITH YOUR PERIPHERAL VISION. THE FULL FACE MASKS ALWAYS SMELL LIKE YOUR BAD BREATH AT ITS WORST. AND NO MATTER WHAT--YOU LOOK KINDA RIDICULOUS.
Desert Rose
Steaks Live Musik
STILL, I NEVER SHOULD'VE STOPPED WEARING A MASK...
...BECAUSE WITHOUT A MASK, EVERYONE KNOWS WHO YOU ARE.
...THANK YOU SO MUCH, MR. BARTON. I CAN'T TELL YOU WHAT AN HONOR IT IS TO MEET A TRUE HERO.
THANKS.
THEY THINK THEY KNOW YOU...
...THINK THEY CAN SAY ANYTHING.
A FEW YEARS BACK, OUTSIDE TULSA, THE HULK WENT ON A RAMPAGE--DESTROYED MY BROTHER'S HOME, BROKE BOTH HIS LEGS. HE SPENT NEARLY A YEAR IN REHAB...
YOU DID A GOOD THING. THE WORLD IS BETTER WITHOUT THE HULK. SAFER. GOD BLESS YOU, MR. BARTON.
IT'S BEEN THIS WAY FOR... OH, HELL, I DON'T KNOW HOW LONG. HOW LONG HAS IT BEEN SINCE I KILLED BRUCE BANNER?
...YOU AREN'T LIKE THOSE OTHERS, RUNNING AROUND IN THEIR SILLY COSTUMES, SHOOTING LASER BEAMS OUT OF THEIR EYES OR TURNING INTO A GIANT BUG. NO, SIR...
SEEMS LIKE A LIFETIME.
CAN'T GO ANYWHERE WITHOUT BEING RECOGNIZED.
CAN'T GO ANYWHERE WITHOUT BEING PRAISED FOR KILLING MY FRIEND--WITHOUT HEARING THE DAVID AND GOLIATH COMPARISONS.
FACT OF THE MATTER IS THAT BRUCE ASKED ME TO DO IT. HE BEGGED ME TO TAKE HIS LIFE.
I DON'T SEE HOW THAT MAKES ME A HERO.
SO CLINT BARTON IS A MEMBER OF THE AVENGERS?
DON'T BE IMPRESSED--THE AVENGERS HAVE A LOW ENTRY THRESHOLD.
HE'S DRAWN AN IMPRESSIVE CROWD, SHERIFF.
YEAH, WELL, I ONCE STOOD IN LINE TO MEET THE BACKSTREET BOYS, WHICH PROVES... WELL...I DON'T KNOW.
LET'S JUST SEE WHAT HE'S DOING IN OUR TOWN, DEPUTY.

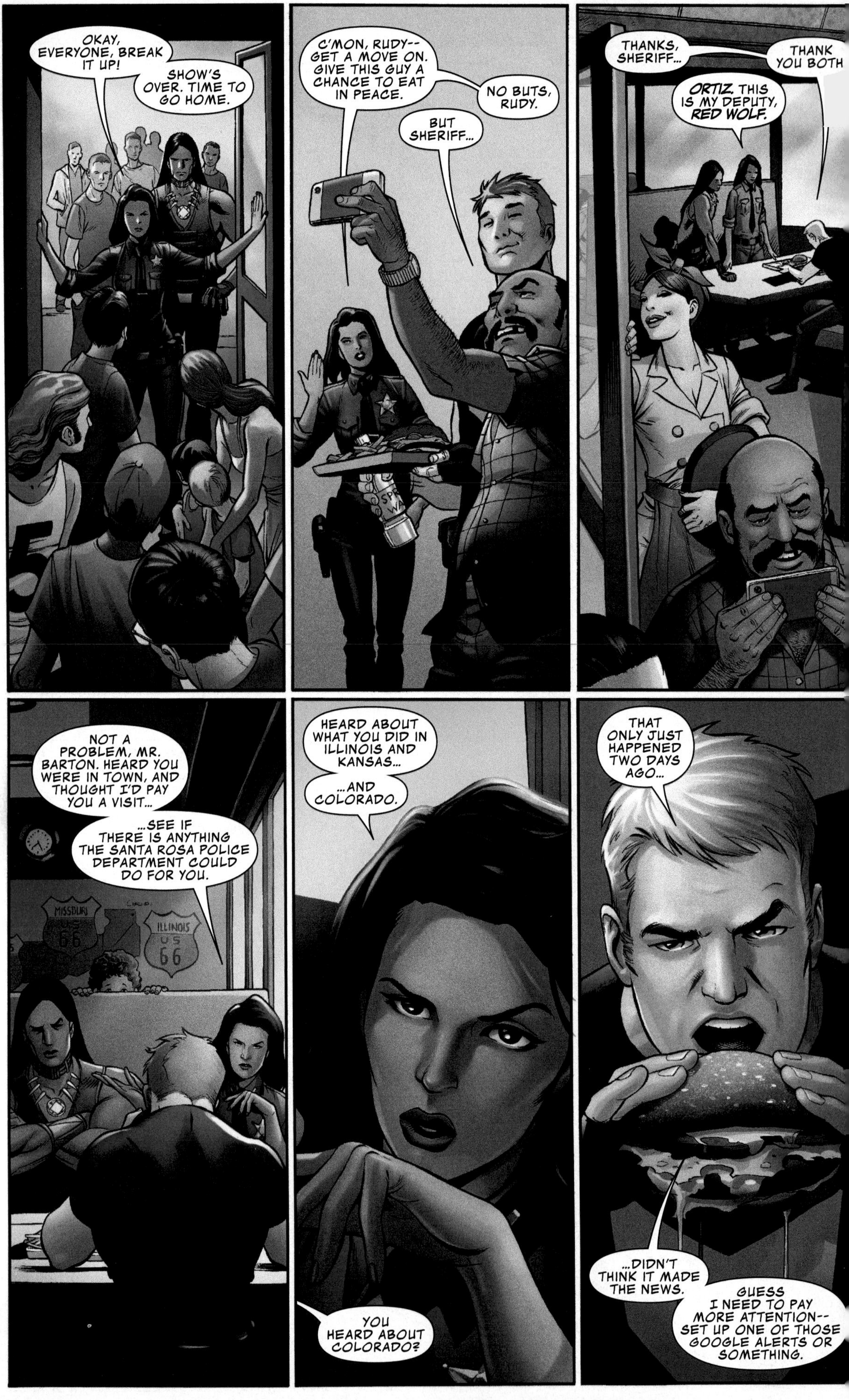
OKAY, EVERYONE, BREAK IT UP!
SHOW'S OVER. TIME TO GO HOME.
C'MON, RUDY-- GET A MOVE ON. GIVE THIS GUY A CHANCE TO EAT IN PEACE.
BUT SHERIFF...
NO BUTS, RUDY.
THANKS, SHERIFF...
THANK YOU BOTH
ORTIZ. THIS IS MY DEPUTY, RED WOLF.
NOT A PROBLEM, MR. BARTON. HEARD YOU WERE IN TOWN, AND THOUGHT I'D PAY YOU A VISIT...
...SEE IF THERE IS ANYTHING THE SANTA ROSA POLICE DEPARTMENT COULD DO FOR YOU.
MISSOURI
US
66
ILLINOIS
US
66
HEARD ABOUT WHAT YOU DID IN ILLINOIS AND KANSAS...
...AND COLORADO.
YOU HEARD ABOUT COLORADO?
THAT ONLY JUST HAPPENED TWO DAYS AGO...
...DIDN'T THINK IT MADE THE NEWS.
GUESS I NEED TO PAY MORE ATTENTION-- SET UP ONE OF THOSE GOOGLE ALERTS OR SOMETHING.

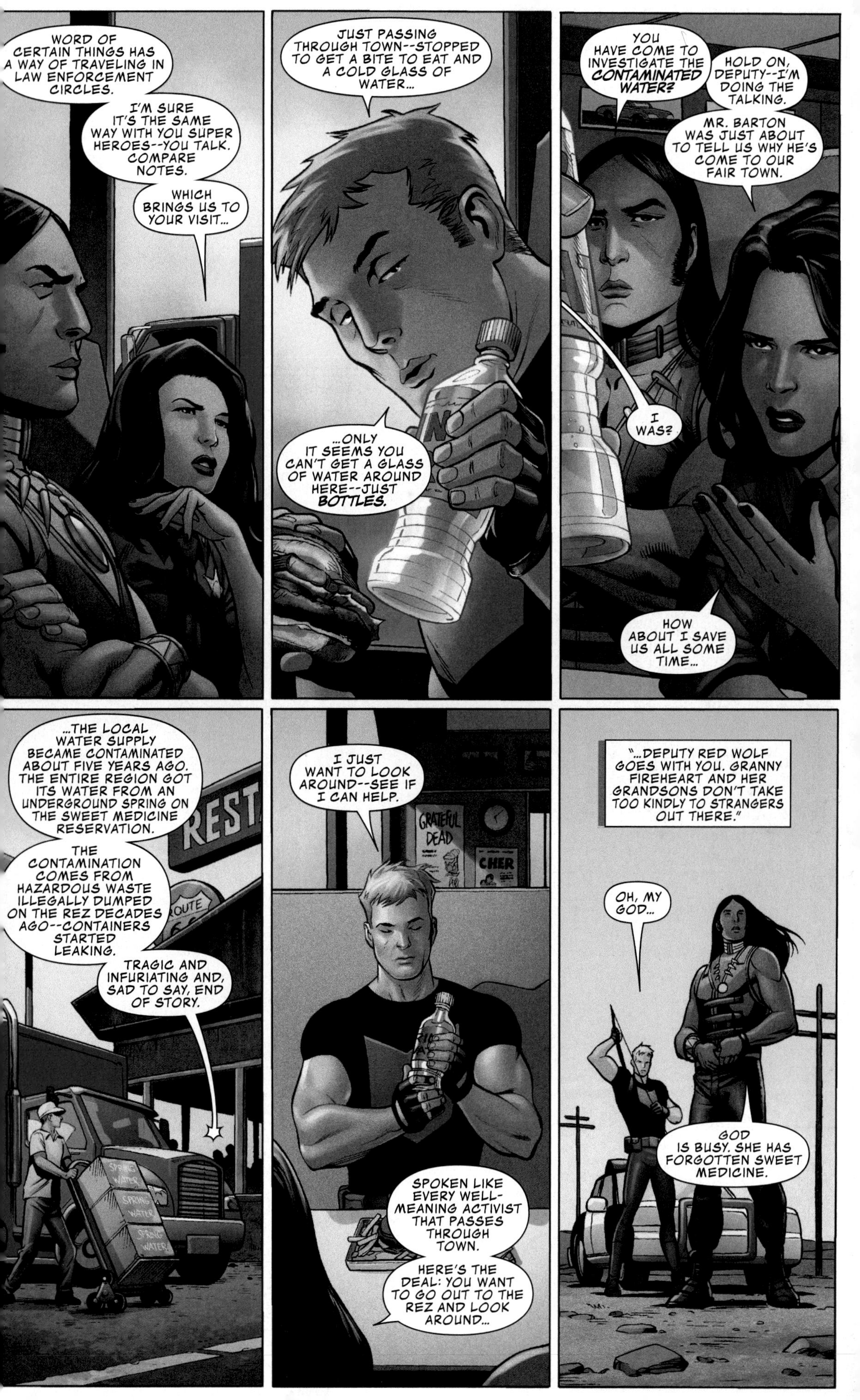
WORD OF CERTAIN THINGS HAS A WAY OF TRAVELING IN LAW ENFORCEMENT CIRCLES.
I'M SURE IT'S THE SAME WAY WITH YOU SUPER HEROES--YOU TALK. COMPARE NOTES.
WHICH BRINGS US TO YOUR VISIT...
JUST PASSING THROUGH TOWN--STOPPED TO GET A BITE TO EAT AND A COLD GLASS OF WATER...
...ONLY IT SEEMS YOU CAN'T GET A GLASS OF WATER AROUND HERE--JUST BOTTLES.
YOU HAVE COME TO INVESTIGATE THE CONTAMINATED WATER?
HOLD ON, DEPUTY--I'M DOING THE TALKING.
MR. BARTON WAS JUST ABOUT TO TELL US WHY HE'S COME TO OUR FAIR TOWN.
I WAS?
HOW ABOUT I SAVE US ALL SOME TIME...
...THE LOCAL WATER SUPPLY BECAME CONTAMINATED ABOUT FIVE YEARS AGO. THE ENTIRE REGION GOT ITS WATER FROM AN UNDERGROUND SPRING ON THE SWEET MEDICINE RESERVATION.
THE CONTAMINATION COMES FROM HAZARDOUS WASTE ILLEGALLY DUMPED ON THE REZ DECADES AGO--CONTAINERS STARTED LEAKING.
TRAGIC AND INFURIATING AND, SAD TO SAY, END OF STORY.
REST
ROUTE 66
SPRING WATER
SPRING WATER
SPRING WATER
I JUST WANT TO LOOK AROUND--SEE IF I CAN HELP.
GRATEFUL DEAD
CHER
SPOKEN LIKE EVERY WELL-MEANING ACTIVIST THAT PASSES THROUGH TOWN.
HERE'S THE DEAL: YOU WANT TO GO OUT TO THE REZ AND LOOK AROUND...
"...DEPUTY RED WOLF GOES WITH YOU. GRANNY FIREHEART AND HER GRANDSONS DON'T TAKE TOO KINDLY TO STRANGERS OUT THERE."
OH, MY GOD...
GOD IS BUSY. SHE HAS FORGOTTEN SWEET MEDICINE.

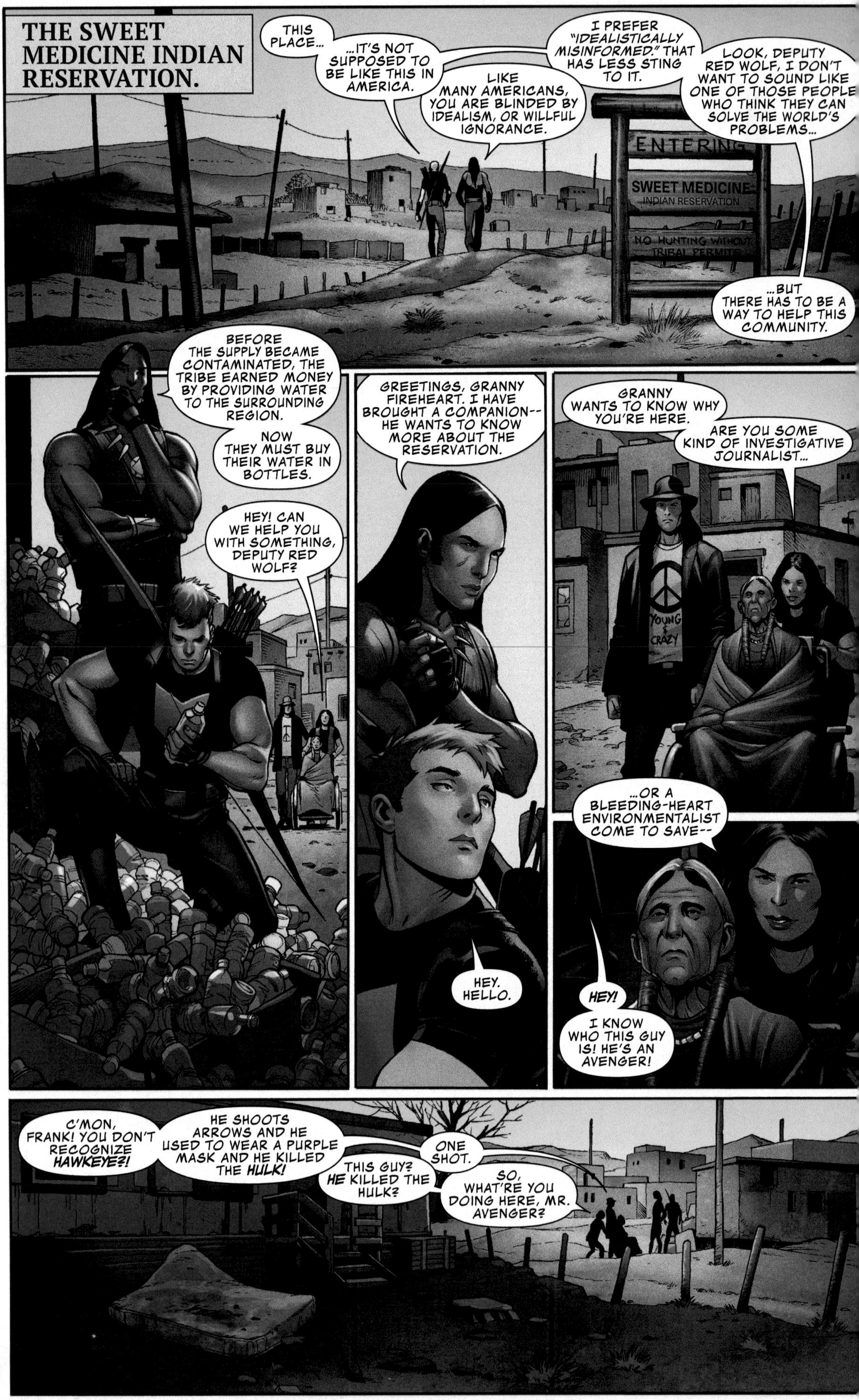
THE SWEET MEDICINE INDIAN RESERVATION.
THIS PLACE...
...IT'S NOT SUPPOSED TO BE LIKE THIS IN AMERICA.
LIKE MANY AMERICANS, YOU ARE BLINDED BY IDEALISM, OR WILLFUL IGNORANCE.
I PREFER "IDEALISTICALLY MISINFORMED." THAT HAS LESS STING TO IT.
LOOK, DEPUTY RED WOLF, I DON'T WANT TO SOUND LIKE ONE OF THOSE PEOPLE WHO THINK THEY CAN SOLVE THE WORLD'S PROBLEMS...
...BUT THERE HAS TO BE A WAY TO HELP THIS COMMUNITY.
ENTERING
SWEET MEDICINE
INDIAN RESERVATION
NO HUNTING WITHOUT TRIBAL PERMITS
BEFORE THE SUPPLY BECAME CONTAMINATED, THE TRIBE EARNED MONEY BY PROVIDING WATER TO THE SURROUNDING REGION.
NOW THEY MUST BUY THEIR WATER IN BOTTLES.
HEY! CAN WE HELP YOU WITH SOMETHING, DEPUTY RED WOLF?
GREETINGS, GRANNY FIREHEART. I HAVE BROUGHT A COMPANION--HE WANTS TO KNOW MORE ABOUT THE RESERVATION.
HEY. HELLO.
GRANNY WANTS TO KNOW WHY YOU'RE HERE.
ARE YOU SOME KIND OF INVESTIGATIVE JOURNALIST...
YOUNG & CRAZY
...OR A BLEEDING-HEART ENVIRONMENTALIST COME TO SAVE--
HEY!
I KNOW WHO THIS GUY IS! HE'S AN AVENGER!
C'MON, FRANK! YOU DON'T RECOGNIZE HAWKEYE?!
HE SHOOTS ARROWS AND HE USED TO WEAR A PURPLE MASK AND HE KILLED THE HULK!
THIS GUY? HE KILLED THE HULK?
ONE SHOT.
SO, WHAT'RE YOU DOING HERE, MR. AVENGER?

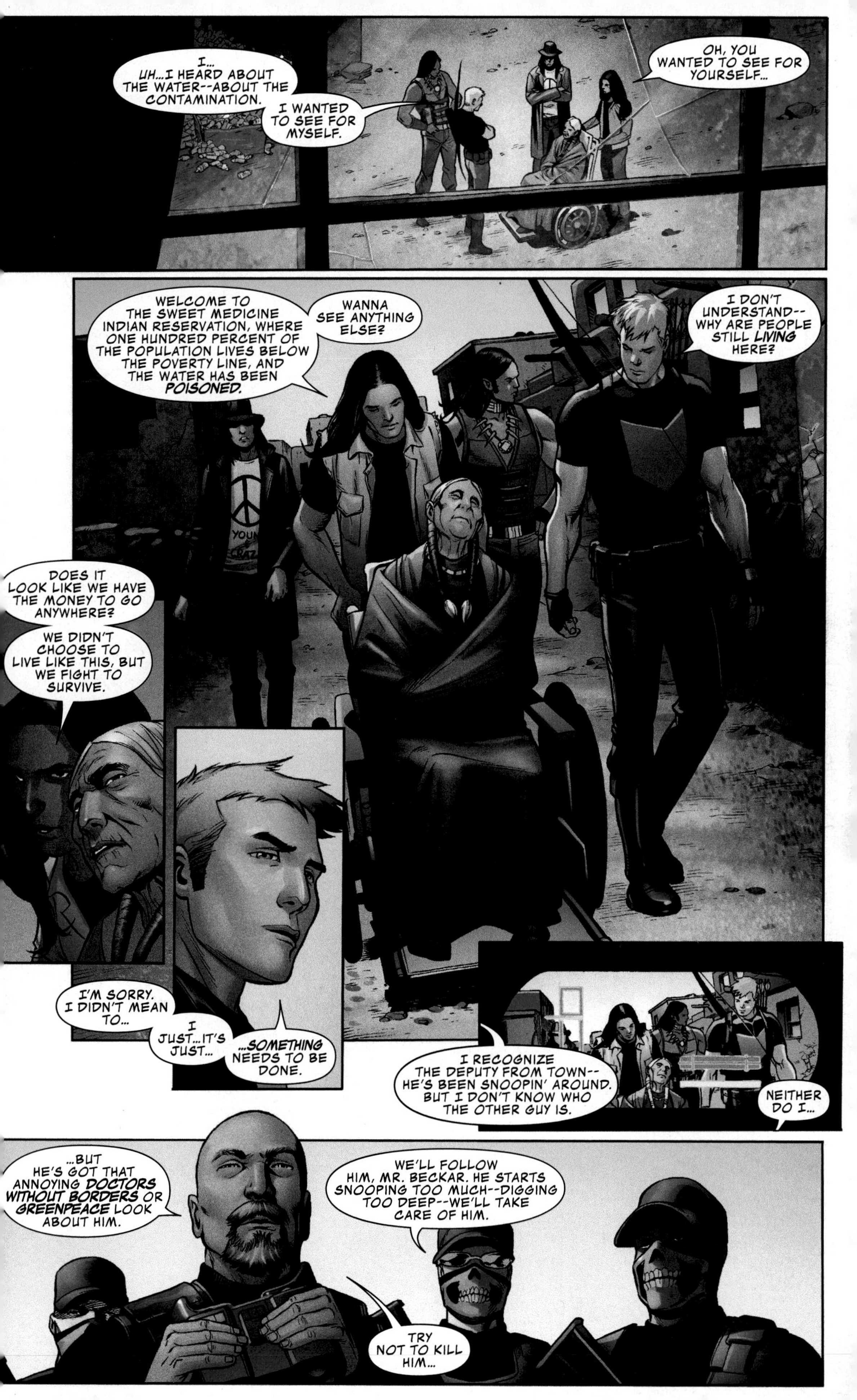
I... UH...I HEARD ABOUT THE WATER--ABOUT THE CONTAMINATION.
I WANTED TO SEE FOR MYSELF.
OH, YOU WANTED TO SEE FOR YOURSELF...
WELCOME TO THE SWEET MEDICINE INDIAN RESERVATION, WHERE ONE HUNDRED PERCENT OF THE POPULATION LIVES BELOW THE POVERTY LINE, AND THE WATER HAS BEEN POISONED.
WANNA SEE ANYTHING ELSE?
I DON'T UNDERSTAND-- WHY ARE PEOPLE STILL LIVING HERE?
DOES IT LOOK LIKE WE HAVE THE MONEY TO GO ANYWHERE?
WE DIDN'T CHOOSE TO LIVE LIKE THIS, BUT WE FIGHT TO SURVIVE.
I'M SORRY. I DIDN'T MEAN TO...
I JUST...IT'S JUST...
...SOMETHING NEEDS TO BE DONE.
I RECOGNIZE THE DEPUTY FROM TOWN-- HE'S BEEN SNOOPIN' AROUND. BUT I DON'T KNOW WHO THE OTHER GUY IS.
NEITHER DO I...
...BUT HE'S GOT THAT ANNOYING DOCTORS WITHOUT BORDERS OR GREENPEACE LOOK ABOUT HIM.
WE'LL FOLLOW HIM, MR. BECKAR. HE STARTS SNOOPING TOO MUCH--DIGGING TOO DEEP--WE'LL TAKE CARE OF HIM.
TRY NOT TO KILL HIM...

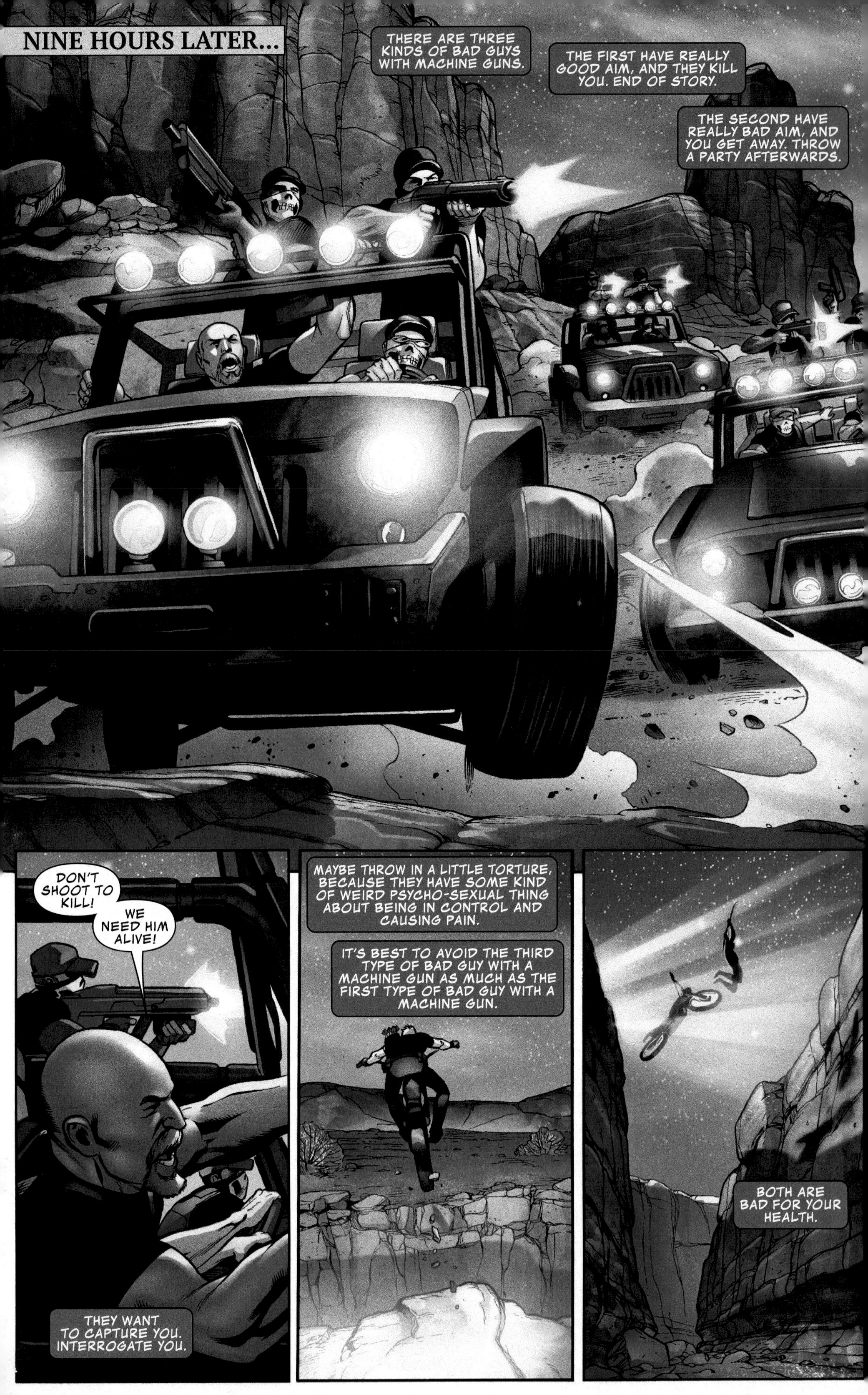
NINE HOURS LATER...
THERE ARE THREE KINDS OF BAD GUYS WITH MACHINE GUNS.
THE FIRST HAVE REALLY GOOD AIM, AND THEY KILL YOU. END OF STORY.
THE SECOND HAVE REALLY BAD AIM, AND YOU GET AWAY. THROW A PARTY AFTERWARDS.
DON'T SHOOT TO KILL!
WE NEED HIM ALIVE!
THEY WANT TO CAPTURE YOU. INTERROGATE YOU.
MAYBE THROW IN A LITTLE TORTURE, BECAUSE THEY HAVE SOME KIND OF WEIRD PSYCHO-SEXUAL THING ABOUT BEING IN CONTROL AND CAUSING PAIN.
IT'S BEST TO AVOID THE THIRD TYPE OF BAD GUY WITH A MACHINE GUN AS MUCH AS THE FIRST TYPE OF BAD GUY WITH A MACHINE GUN.
BOTH ARE BAD FOR YOUR HEALTH.

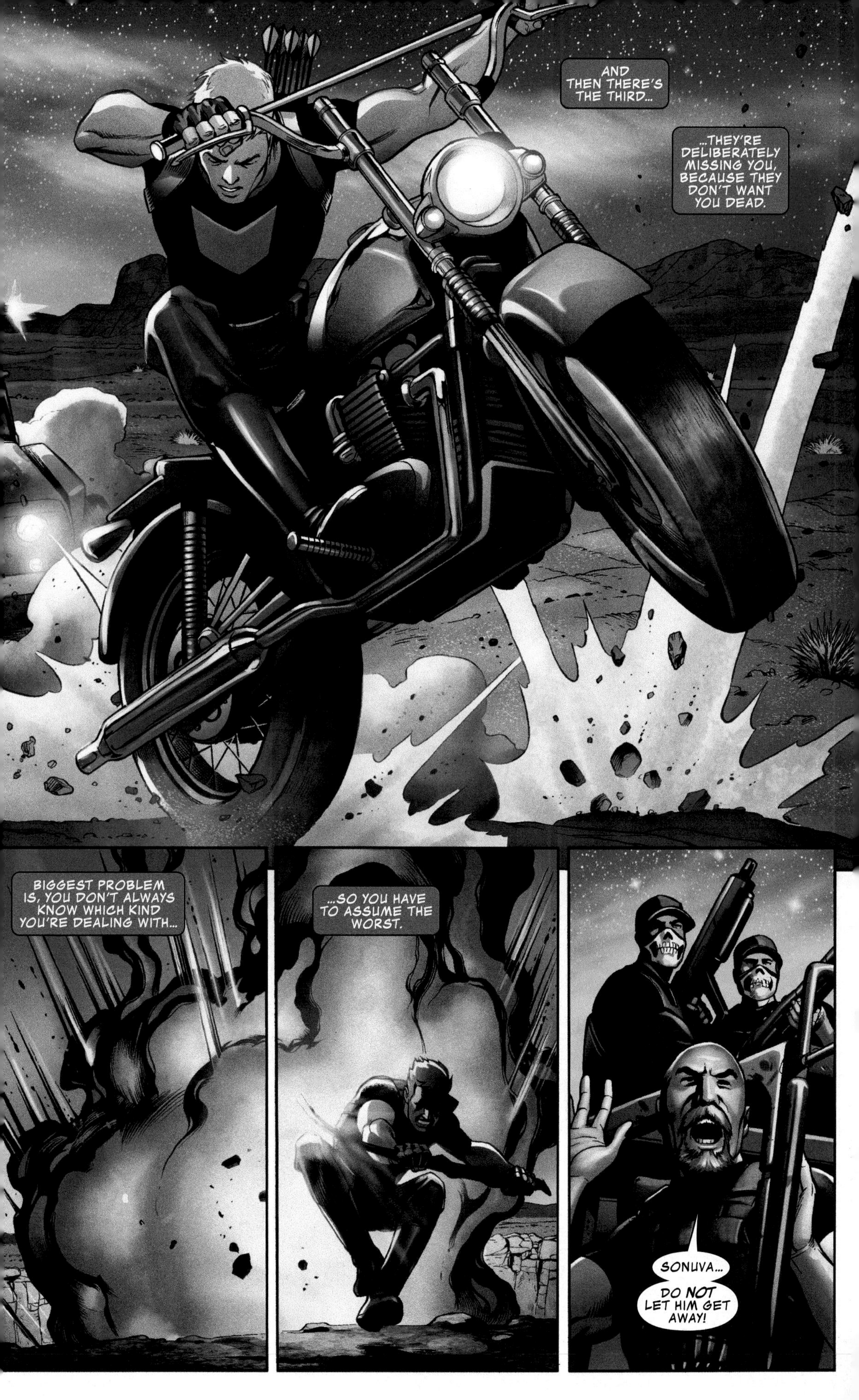
AND THEN THERE'S THE THIRD...
...THEY'RE DELIBERATELY MISSING YOU, BECAUSE THEY DON'T WANT YOU DEAD.
BIGGEST PROBLEM IS, YOU DON'T ALWAYS KNOW WHICH KIND YOU'RE DEALING WITH...
...SO YOU HAVE TO ASSUME THE WORST.
SONUVA...
DO NOT LET HIM GET AWAY!

DON'T THINK FOR A SECOND THAT I DON'T KNOW WHAT PEOPLE SAY ABOUT ME...

...I'M THE GUY WHO BRINGS A BOW AND ARROW TO A GUN FIGHT.

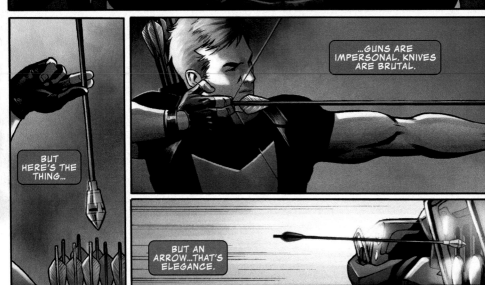

...GUNS ARE IMPERSONAL. KNIVES ARE BRUTAL.

BUT HERE'S THE THING...

BUT AN ARROW...THAT'S ELEGANCE.

IT IS A HANDWRITTEN LETTER IN AN AGE OF TEXT MESSAGES.

A BOW AND ARROW REALLY SAYS "FROM ME, TO YOU, WITH LOVE AND KISSES."

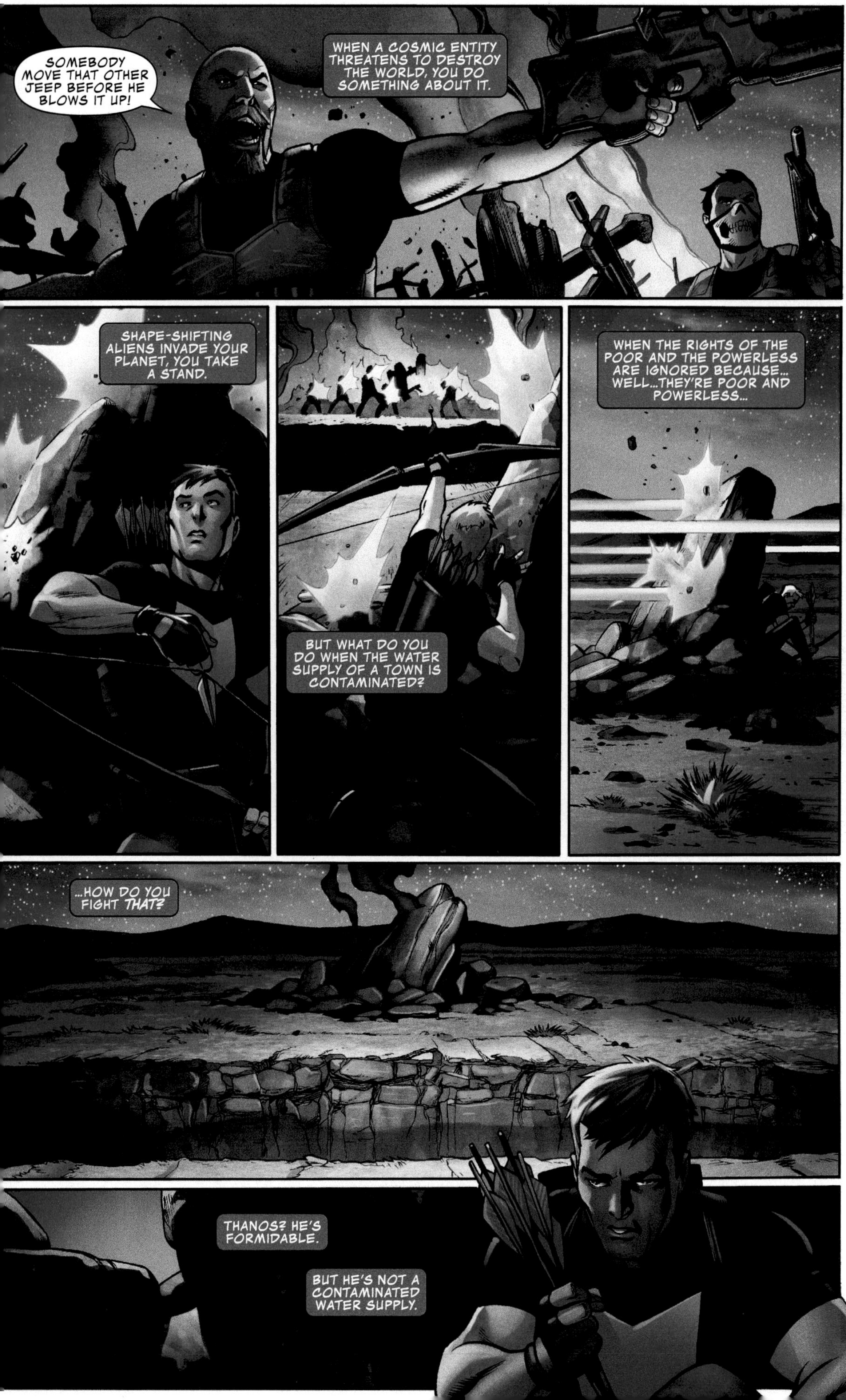
WHEN A COSMIC ENTITY THREATENS TO DESTROY THE WORLD, YOU DO SOMETHING ABOUT IT.
SOMEBODY MOVE THAT OTHER JEEP BEFORE HE BLOWS IT UP!
SHAPE-SHIFTING ALIENS INVADE YOUR PLANET, YOU TAKE A STAND.
WHEN THE RIGHTS OF THE POOR AND THE POWERLESS ARE IGNORED BECAUSE... WELL...THEY'RE POOR AND POWERLESS...
BUT WHAT DO YOU DO WHEN THE WATER SUPPLY OF A TOWN IS CONTAMINATED?
...HOW DO YOU FIGHT *THAT?*
THANOS? HE'S FORMIDABLE.
BUT HE'S NOT A CONTAMINATED WATER SUPPLY.

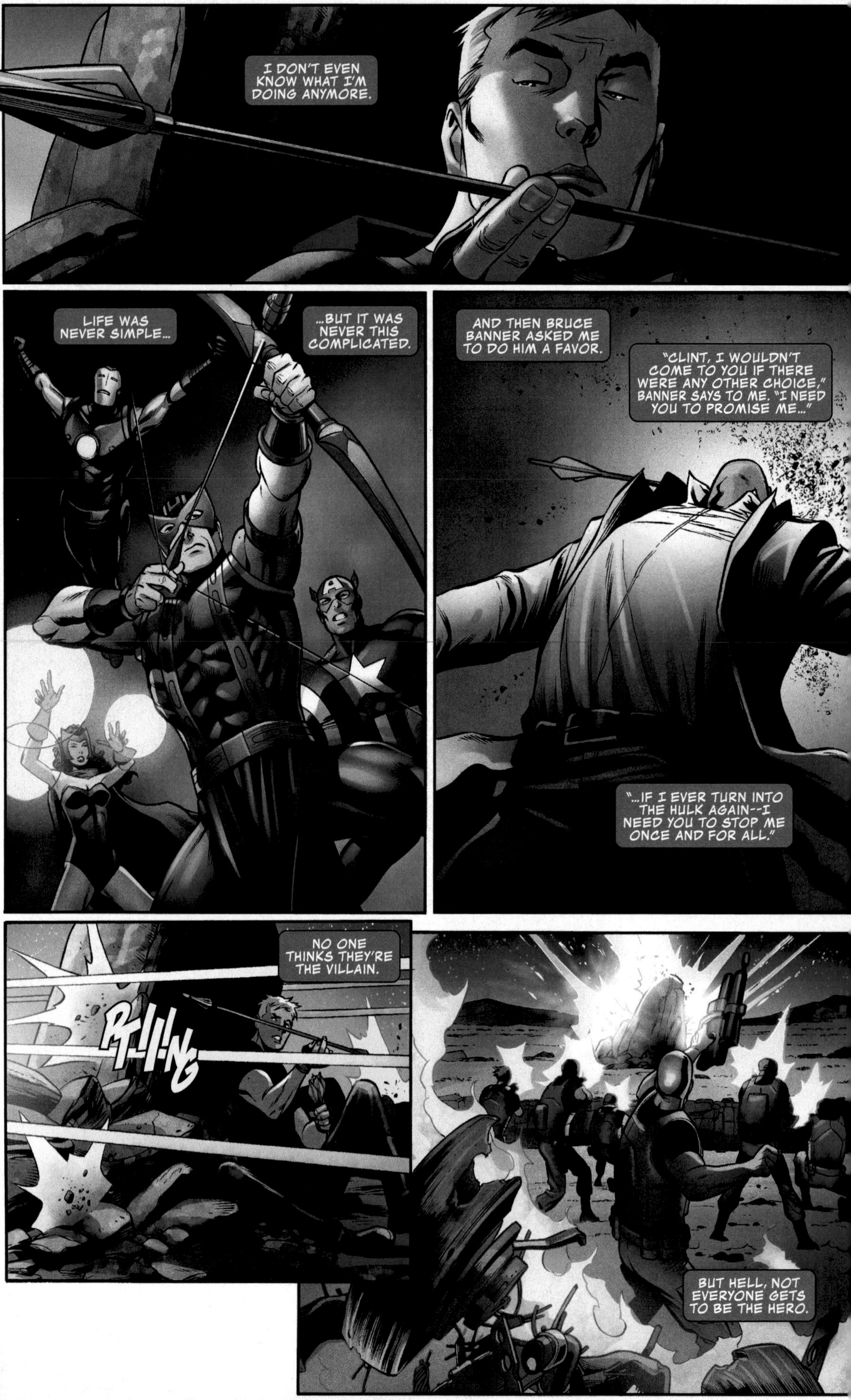
I DON'T EVEN KNOW WHAT I'M DOING ANYMORE.
LIFE WAS NEVER SIMPLE...
...BUT IT WAS NEVER THIS COMPLICATED.
AND THEN BRUCE BANNER ASKED ME TO DO HIM A FAVOR.
"CLINT, I WOULDN'T COME TO YOU IF THERE WERE ANY OTHER CHOICE," BANNER SAYS TO ME. "I NEED YOU TO PROMISE ME..."
"...IF I EVER TURN INTO THE HULK AGAIN--I NEED YOU TO STOP ME ONCE AND FOR ALL."
NO ONE THINKS THEY'RE THE VILLAIN.
PT-I-I-I-NG
BUT HELL, NOT EVERYONE GETS TO BE THE HERO.

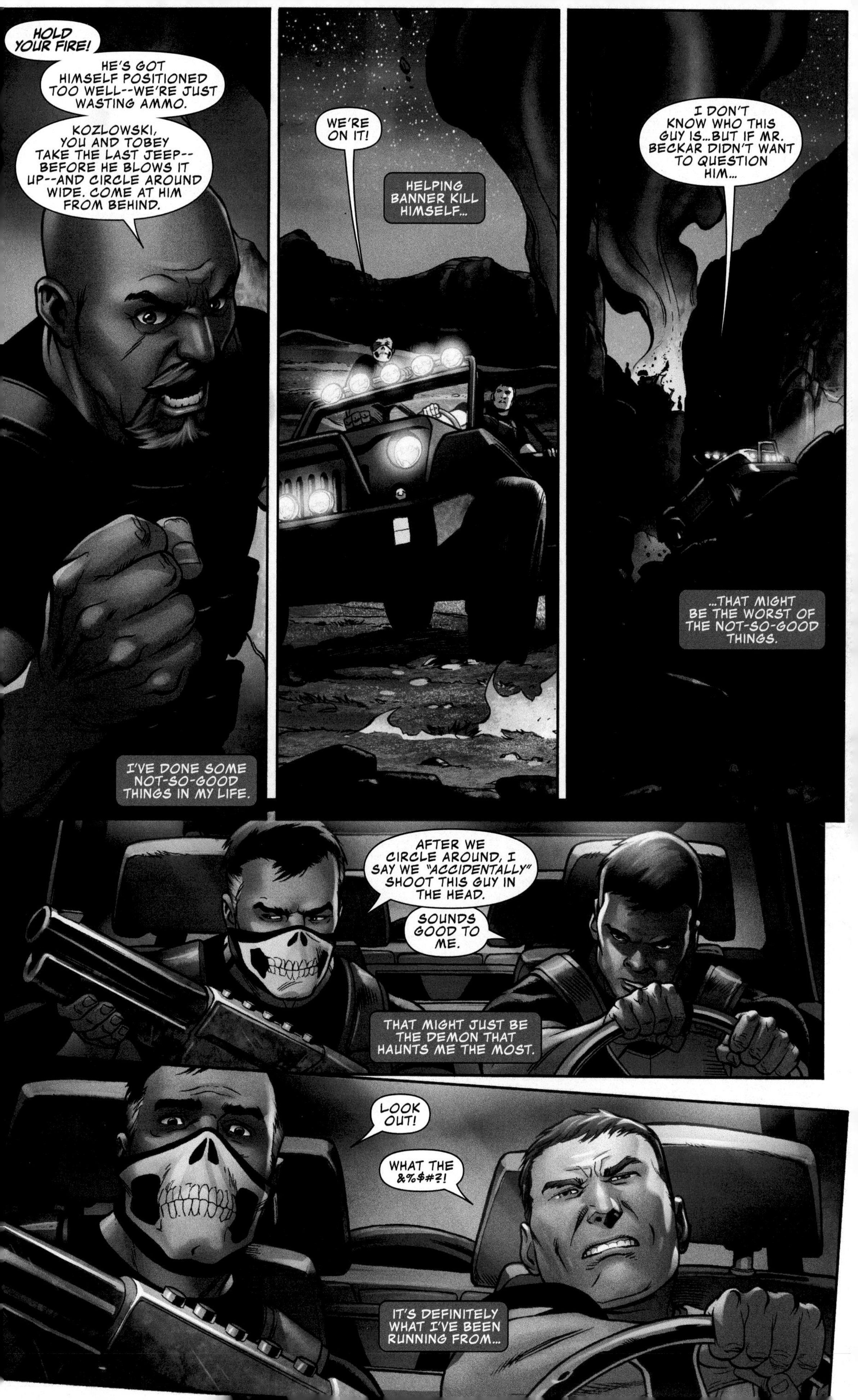
HOLD YOUR FIRE!
HE'S GOT HIMSELF POSITIONED TOO WELL--WE'RE JUST WASTING AMMO.
KOZLOWSKI, YOU AND TOBEY TAKE THE LAST JEEP--BEFORE HE BLOWS IT UP--AND CIRCLE AROUND WIDE. COME AT HIM FROM BEHIND.
I'VE DONE SOME NOT-SO-GOOD THINGS IN MY LIFE.
WE'RE ON IT!
HELPING BANNER KILL HIMSELF...
I DON'T KNOW WHO THIS GUY IS...BUT IF MR. BECKAR DIDN'T WANT TO QUESTION HIM...
...THAT MIGHT BE THE WORST OF THE NOT-SO-GOOD THINGS.
AFTER WE CIRCLE AROUND, I SAY WE "ACCIDENTALLY" SHOOT THIS GUY IN THE HEAD.
SOUNDS GOOD TO ME.
THAT MIGHT JUST BE THE DEMON THAT HAUNTS ME THE MOST.
LOOK OUT!
WHAT THE &%$#?!
IT'S DEFINITELY WHAT I'VE BEEN RUNNING FROM...

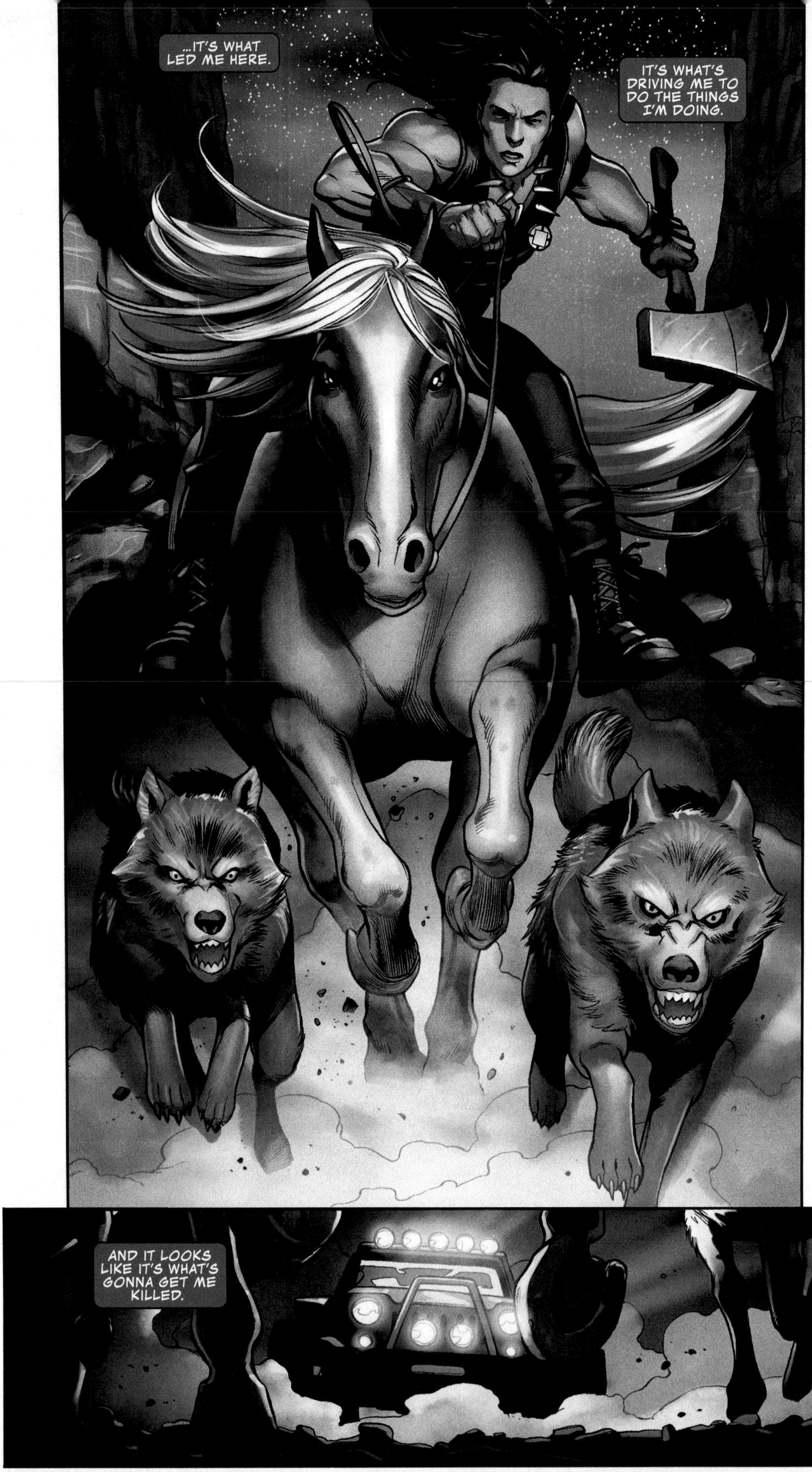
...IT'S WHAT
LED ME HERE.
IT'S WHAT'S
DRIVING ME TO
DO THE THINGS
I'M DOING.
AND IT LOOKS
LIKE IT'S WHAT'S
GONNA GET ME
KILLED.

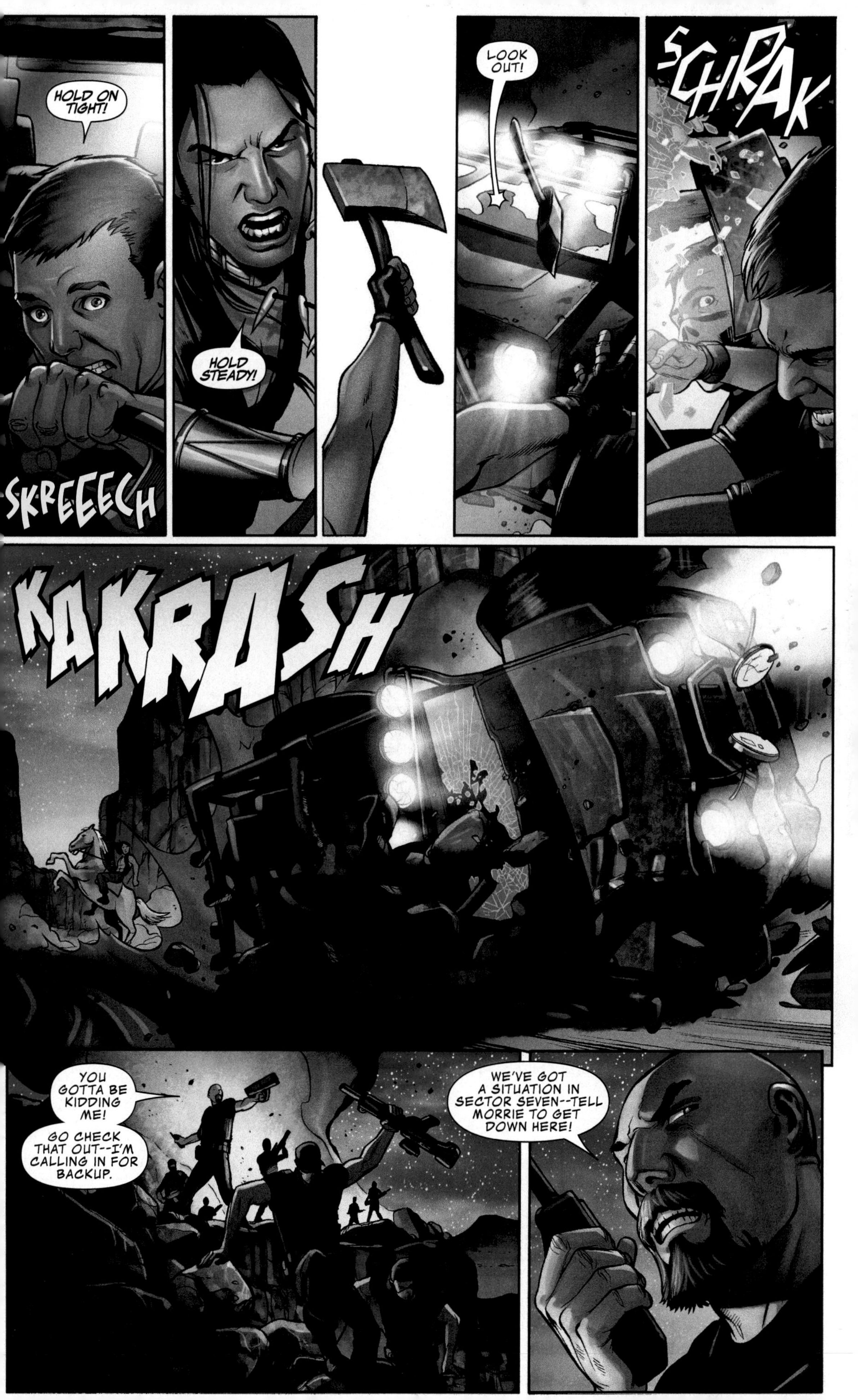
HOLD ON TIGHT!
SKREEECH
HOLD STEADY!
LOOK OUT!
SCHRAK
KAKRASH
YOU GOTTA BE KIDDING ME!
GO CHECK THAT OUT--I'M CALLING IN FOR BACKUP.
WE'VE GOT A SITUATION IN SECTOR SEVEN--TELL MORRIE TO GET DOWN HERE!

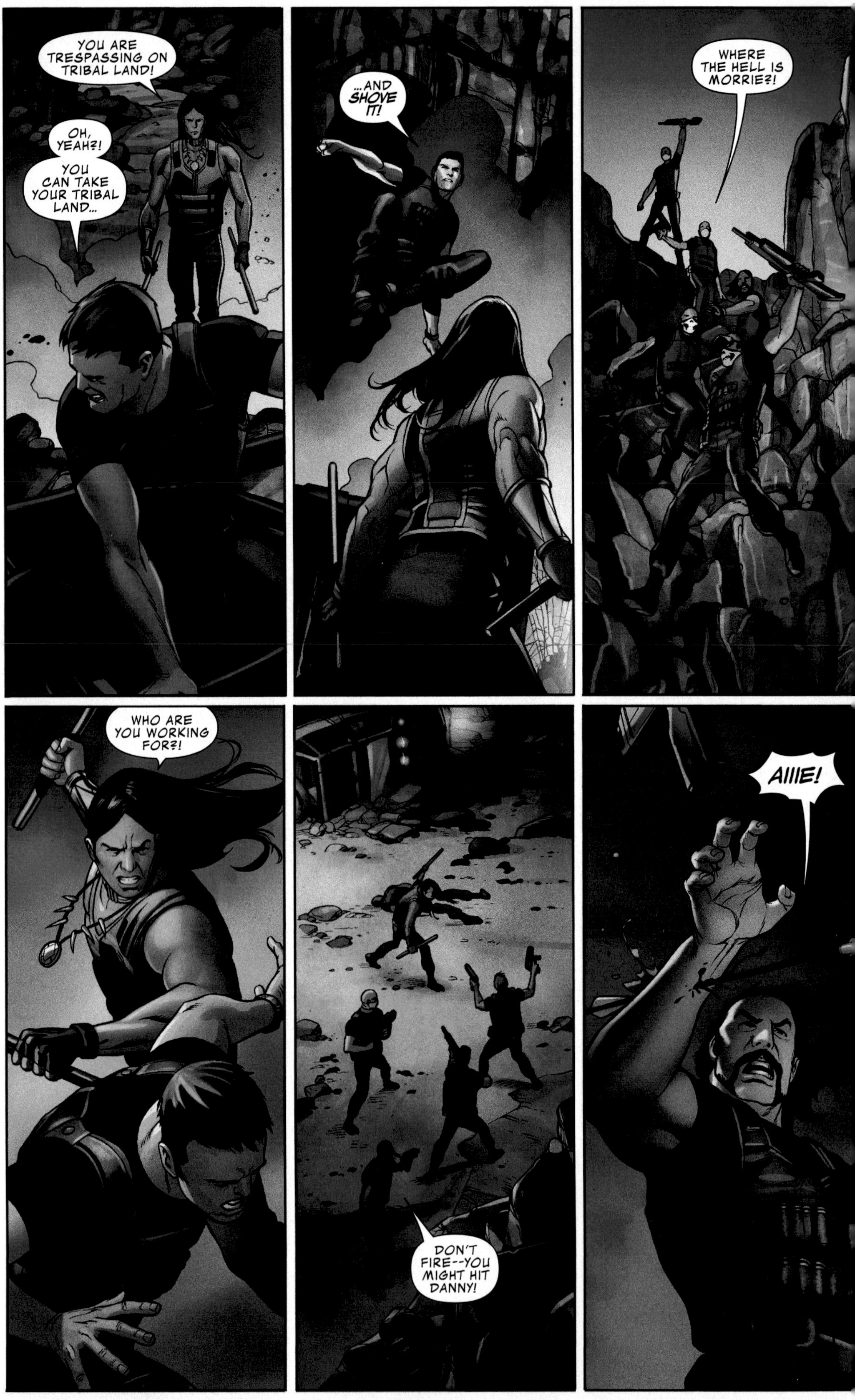
YOU ARE TRESPASSING ON TRIBAL LAND!
OH, YEAH?!
YOU CAN TAKE YOUR TRIBAL LAND...
...AND SHOVE IT!
WHERE THE HELL IS MORRIE?!
WHO ARE YOU WORKING FOR?!
DON'T FIRE--YOU MIGHT HIT DANNY!
AIIIE!

I'M READY TO FACE MY DEMONS-- TO ANSWER FOR ALL MY SINS.

BUT THERE'S A GUARDIAN ANGEL WITH OTHER PLANS...

...WHICH MEANS THIS ISN'T MY TIME TO DIE.

IT'S MY TIME TO FIGHT.

I CAN'T DIE. NOT AGAIN. AND DEFINITELY NOT NOW.

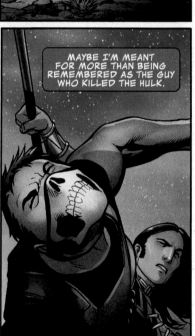

MAYBE I'M MEANT FOR MORE THAN BEING REMEMBERED AS THE GUY WHO KILLED THE HULK.

MAYBE.

I DON'T KNOW.

ALL I KNOW IS ONE THING...

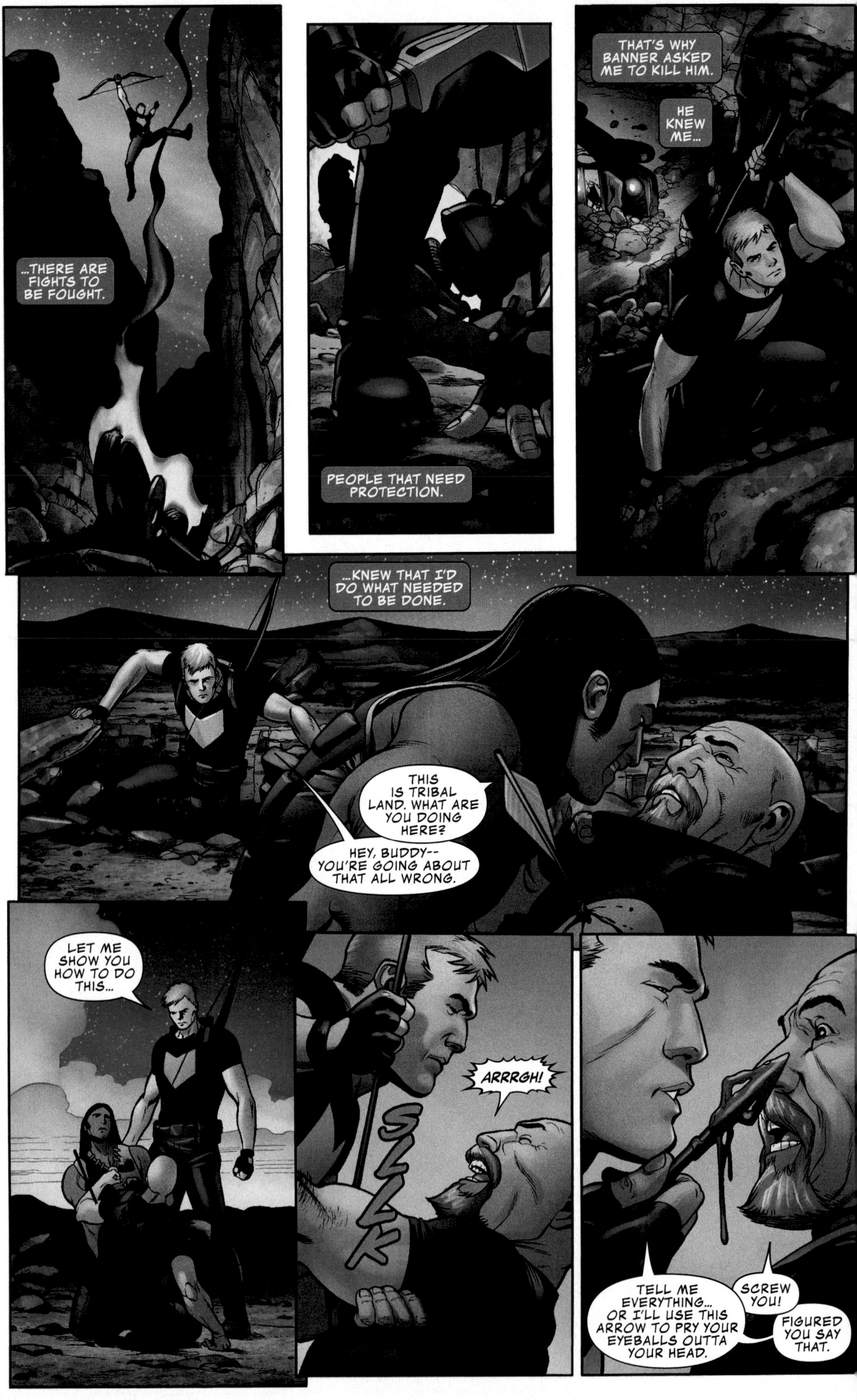

...THERE ARE FIGHTS TO BE FOUGHT.
PEOPLE THAT NEED PROTECTION.
THAT'S WHY BANNER ASKED ME TO KILL HIM.
HE KNEW ME...
...KNEW THAT I'D DO WHAT NEEDED TO BE DONE.
THIS IS TRIBAL LAND. WHAT ARE YOU DOING HERE?
HEY, BUDDY-- YOU'RE GOING ABOUT THAT ALL WRONG.
LET ME SHOW YOU HOW TO DO THIS...
ARRRGH!
SLLK
TELL ME EVERYTHING... OR I'LL USE THIS ARROW TO PRY YOUR EYEBALLS OUTTA YOUR HEAD.
SCREW YOU!
FIGURED YOU SAY THAT.

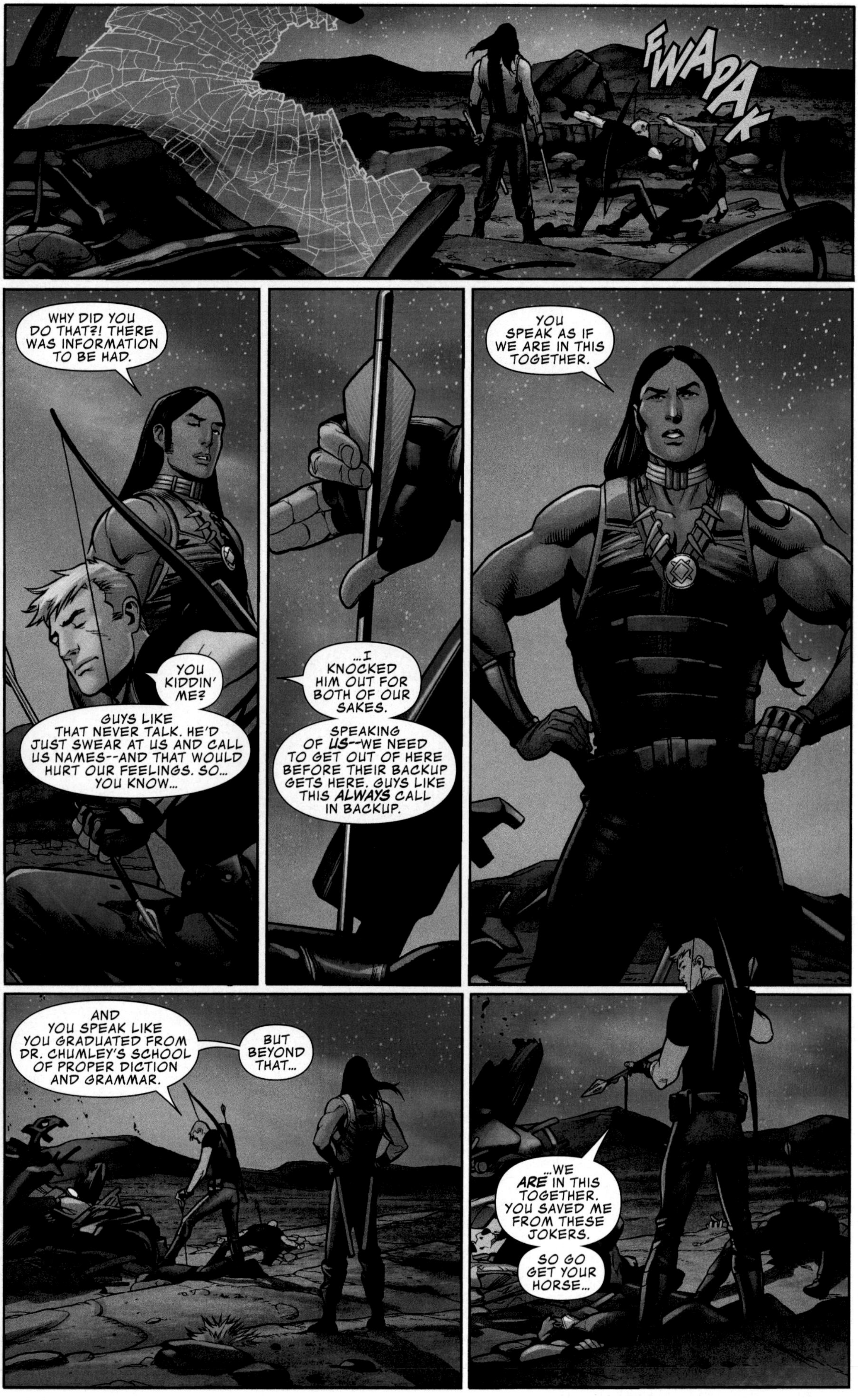
FWAPAK
WHY DID YOU DO THAT?! THERE WAS INFORMATION TO BE HAD.
YOU KIDDIN' ME?
GUYS LIKE THAT NEVER TALK. HE'D JUST SWEAR AT US AND CALL US NAMES--AND THAT WOULD HURT OUR FEELINGS. SO... YOU KNOW...
...I KNOCKED HIM OUT FOR BOTH OF OUR SAKES.
SPEAKING OF US--WE NEED TO GET OUT OF HERE BEFORE THEIR BACKUP GETS HERE. GUYS LIKE THIS ALWAYS CALL IN BACKUP.
YOU SPEAK AS IF WE ARE IN THIS TOGETHER.
AND YOU SPEAK LIKE YOU GRADUATED FROM DR. CHUMLEY'S SCHOOL OF PROPER DICTION AND GRAMMAR.
BUT BEYOND THAT...
...WE ARE IN THIS TOGETHER. YOU SAVED ME FROM THESE JOKERS.
SO GO GET YOUR HORSE...

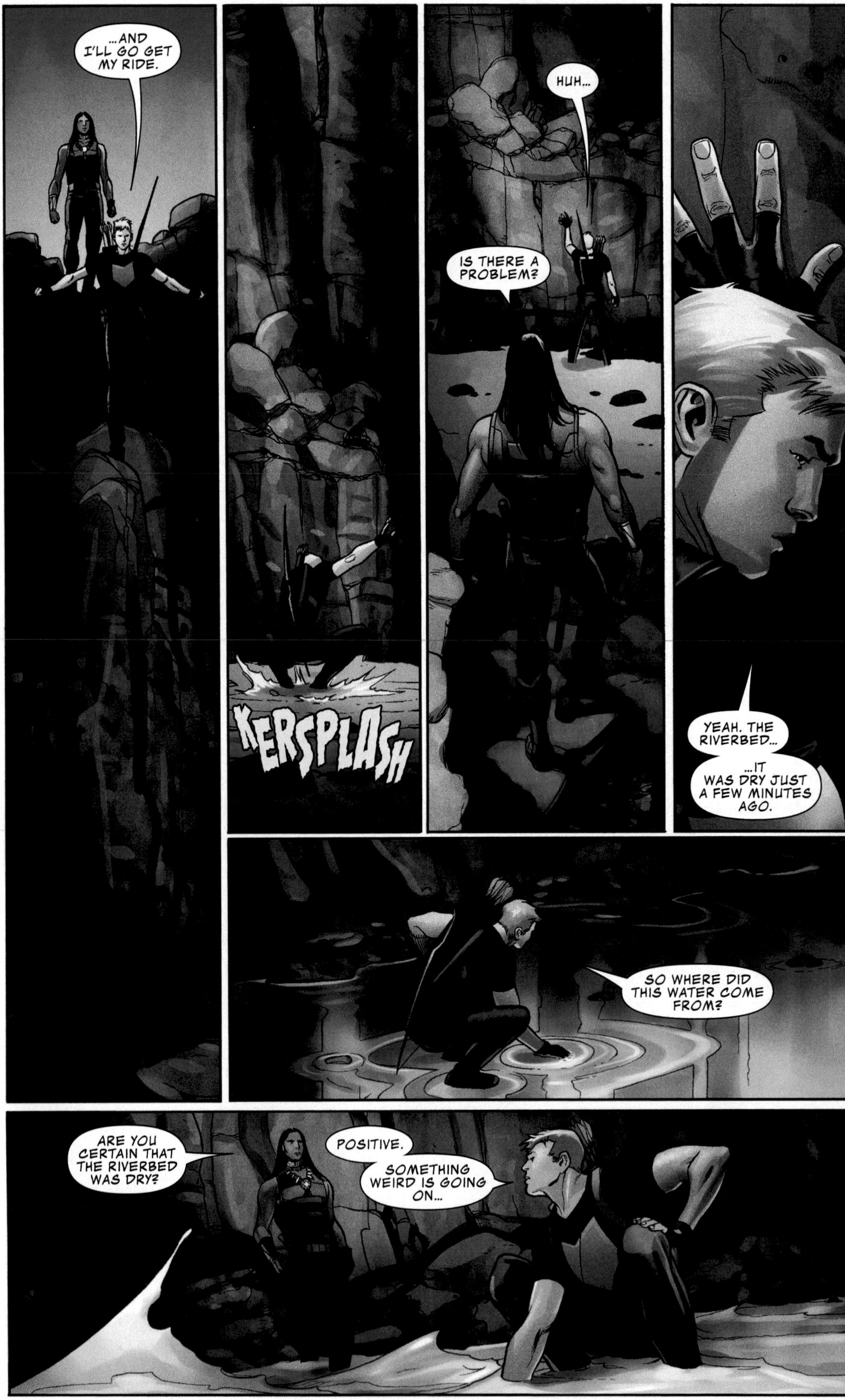
...AND I'LL GO GET MY RIDE.
KERSPLASH
HUH...
IS THERE A PROBLEM?
YEAH. THE RIVERBED...
...IT WAS DRY JUST A FEW MINUTES AGO.
SO WHERE DID THIS WATER COME FROM?
ARE YOU CERTAIN THAT THE RIVERBED WAS DRY?
POSITIVE.
SOMETHING WEIRD IS GOING ON...

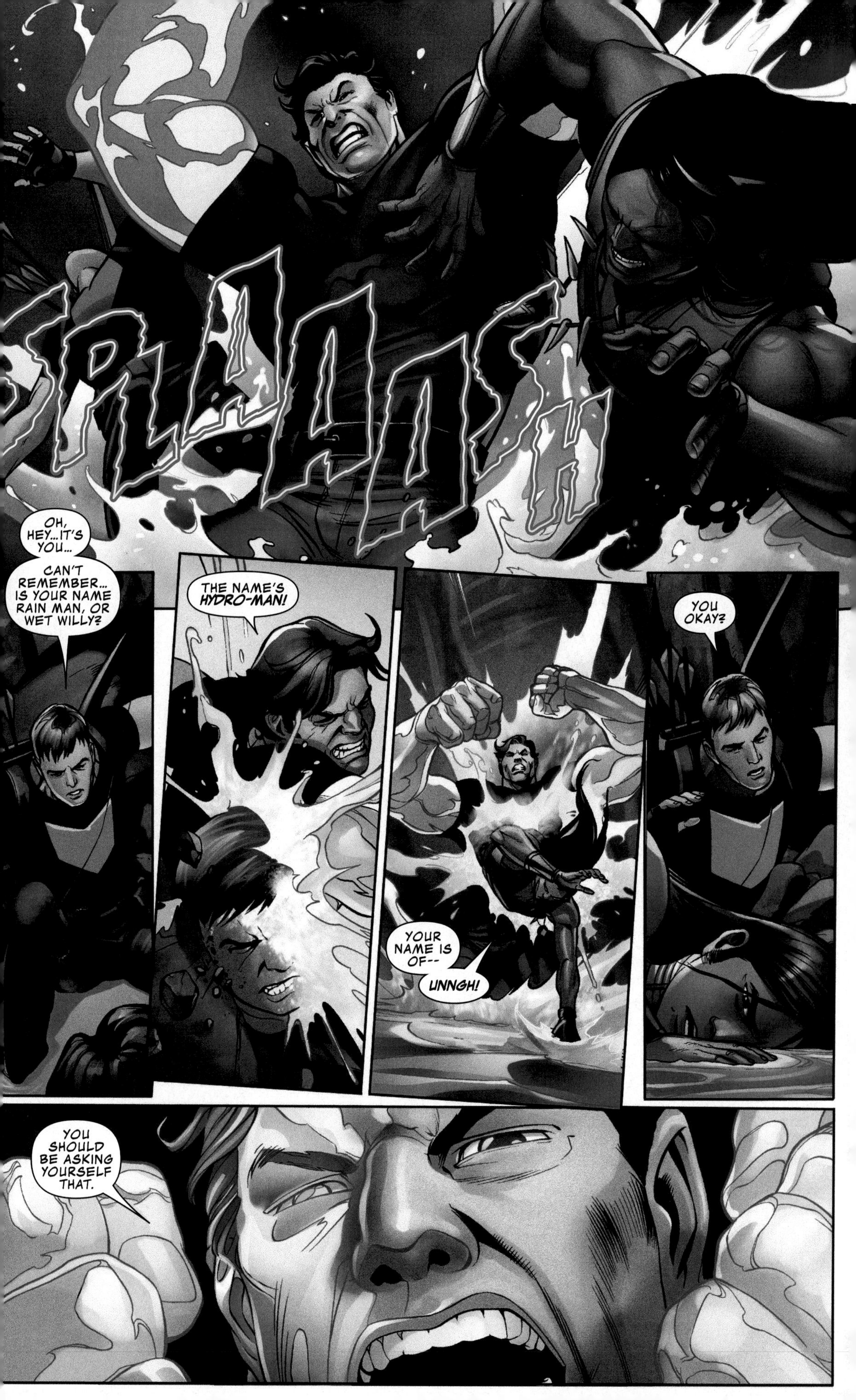
SPLAASH
OH, HEY...IT'S YOU...
CAN'T REMEMBER... IS YOUR NAME RAIN MAN, OR WET WILLY?
THE NAME'S HYDRO-MAN!
YOUR NAME IS OF--
UNNGH!
YOU OKAY?
YOU SHOULD BE ASKING YOURSELF THAT.

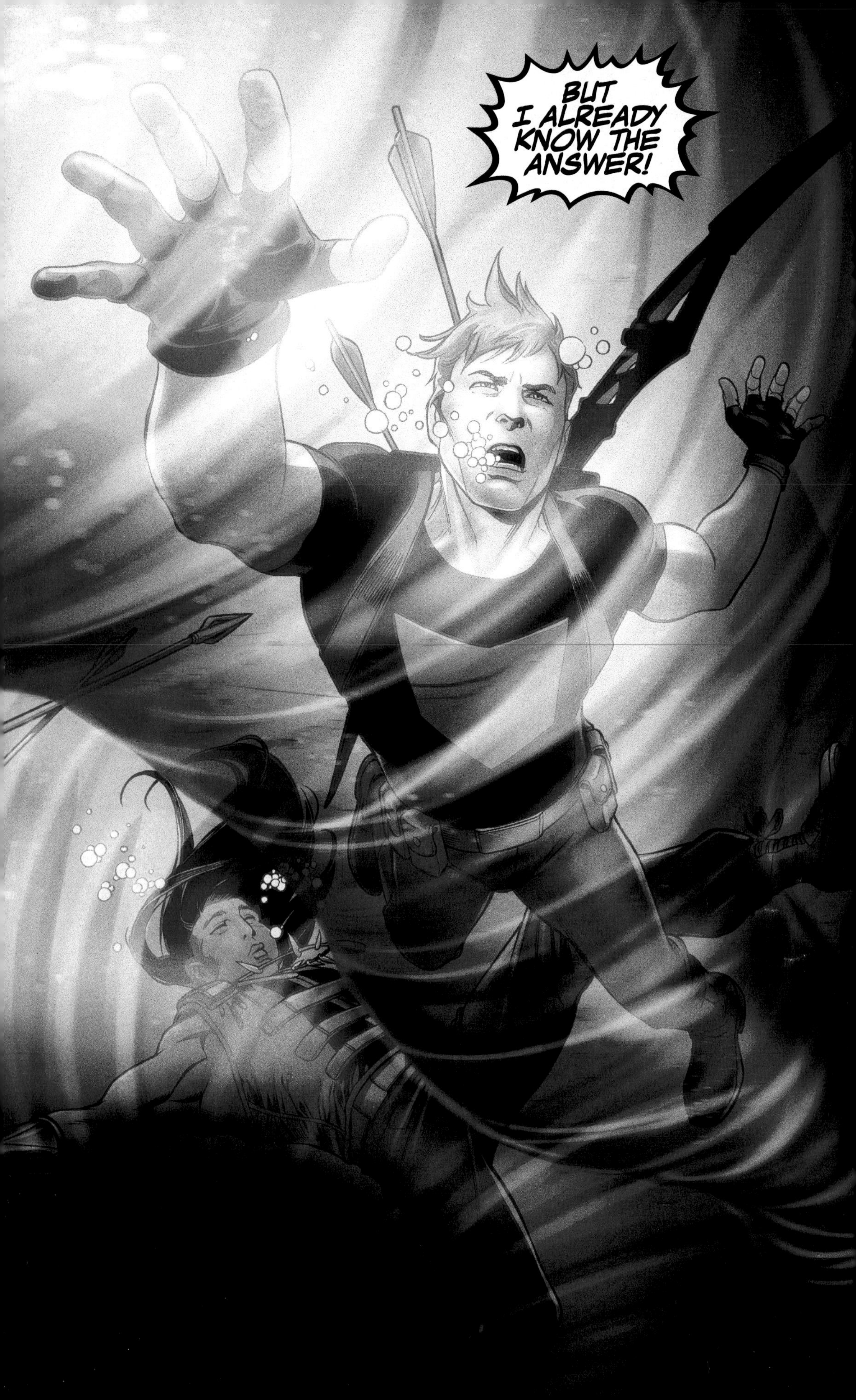
BUT I ALREADY KNOW THE ANSWER!

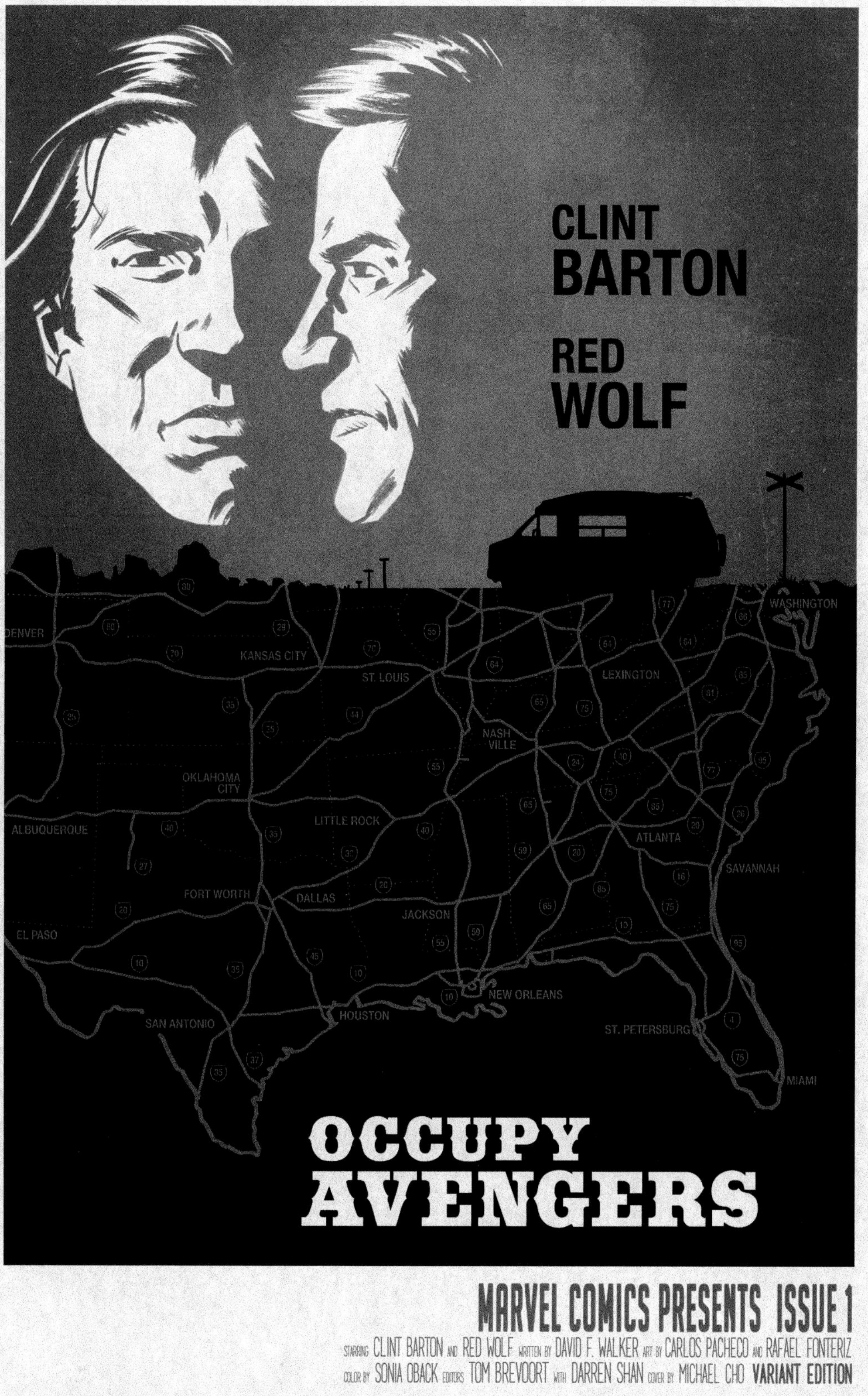
CLINT
BARTON
RED
WOLF
WASHINGTON
DENVER
KANSAS CITY
ST. LOUIS
LEXINGTON
NASH VILLE
OKLAHOMA CITY
ALBUQUERQUE
LITTLE ROCK
ATLANTA
SAVANNAH
FORT WORTH
DALLAS
JACKSON
EL PASO
NEW ORLEANS
SAN ANTONIO
HOUSTON
ST. PETERSBURG
MIAMI
OCCUPY
AVENGERS
MARVEL COMICS PRESENTS ISSUE 1
STARRING CLINT BARTON AND RED WOLF WRITTEN BY DAVID F. WALKER ART BY CARLOS PACHECO AND RAFAEL FONTERIZ
COLOR BY SONIA OBACK EDITORS TOM BREVOORT WITH DARREN SHAN COVER BY MICHAEL CHO VARIANT EDITION

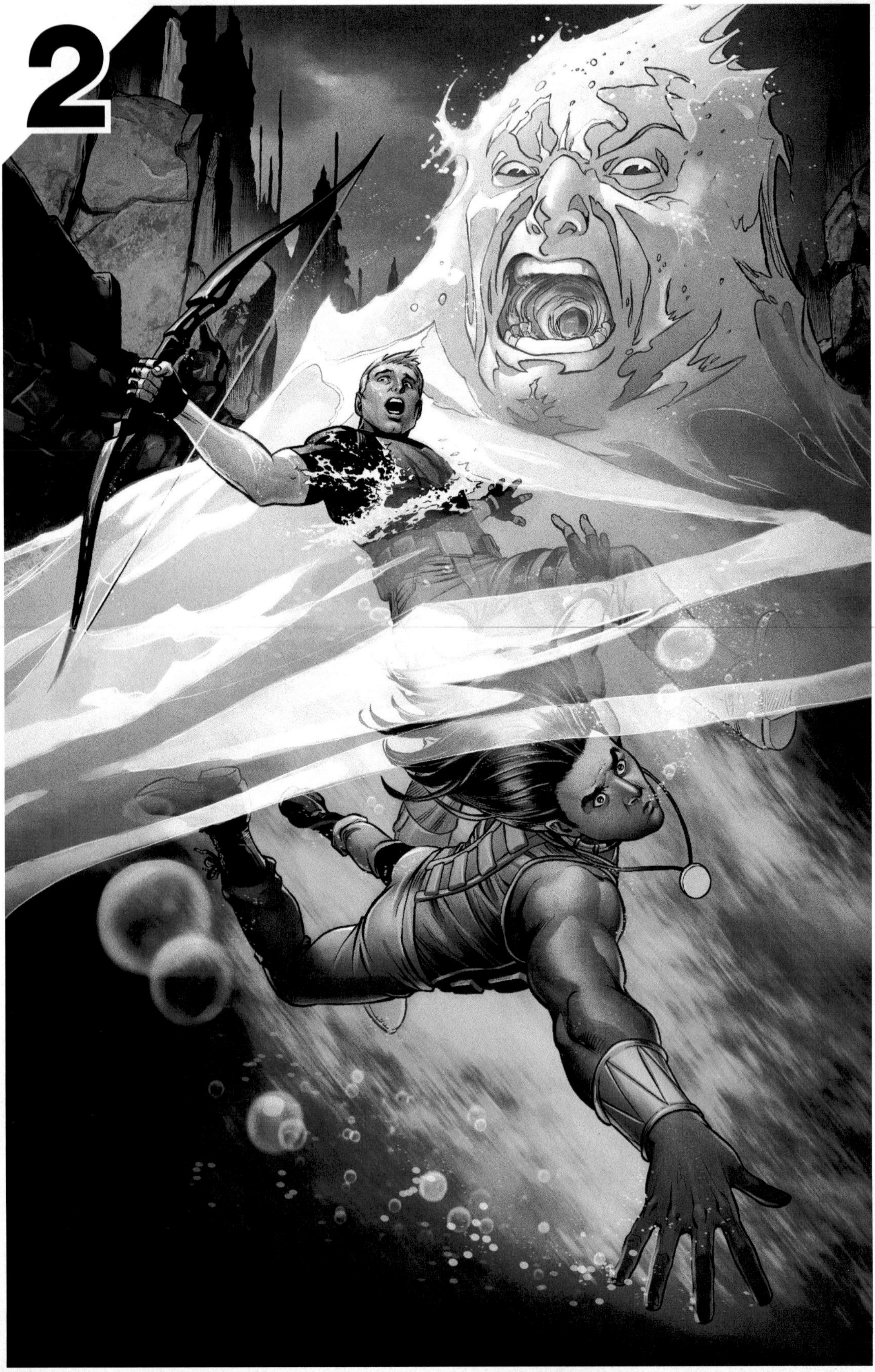
2

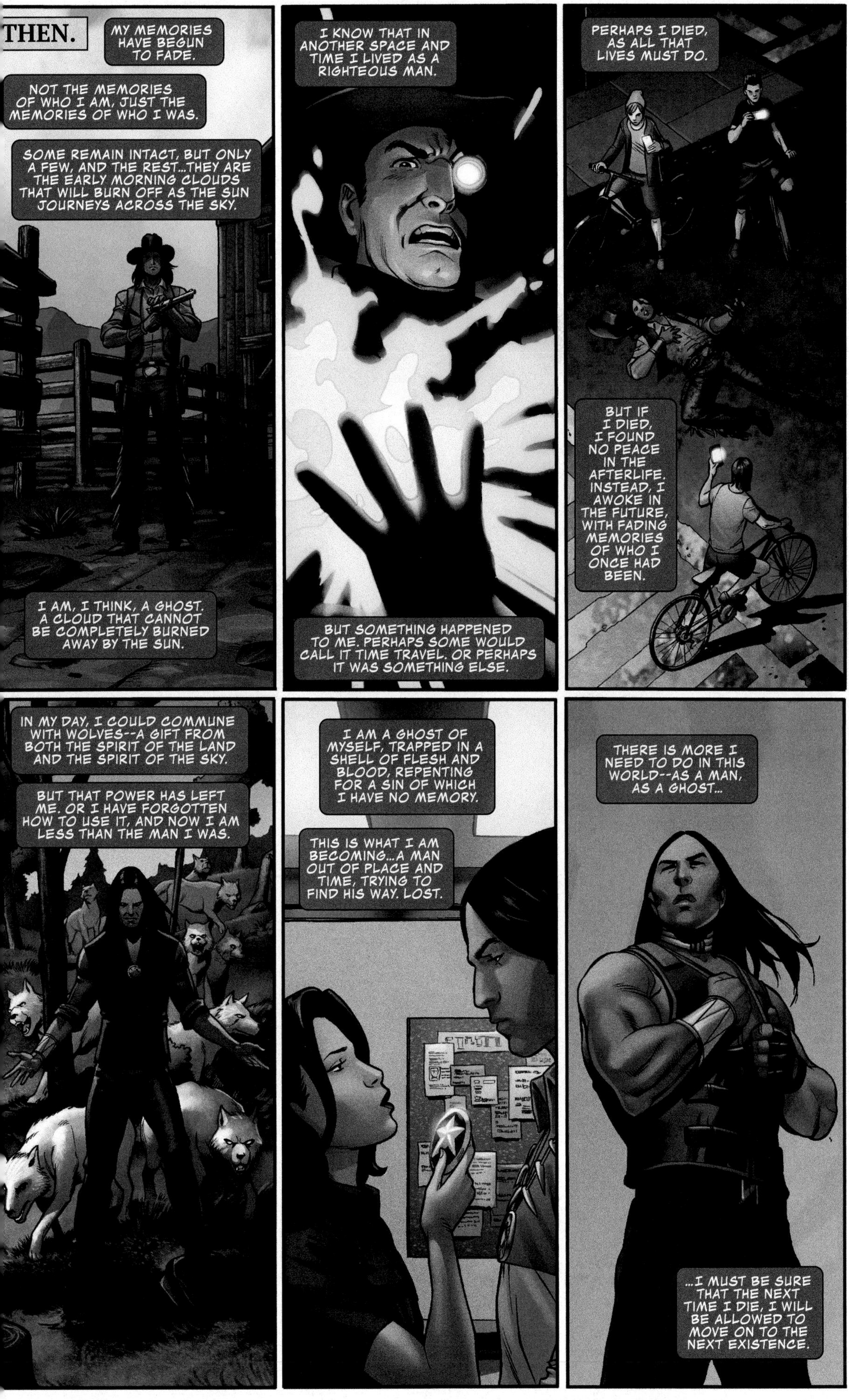
THEN.
MY MEMORIES HAVE BEGUN TO FADE.
NOT THE MEMORIES OF WHO I AM, JUST THE MEMORIES OF WHO I WAS.
SOME REMAIN INTACT, BUT ONLY A FEW, AND THE REST...THEY ARE THE EARLY MORNING CLOUDS THAT WILL BURN OFF AS THE SUN JOURNEYS ACROSS THE SKY.
I AM, I THINK, A GHOST. A CLOUD THAT CANNOT BE COMPLETELY BURNED AWAY BY THE SUN.
I KNOW THAT IN ANOTHER SPACE AND TIME I LIVED AS A RIGHTEOUS MAN.
BUT SOMETHING HAPPENED TO ME. PERHAPS SOME WOULD CALL IT TIME TRAVEL. OR PERHAPS IT WAS SOMETHING ELSE.
PERHAPS I DIED, AS ALL THAT LIVES MUST DO.
BUT IF I DIED, I FOUND NO PEACE IN THE AFTERLIFE. INSTEAD, I AWOKE IN THE FUTURE, WITH FADING MEMORIES OF WHO I ONCE HAD BEEN.
IN MY DAY, I COULD COMMUNE WITH WOLVES--A GIFT FROM BOTH THE SPIRIT OF THE LAND AND THE SPIRIT OF THE SKY.
BUT THAT POWER HAS LEFT ME. OR I HAVE FORGOTTEN HOW TO USE IT, AND NOW I AM LESS THAN THE MAN I WAS.
I AM A GHOST OF MYSELF, TRAPPED IN A SHELL OF FLESH AND BLOOD, REPENTING FOR A SIN OF WHICH I HAVE NO MEMORY.
THIS IS WHAT I AM BECOMING...A MAN OUT OF PLACE AND TIME, TRYING TO FIND HIS WAY. LOST.
THERE IS MORE I NEED TO DO IN THIS WORLD--AS A MAN, AS A GHOST...
...I MUST BE SURE THAT THE NEXT TIME I DIE, I WILL BE ALLOWED TO MOVE ON TO THE NEXT EXISTENCE.

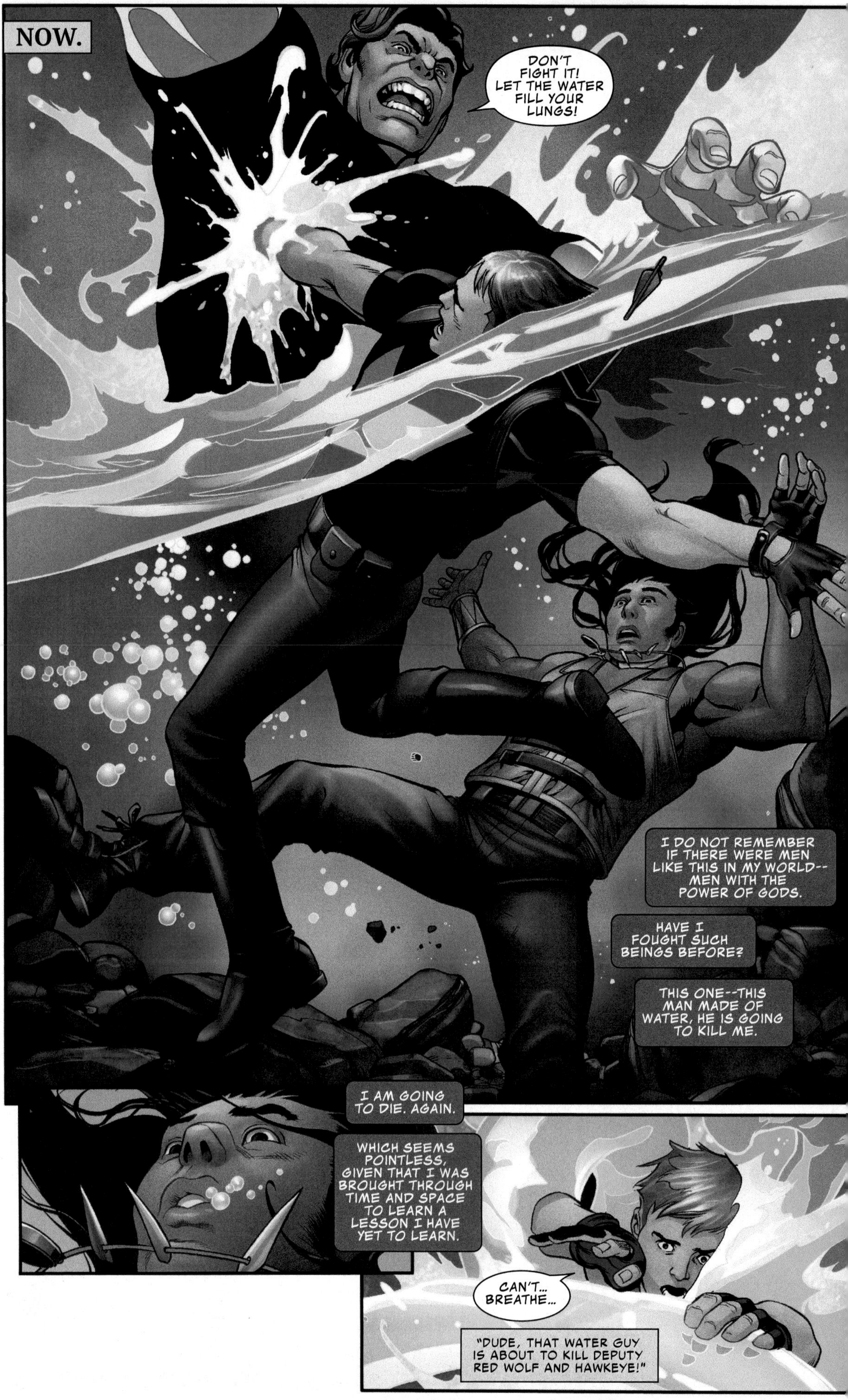
NOW.
DON'T FIGHT IT! LET THE WATER FILL YOUR LUNGS!
I DO NOT REMEMBER IF THERE WERE MEN LIKE THIS IN MY WORLD-- MEN WITH THE POWER OF GODS.
HAVE I FOUGHT SUCH BEINGS BEFORE?
THIS ONE--THIS MAN MADE OF WATER, HE IS GOING TO KILL ME.
I AM GOING TO DIE. AGAIN.
WHICH SEEMS POINTLESS, GIVEN THAT I WAS BROUGHT THROUGH TIME AND SPACE TO LEARN A LESSON I HAVE YET TO LEARN.
CAN'T... BREATHE...
"DUDE, THAT WATER GUY IS ABOUT TO KILL DEPUTY RED WOLF AND HAWKEYE!"

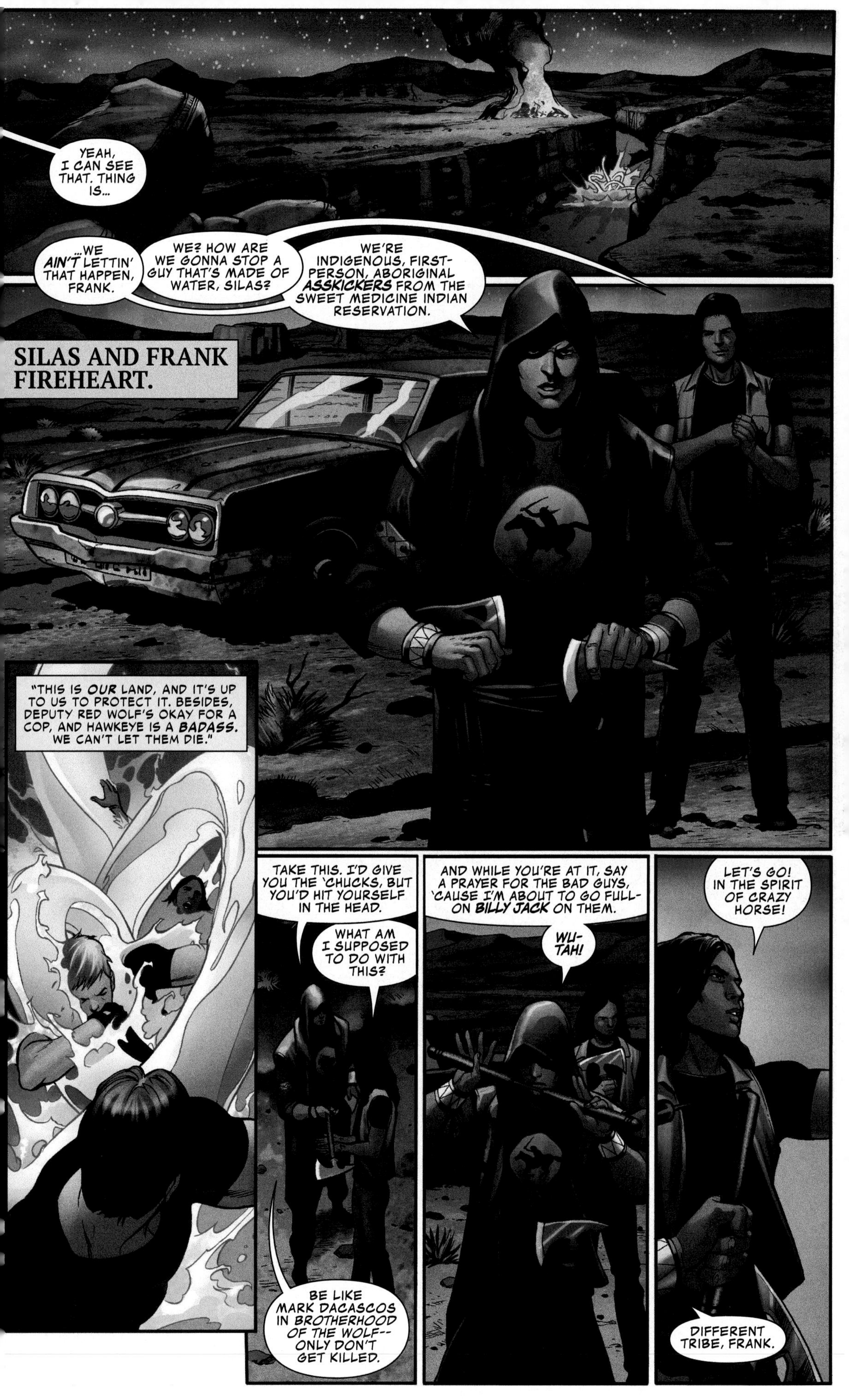

YEAH, I CAN SEE THAT. THING IS...
...WE AIN'T LETTIN' THAT HAPPEN, FRANK.
WE? HOW ARE WE GONNA STOP A GUY THAT'S MADE OF WATER, SILAS?
WE'RE INDIGENOUS, FIRST-PERSON, ABORIGINAL ASSKICKERS FROM THE SWEET MEDICINE INDIAN RESERVATION.
SILAS AND FRANK FIREHEART.
"THIS IS OUR LAND, AND IT'S UP TO US TO PROTECT IT. BESIDES, DEPUTY RED WOLF'S OKAY FOR A COP, AND HAWKEYE IS A BADASS. WE CAN'T LET THEM DIE."
TAKE THIS. I'D GIVE YOU THE 'CHUCKS, BUT YOU'D HIT YOURSELF IN THE HEAD.
WHAT AM I SUPPOSED TO DO WITH THIS?
BE LIKE MARK DACASCOS IN BROTHERHOOD OF THE WOLF-- ONLY DON'T GET KILLED.
AND WHILE YOU'RE AT IT, SAY A PRAYER FOR THE BAD GUYS, 'CAUSE I'M ABOUT TO GO FULL-ON BILLY JACK ON THEM.
WU-TAH!
LET'S GO! IN THE SPIRIT OF CRAZY HORSE!
DIFFERENT TRIBE, FRANK.

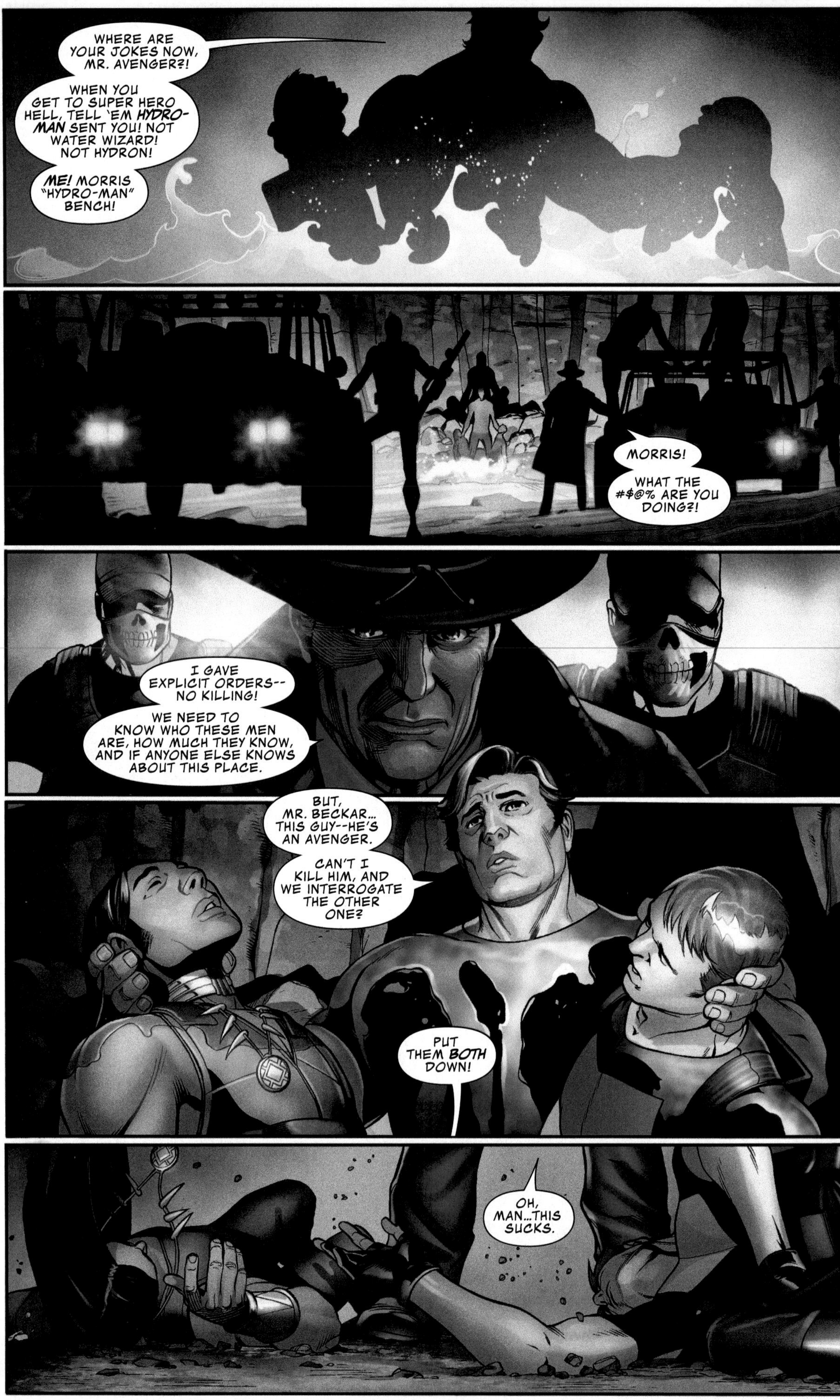
WHERE ARE YOUR JOKES NOW, MR. AVENGER?!
WHEN YOU GET TO SUPER HERO HELL, TELL 'EM HYDRO-MAN SENT YOU! NOT WATER WIZARD! NOT HYDRON!
ME! MORRIS "HYDRO-MAN" BENCH!
MORRIS!
WHAT THE #$@% ARE YOU DOING?!
I GAVE EXPLICIT ORDERS-- NO KILLING!
WE NEED TO KNOW WHO THESE MEN ARE, HOW MUCH THEY KNOW, AND IF ANYONE ELSE KNOWS ABOUT THIS PLACE.
BUT, MR. BECKAR... THIS GUY--HE'S AN AVENGER.
CAN'T I KILL HIM, AND WE INTERROGATE THE OTHER ONE?
PUT THEM BOTH DOWN!
OH, MAN...THIS SUCKS.

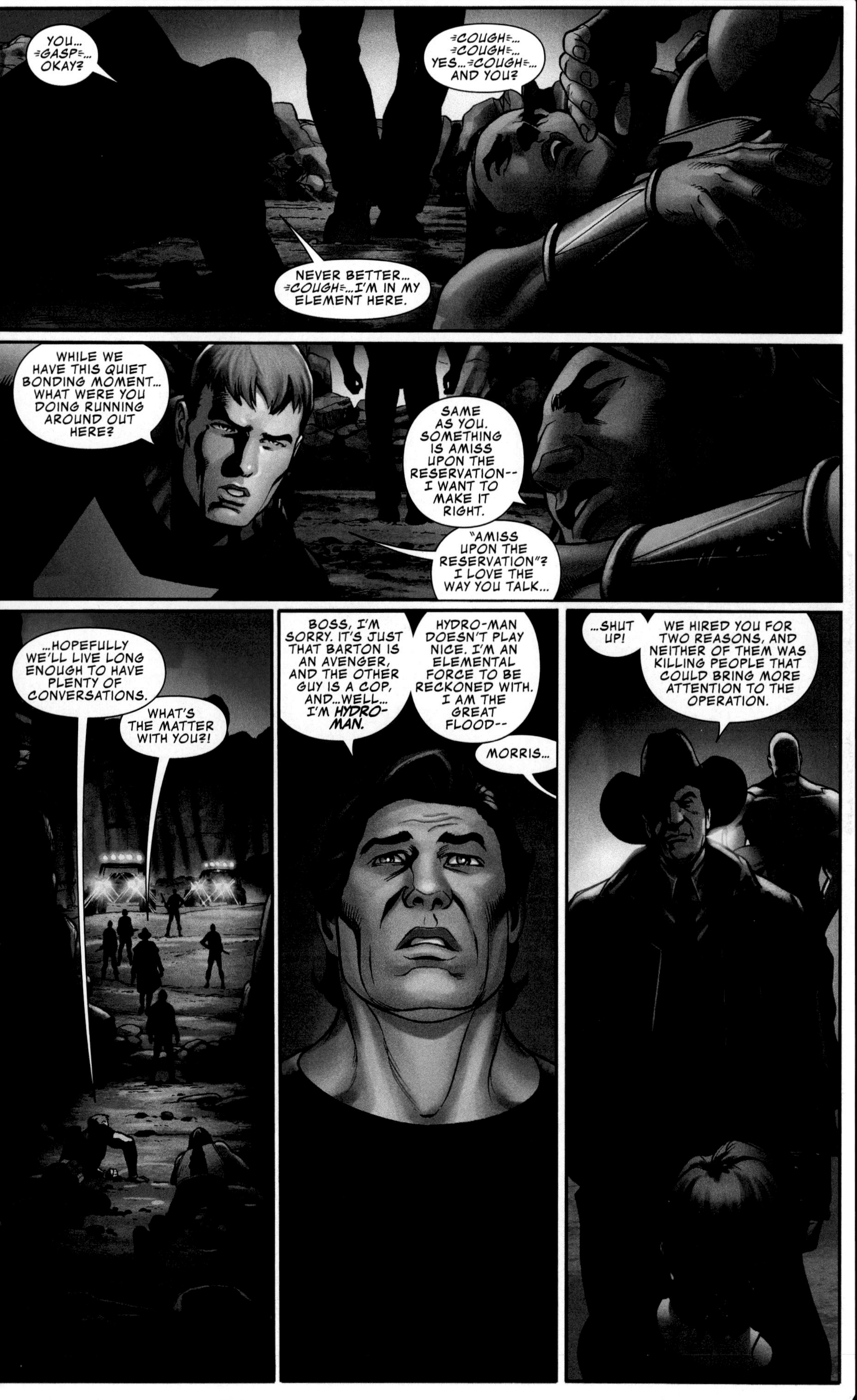
YOU... ≡GASP≡... OKAY?
≡COUGH≡... ≡COUGH≡... YES... ≡COUGH≡... AND YOU?
NEVER BETTER... ≡COUGH≡... I'M IN MY ELEMENT HERE.
WHILE WE HAVE THIS QUIET BONDING MOMENT... WHAT WERE YOU DOING RUNNING AROUND OUT HERE?
SAME AS YOU. SOMETHING IS AMISS UPON THE RESERVATION-- I WANT TO MAKE IT RIGHT.
"AMISS UPON THE RESERVATION"? I LOVE THE WAY YOU TALK...
...HOPEFULLY WE'LL LIVE LONG ENOUGH TO HAVE PLENTY OF CONVERSATIONS.
WHAT'S THE MATTER WITH YOU?!
BOSS, I'M SORRY. IT'S JUST THAT BARTON IS AN AVENGER, AND THE OTHER GUY IS A COP, AND...WELL... I'M HYDRO-MAN.
HYDRO-MAN DOESN'T PLAY NICE. I'M AN ELEMENTAL FORCE TO BE RECKONED WITH. I AM THE GREAT FLOOD--
MORRIS...
...SHUT UP!
WE HIRED YOU FOR TWO REASONS, AND NEITHER OF THEM WAS KILLING PEOPLE THAT COULD BRING MORE ATTENTION TO THE OPERATION.

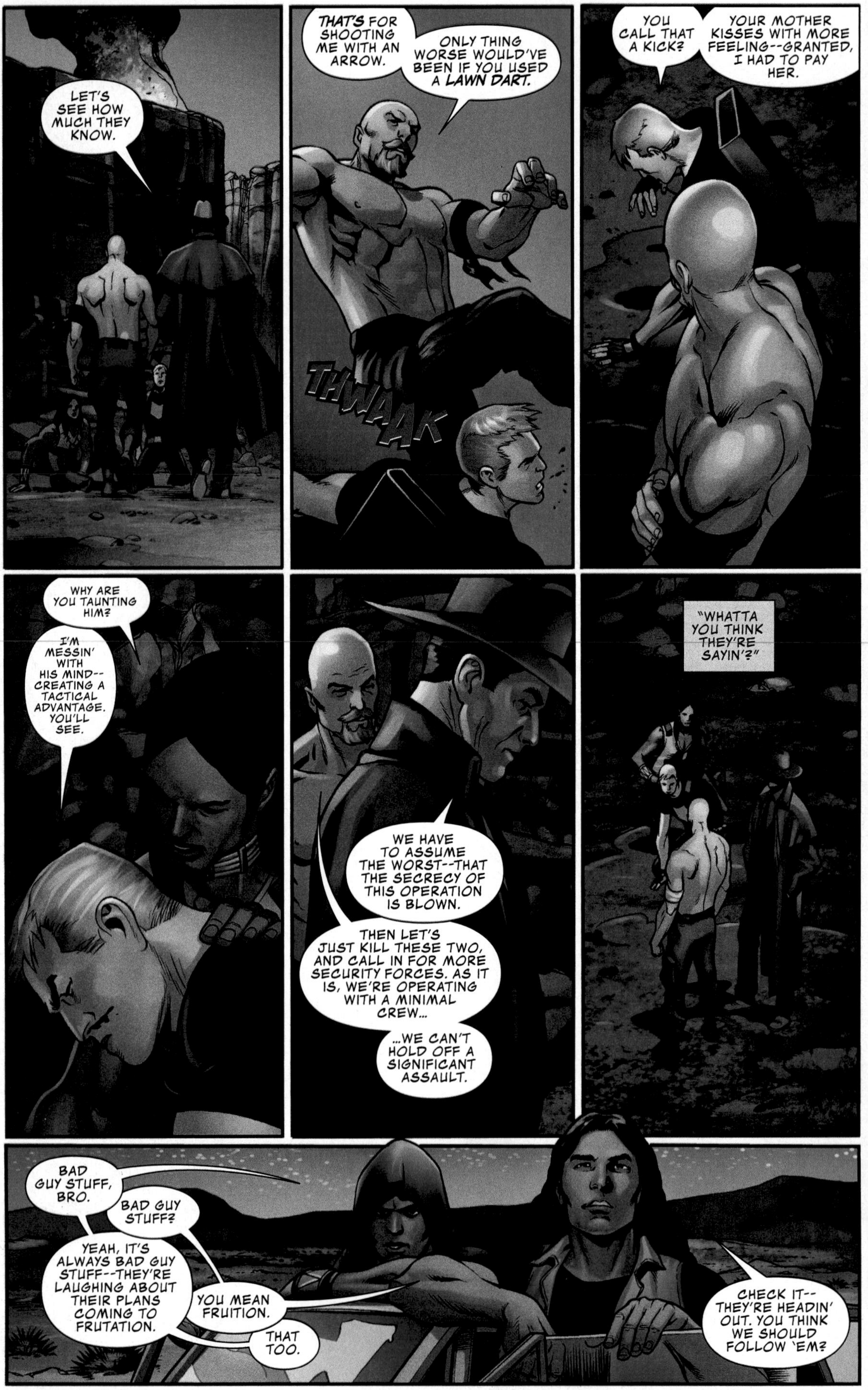
LET'S SEE HOW MUCH THEY KNOW.
THAT'S FOR SHOOTING ME WITH AN ARROW.
ONLY THING WORSE WOULD'VE BEEN IF YOU USED A LAWN DART.
THWAAAK
YOU CALL THAT A KICK?
YOUR MOTHER KISSES WITH MORE FEELING--GRANTED, I HAD TO PAY HER.
WHY ARE YOU TAUNTING HIM?
I'M MESSIN' WITH HIS MIND--CREATING A TACTICAL ADVANTAGE. YOU'LL SEE.
WE HAVE TO ASSUME THE WORST--THAT THE SECRECY OF THIS OPERATION IS BLOWN.
THEN LET'S JUST KILL THESE TWO, AND CALL IN FOR MORE SECURITY FORCES. AS IT IS, WE'RE OPERATING WITH A MINIMAL CREW...
...WE CAN'T HOLD OFF A SIGNIFICANT ASSAULT.
"WHATTA YOU THINK THEY'RE SAYIN'?"
BAD GUY STUFF, BRO.
BAD GUY STUFF?
YEAH, IT'S ALWAYS BAD GUY STUFF--THEY'RE LAUGHING ABOUT THEIR PLANS COMING TO FRUTATION.
YOU MEAN FRUITION.
THAT TOO.
CHECK IT--THEY'RE HEADIN' OUT. YOU THINK WE SHOULD FOLLOW 'EM?

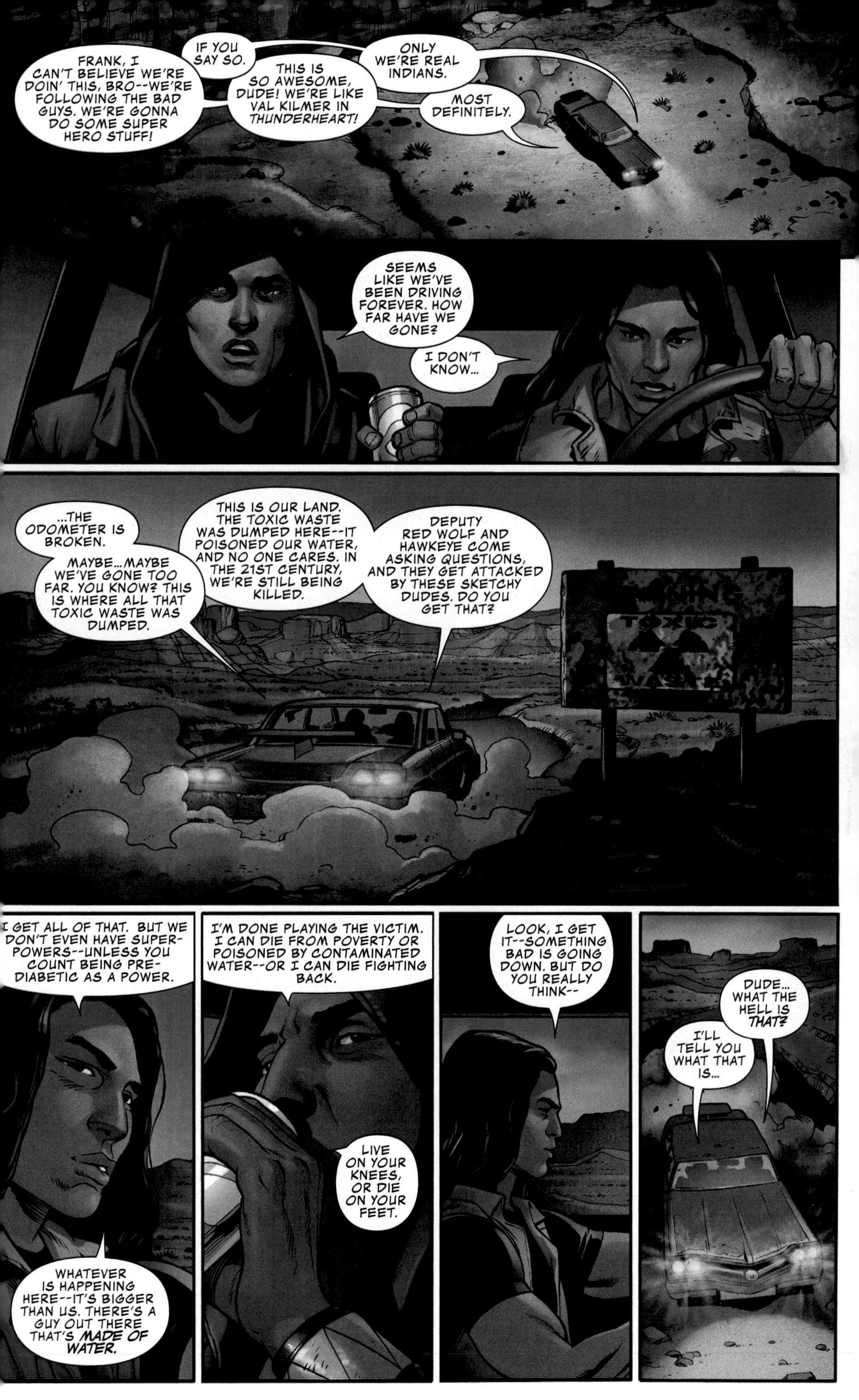
FRANK, I CAN'T BELIEVE WE'RE DOIN' THIS, BRO--WE'RE FOLLOWING THE BAD GUYS. WE'RE GONNA DO SOME SUPER HERO STUFF!
IF YOU SAY SO.
THIS IS SO AWESOME, DUDE! WE'RE LIKE VAL KILMER IN *THUNDERHEART!*
ONLY WE'RE REAL INDIANS.
MOST DEFINITELY.
SEEMS LIKE WE'VE BEEN DRIVING FOREVER. HOW FAR HAVE WE GONE?
I DON'T KNOW...
...THE ODOMETER IS BROKEN.
MAYBE...MAYBE WE'VE GONE TOO FAR. YOU KNOW? THIS IS WHERE ALL THAT TOXIC WASTE WAS DUMPED.
THIS IS OUR LAND. THE TOXIC WASTE WAS DUMPED HERE--IT POISONED OUR WATER, AND NO ONE CARES. IN THE 21ST CENTURY, WE'RE STILL BEING KILLED.
DEPUTY RED WOLF AND HAWKEYE COME ASKING QUESTIONS, AND THEY GET ATTACKED BY THESE SKETCHY DUDES. DO YOU GET THAT?
TOXIC
I GET ALL OF THAT. BUT WE DON'T EVEN HAVE SUPER-POWERS--UNLESS YOU COUNT BEING PRE-DIABETIC AS A POWER.
WHATEVER IS HAPPENING HERE--IT'S BIGGER THAN US. THERE'S A GUY OUT THERE THAT'S ***MADE OF WATER.***
I'M DONE PLAYING THE VICTIM. I CAN DIE FROM POVERTY OR POISONED BY CONTAMINATED WATER--OR I CAN DIE FIGHTING BACK.
LIVE ON YOUR KNEES, OR DIE ON YOUR FEET.
LOOK, I GET IT--SOMETHING BAD IS GOING DOWN. BUT DO YOU REALLY THINK--
DUDE... WHAT THE HELL IS ***THAT?***
I'LL TELL YOU WHAT THAT IS...

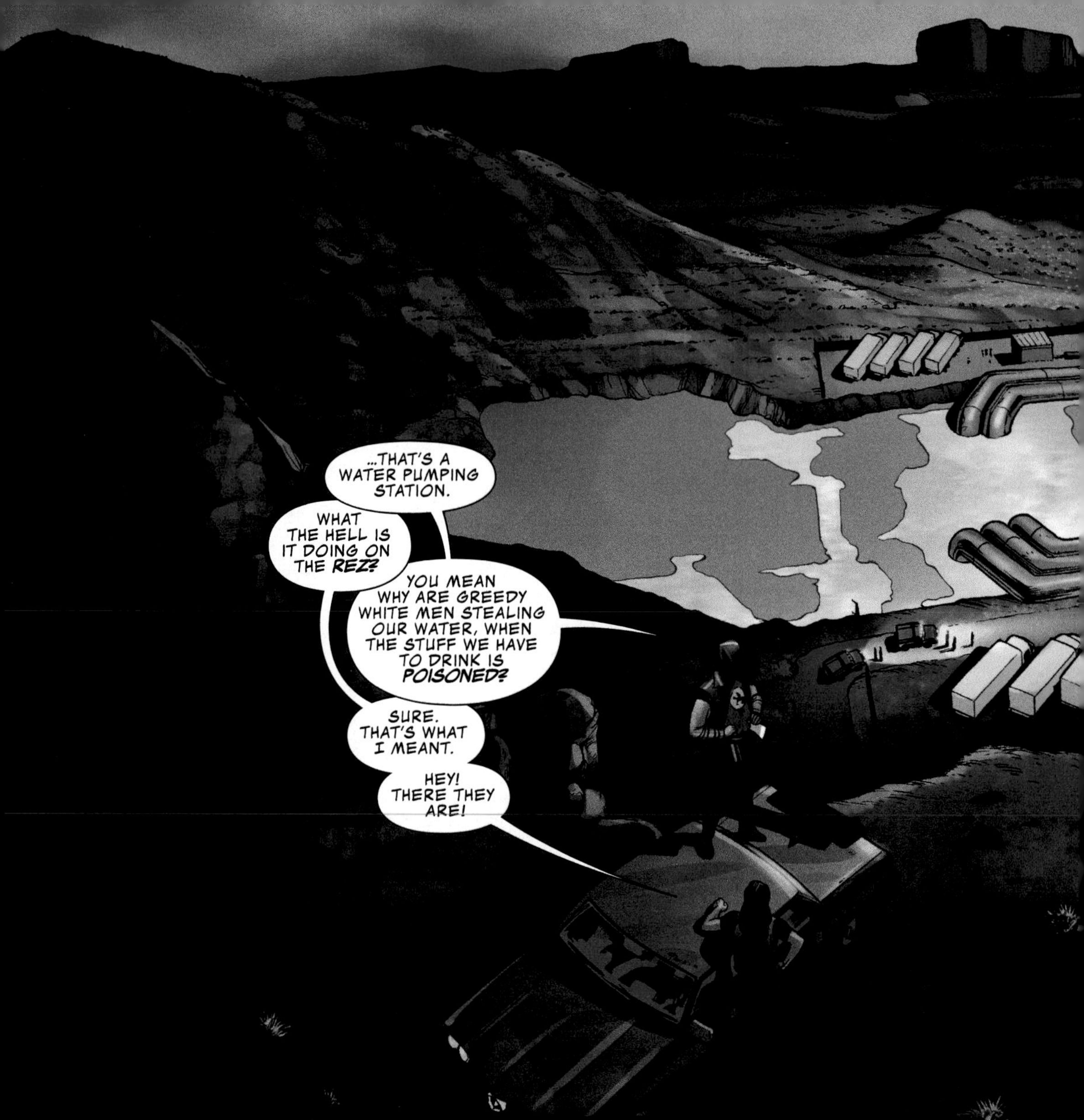
...THAT'S A WATER PUMPING STATION.
WHAT THE HELL IS IT DOING ON THE *REZ?*
YOU MEAN WHY ARE GREEDY WHITE MEN STEALING OUR WATER, WHEN THE STUFF WE HAVE TO DRINK IS *POISONED?*
SURE. THAT'S WHAT I MEANT.
HEY! THERE THEY ARE!

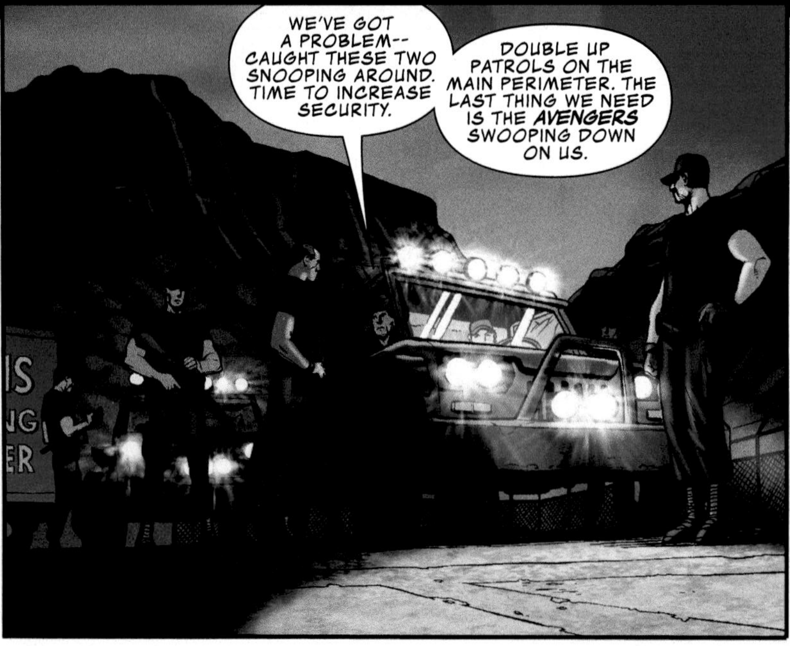
WE'VE GOT A PROBLEM-- CAUGHT THESE TWO SNOOPING AROUND. TIME TO INCREASE SECURITY.
DOUBLE UP PATROLS ON THE MAIN PERIMETER. THE LAST THING WE NEED IS THE *AVENGERS* SWOOPING DOWN ON US.

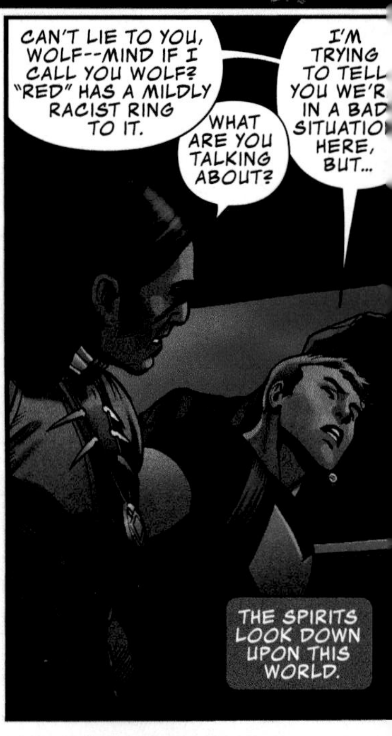
I'M TRYING TO TELL YOU WE'R IN A BAD SITUATIO HERE, BUT...
CAN'T LIE TO YOU, WOLF--MIND IF I CALL YOU WOLF? "RED" HAS A MILDLY RACIST RING TO IT.
WHAT ARE YOU TALKING ABOUT?
THE SPIRITS LOOK DOWN UPON THIS WORLD.

HEY!

QUIT YACKIN'!

THEY GIVE LIFE TO EVERYTHING FOR A PURPOSE.

THEY GAVE LIFE TO ME FOR A PURPOSE.

ARGH!

OOOF!

KERSLAM

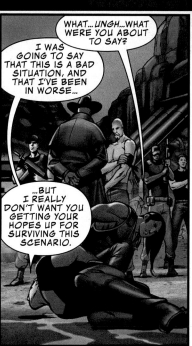

WHAT... UNGH... WHAT WERE YOU ABOUT TO SAY?

I WAS GOING TO SAY THAT THIS IS A BAD SITUATION, AND THAT I'VE BEEN IN WORSE...

...BUT I REALLY DON'T WANT YOU GETTING YOUR HOPES UP FOR SURVIVING THIS SCENARIO.

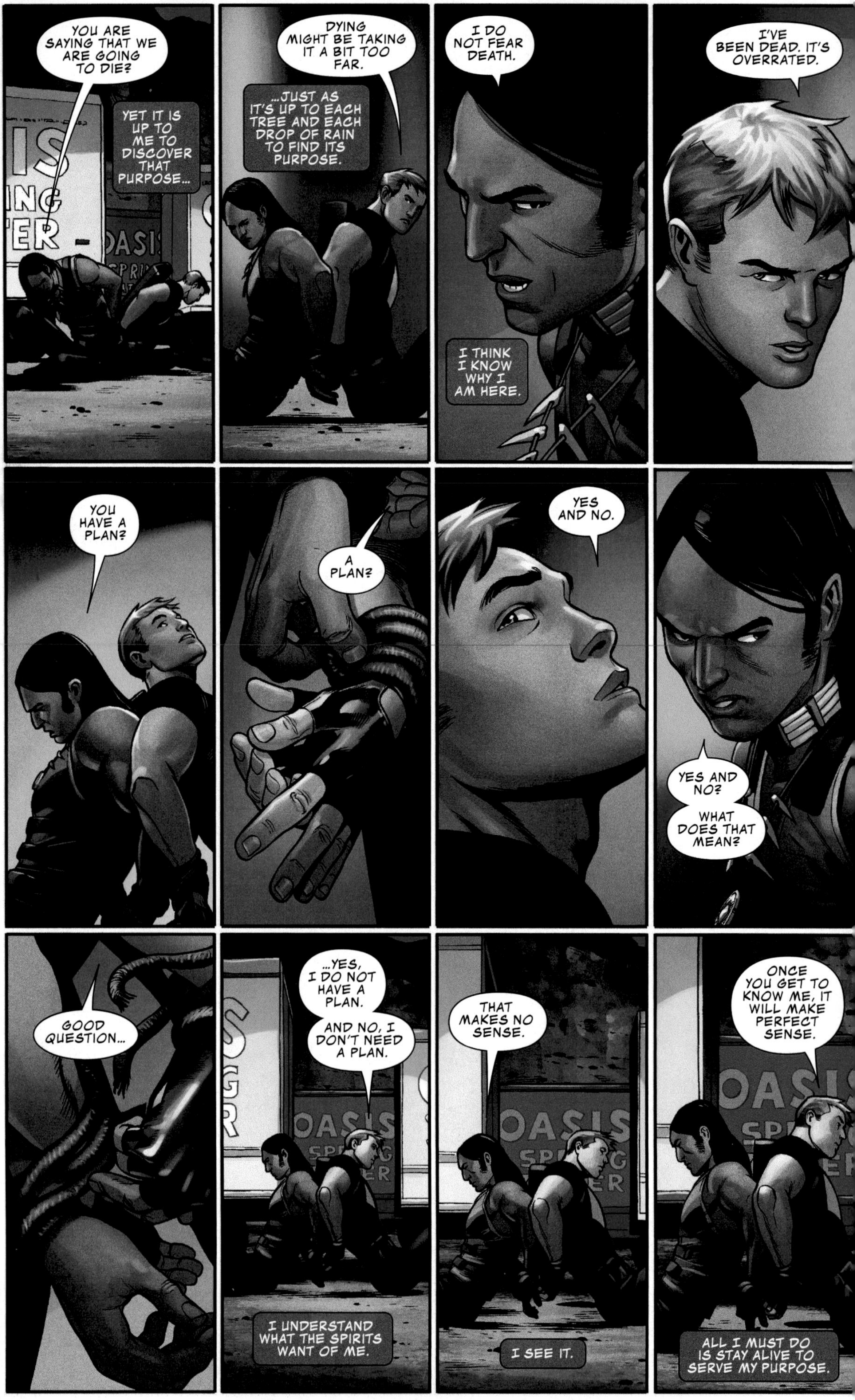
YOU ARE SAYING THAT WE ARE GOING TO DIE?
YET IT IS UP TO ME TO DISCOVER THAT PURPOSE...
OASIS
DYING MIGHT BE TAKING IT A BIT TOO FAR.
...JUST AS IT'S UP TO EACH TREE AND EACH DROP OF RAIN TO FIND ITS PURPOSE.
I DO NOT FEAR DEATH.
I THINK I KNOW WHY I AM HERE.
I'VE BEEN DEAD. IT'S OVERRATED.
YOU HAVE A PLAN?
A PLAN?
YES AND NO.
YES AND NO?
WHAT DOES THAT MEAN?
GOOD QUESTION...
...YES, I DO NOT HAVE A PLAN.
AND NO, I DON'T NEED A PLAN.
OASIS
I UNDERSTAND WHAT THE SPIRITS WANT OF ME.
THAT MAKES NO SENSE.
OASIS
I SEE IT.
ONCE YOU GET TO KNOW ME, IT WILL MAKE PERFECT SENSE.
ALL I MUST DO IS STAY ALIVE TO SERVE MY PURPOSE.

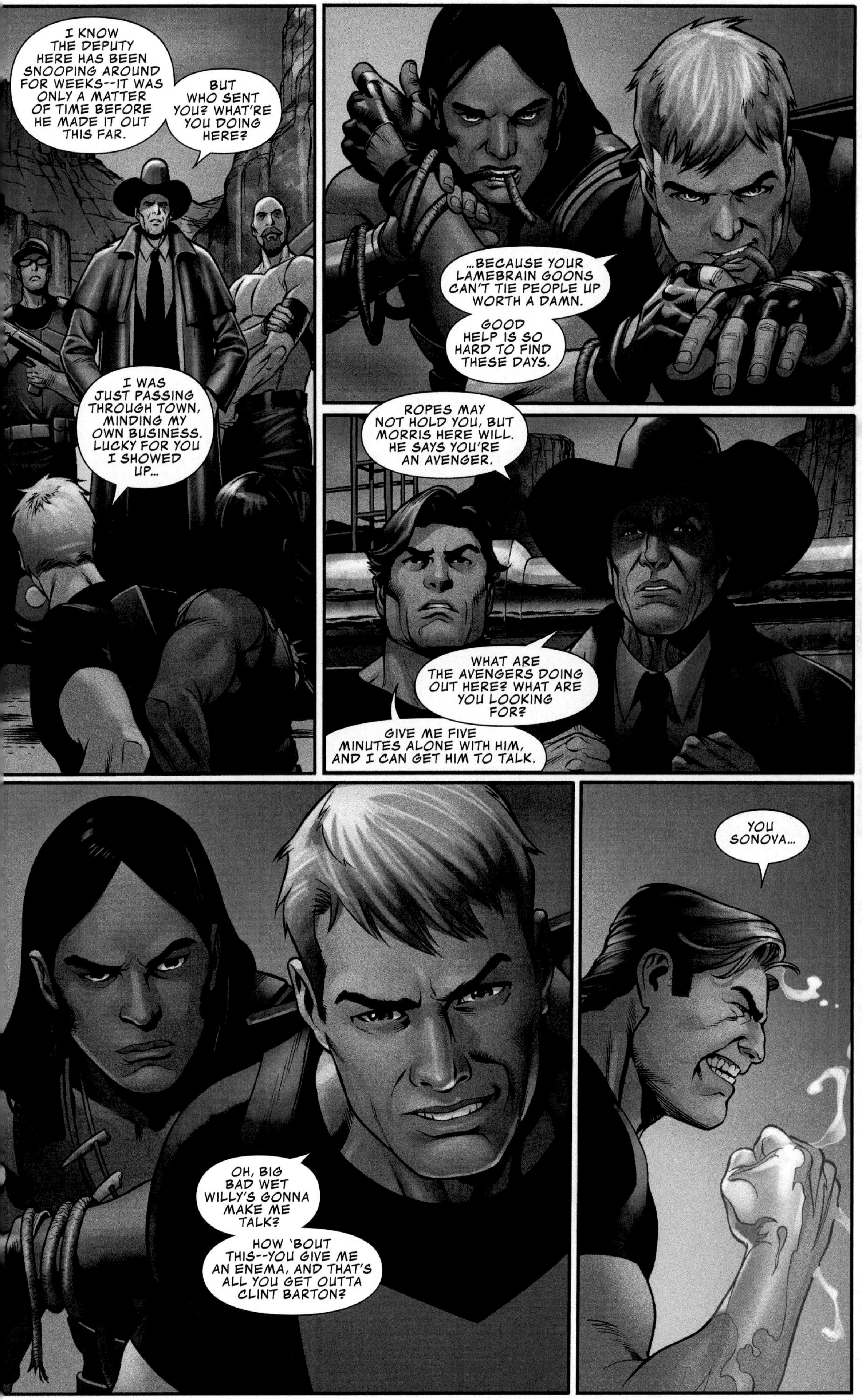
I KNOW THE DEPUTY HERE HAS BEEN SNOOPING AROUND FOR WEEKS--IT WAS ONLY A MATTER OF TIME BEFORE HE MADE IT OUT THIS FAR.
BUT WHO SENT YOU? WHAT'RE YOU DOING HERE?
I WAS JUST PASSING THROUGH TOWN, MINDING MY OWN BUSINESS. LUCKY FOR YOU I SHOWED UP...
...BECAUSE YOUR LAMEBRAIN GOONS CAN'T TIE PEOPLE UP WORTH A DAMN.
GOOD HELP IS SO HARD TO FIND THESE DAYS.
ROPES MAY NOT HOLD YOU, BUT MORRIS HERE WILL. HE SAYS YOU'RE AN AVENGER.
WHAT ARE THE AVENGERS DOING OUT HERE? WHAT ARE YOU LOOKING FOR?
GIVE ME FIVE MINUTES ALONE WITH HIM, AND I CAN GET HIM TO TALK.
OH, BIG BAD WET WILLY'S GONNA MAKE ME TALK?
HOW 'BOUT THIS--YOU GIVE ME AN ENEMA, AND THAT'S ALL YOU GET OUTTA CLINT BARTON?
YOU SONOVA...

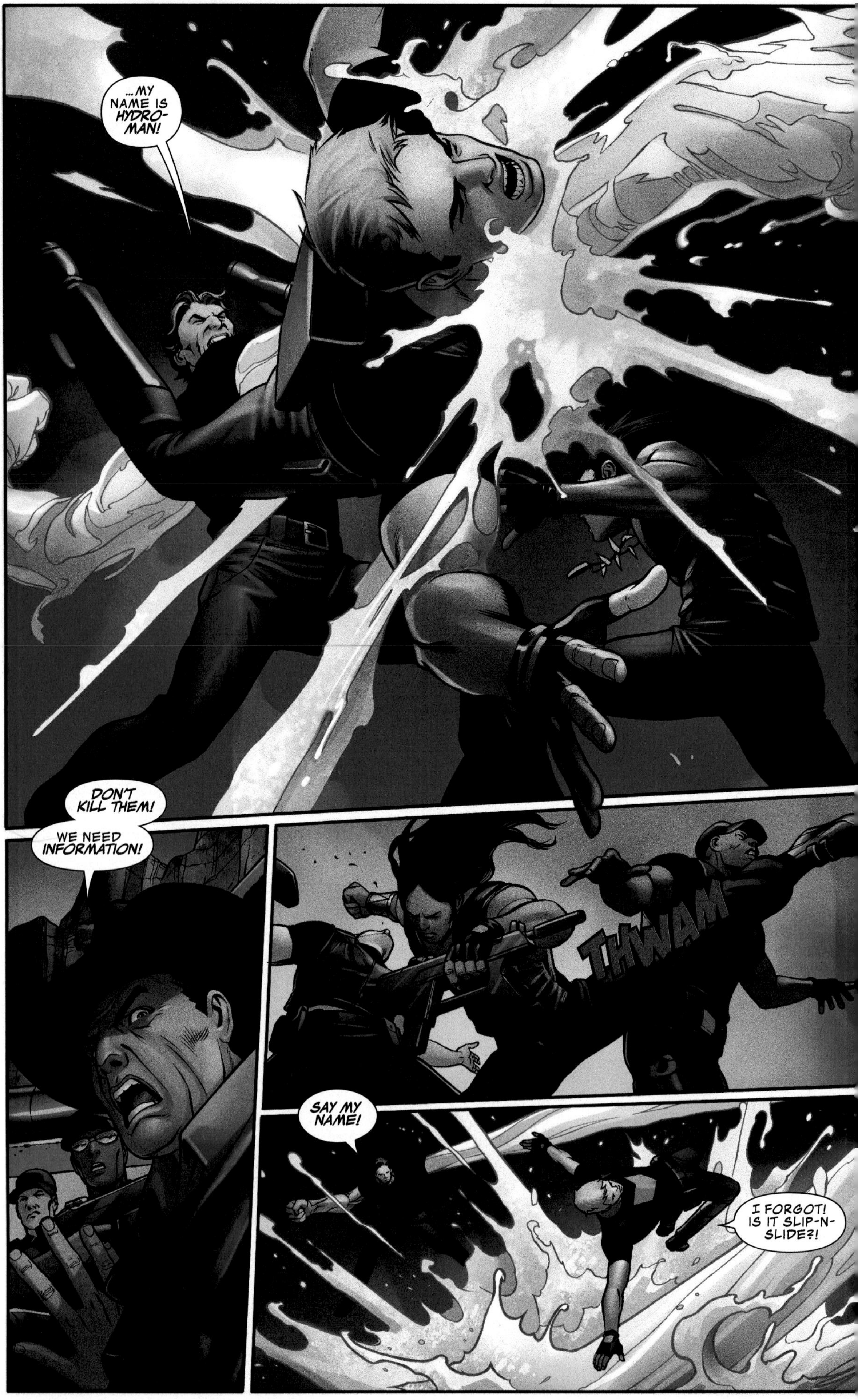
...MY NAME IS HYDRO-MAN!
DON'T KILL THEM!
WE NEED INFORMATION!
THWAM
SAY MY NAME!
I FORGOT! IS IT SLIP-N-SLIDE?!

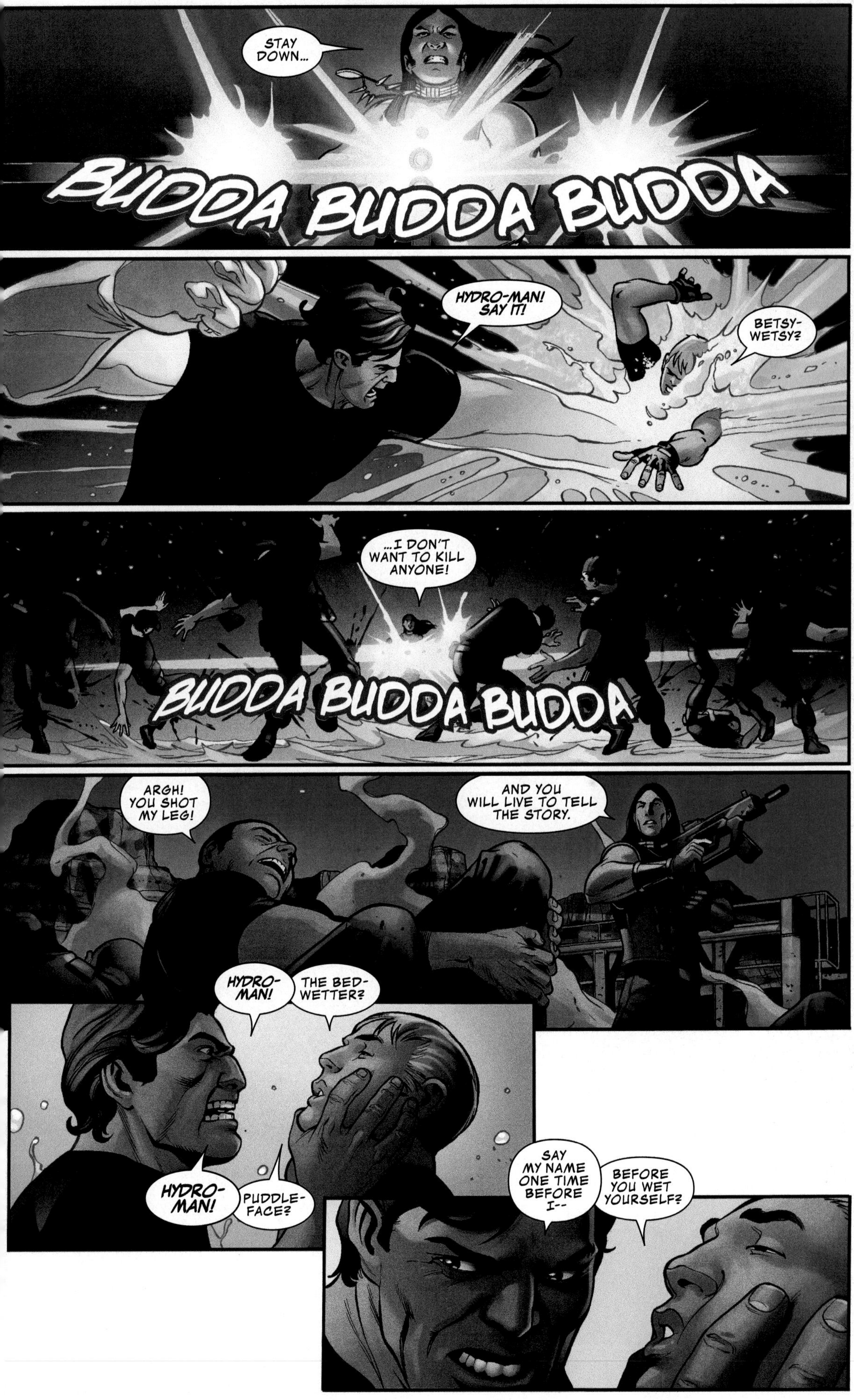
STAY DOWN...
BUDDA BUDDA BUDDA
HYDRO-MAN! SAY IT!
BETSY-WETSY?
...I DON'T WANT TO KILL ANYONE!
BUDDA BUDDA BUDDA
ARGH! YOU SHOT MY LEG!
AND YOU WILL LIVE TO TELL THE STORY.
HYDRO-MAN!
THE BED-WETTER?
HYDRO-MAN!
PUDDLE-FACE?
SAY MY NAME ONE TIME BEFORE I--
BEFORE YOU WET YOURSELF?

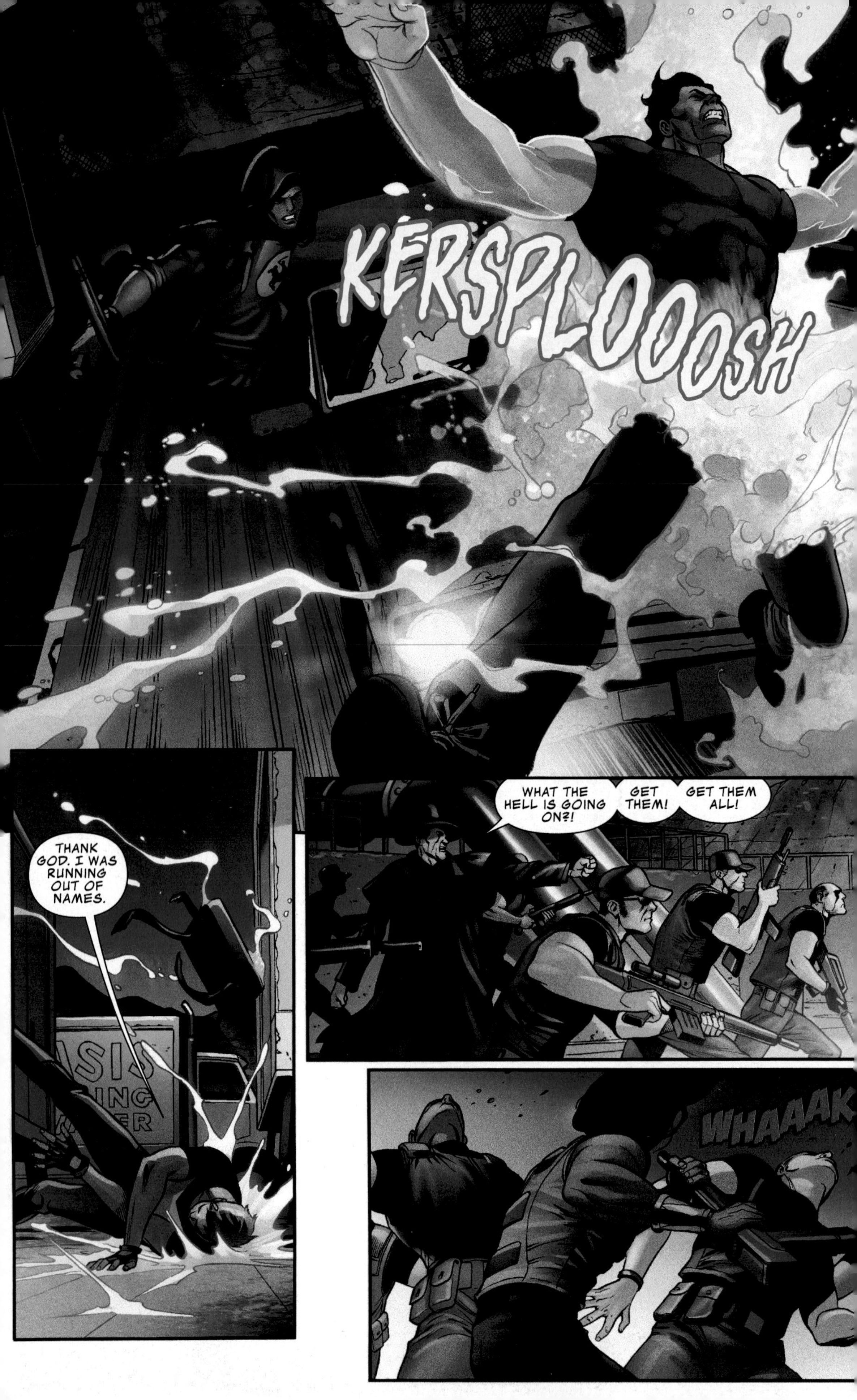
KERSPLOOOSH
THANK GOD. I WAS RUNNING OUT OF NAMES.
WHAT THE HELL IS GOING ON?!
GET THEM!
GET THEM ALL!
WHAAAK

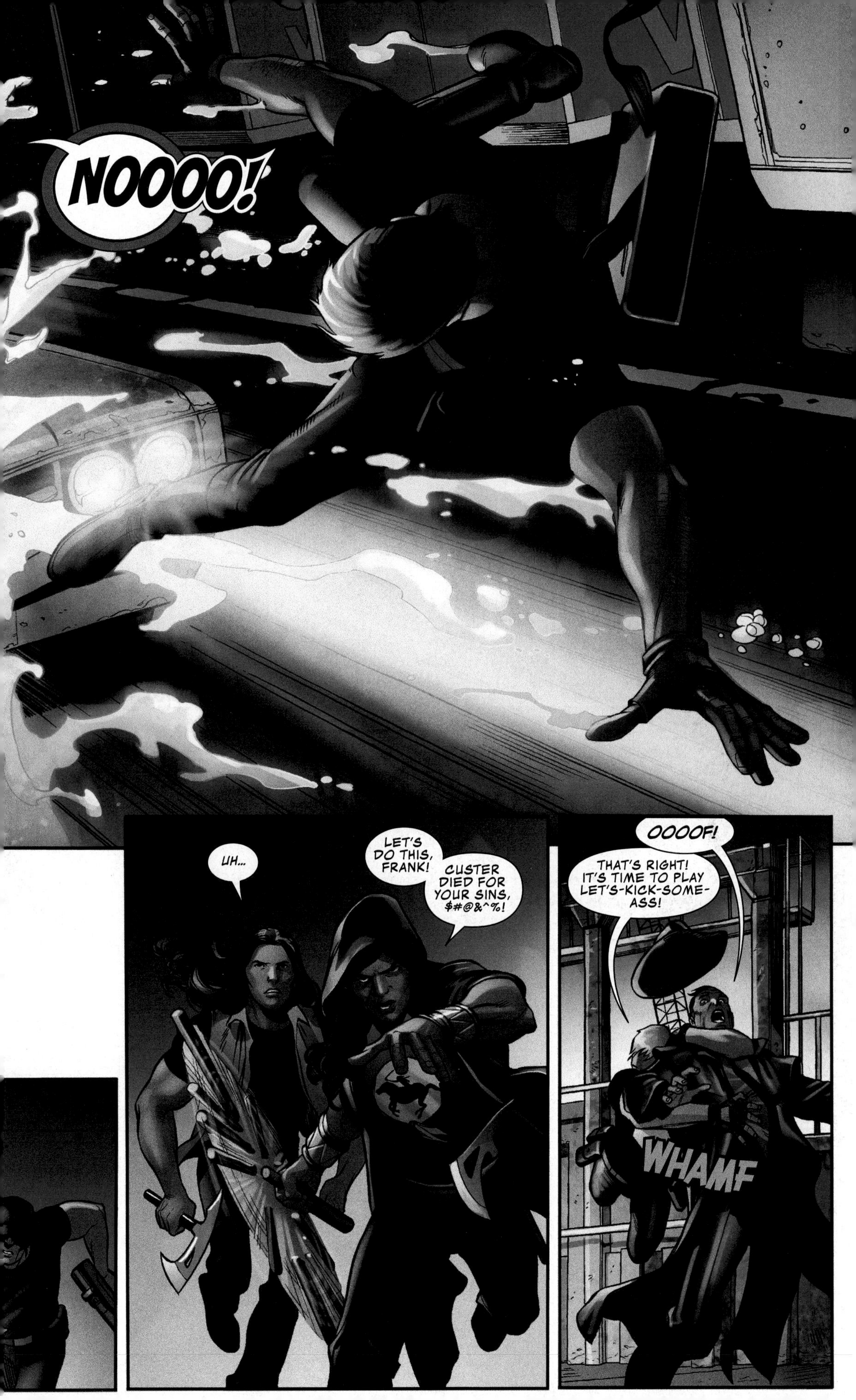

NOOOO!
UH...
LET'S DO THIS, FRANK!
CUSTER DIED FOR YOUR SINS, $#@&^%!
OOOOF!
THAT'S RIGHT! IT'S TIME TO PLAY LET'S-KICK-SOME-ASS!
WHAMF

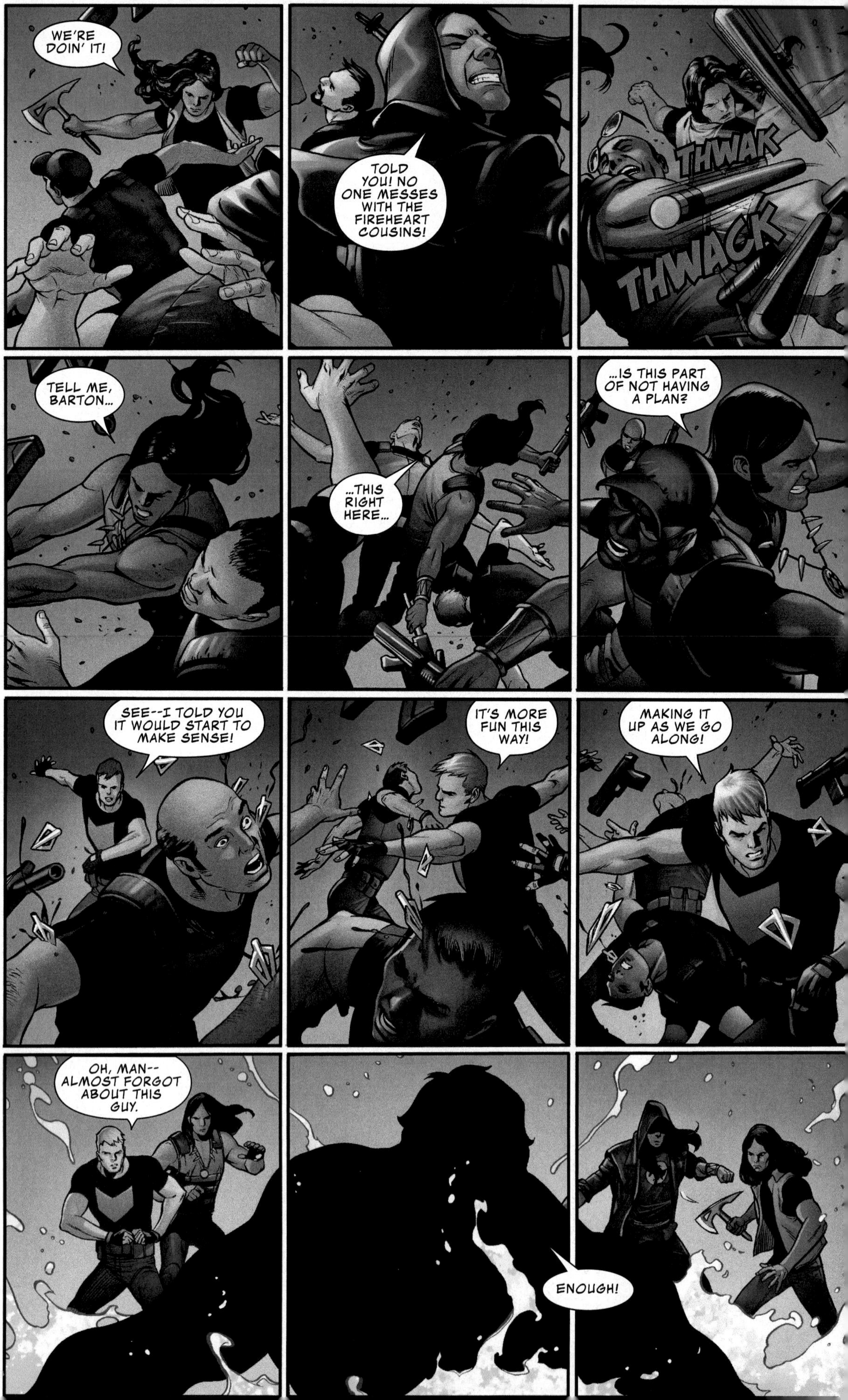
WE'RE DOIN' IT!
TOLD YOU! NO ONE MESSES WITH THE FIREHEART COUSINS!
THWAK
THWACK
TELL ME, BARTON...
...THIS RIGHT HERE...
...IS THIS PART OF NOT HAVING A PLAN?
SEE--I TOLD YOU IT WOULD START TO MAKE SENSE!
IT'S MORE FUN THIS WAY!
MAKING IT UP AS WE GO ALONG!
OH, MAN--ALMOST FORGOT ABOUT THIS GUY.
ENOUGH!

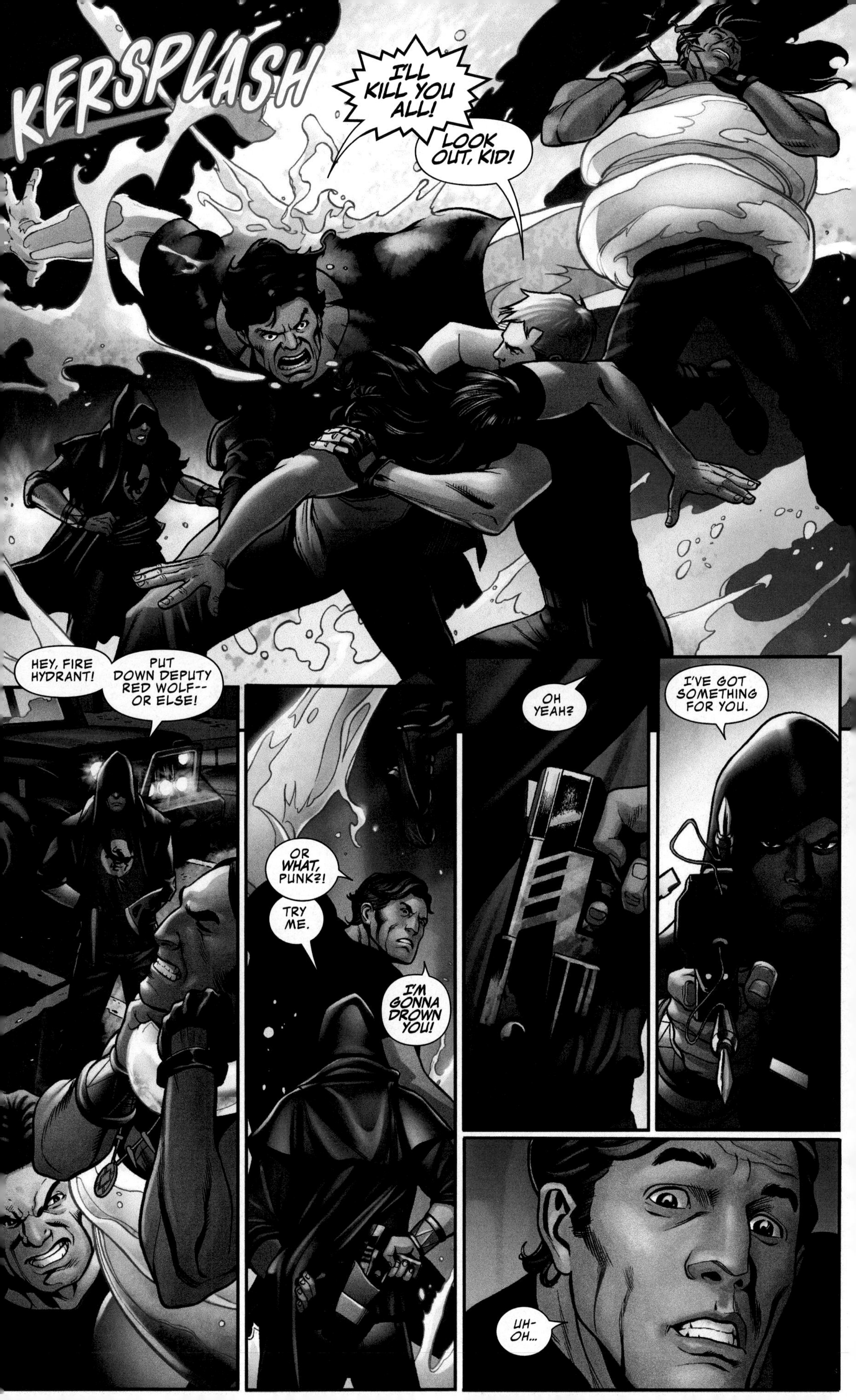
KERSPLASH
I'LL KILL YOU ALL!
LOOK OUT, KID!
HEY, FIRE HYDRANT!
PUT DOWN DEPUTY RED WOLF-- OR ELSE!
OR WHAT, PUNK?!
TRY ME.
I'M GONNA DROWN YOU!
OH YEAH?
I'VE GOT SOMETHING FOR YOU.
UH-OH...

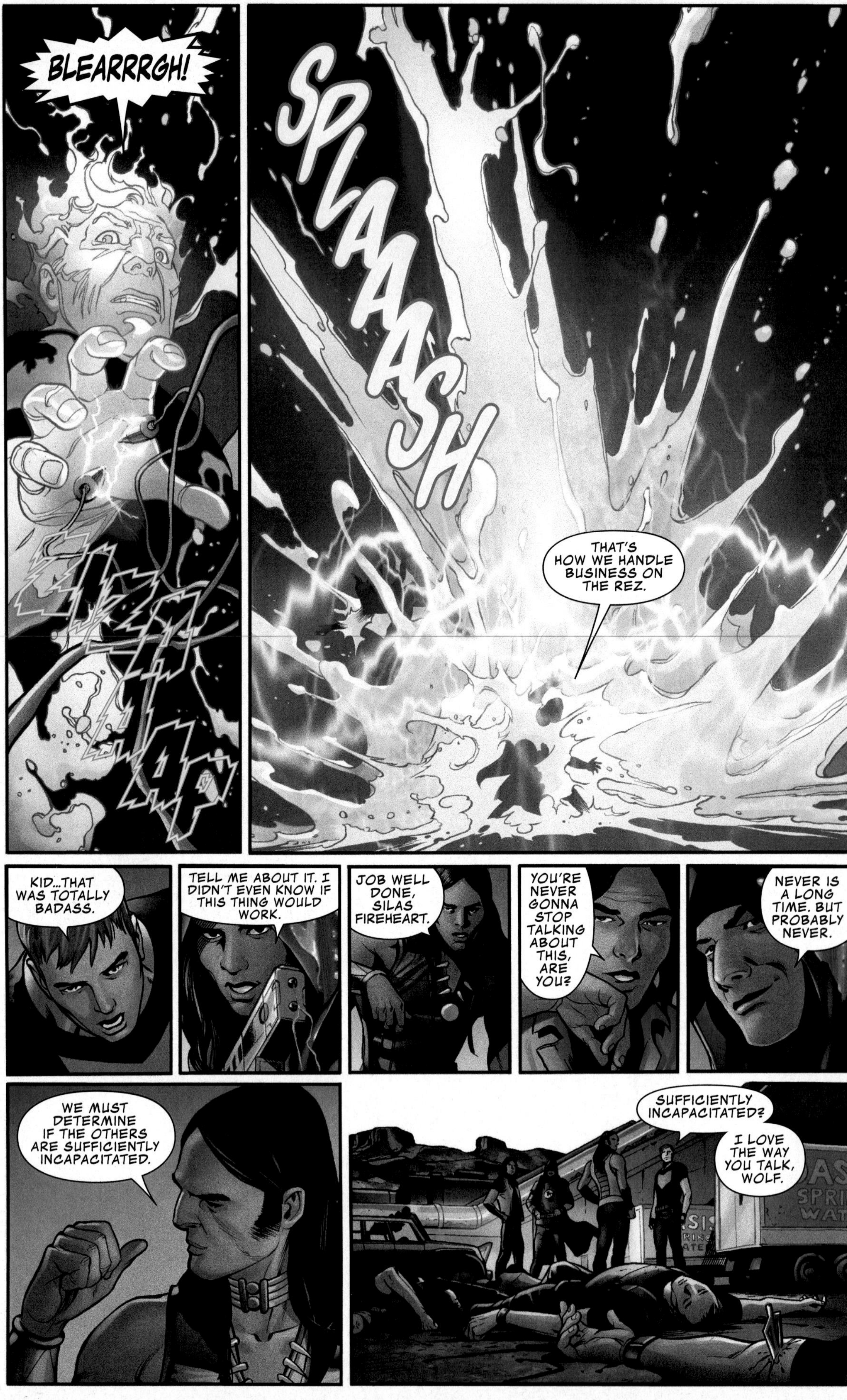
BLEARRRGH!
ZZAP
SPLAAASH
THAT'S HOW WE HANDLE BUSINESS ON THE REZ.
KID...THAT WAS TOTALLY BADASS.
TELL ME ABOUT IT. I DIDN'T EVEN KNOW IF THIS THING WOULD WORK.
JOB WELL DONE, SILAS FIREHEART.
YOU'RE NEVER GONNA STOP TALKING ABOUT THIS, ARE YOU?
NEVER IS A LONG TIME. BUT PROBABLY NEVER.
WE MUST DETERMINE IF THE OTHERS ARE SUFFICIENTLY INCAPACITATED.
SUFFICIENTLY INCAPACITATED?
I LOVE THE WAY YOU TALK, WOLF.

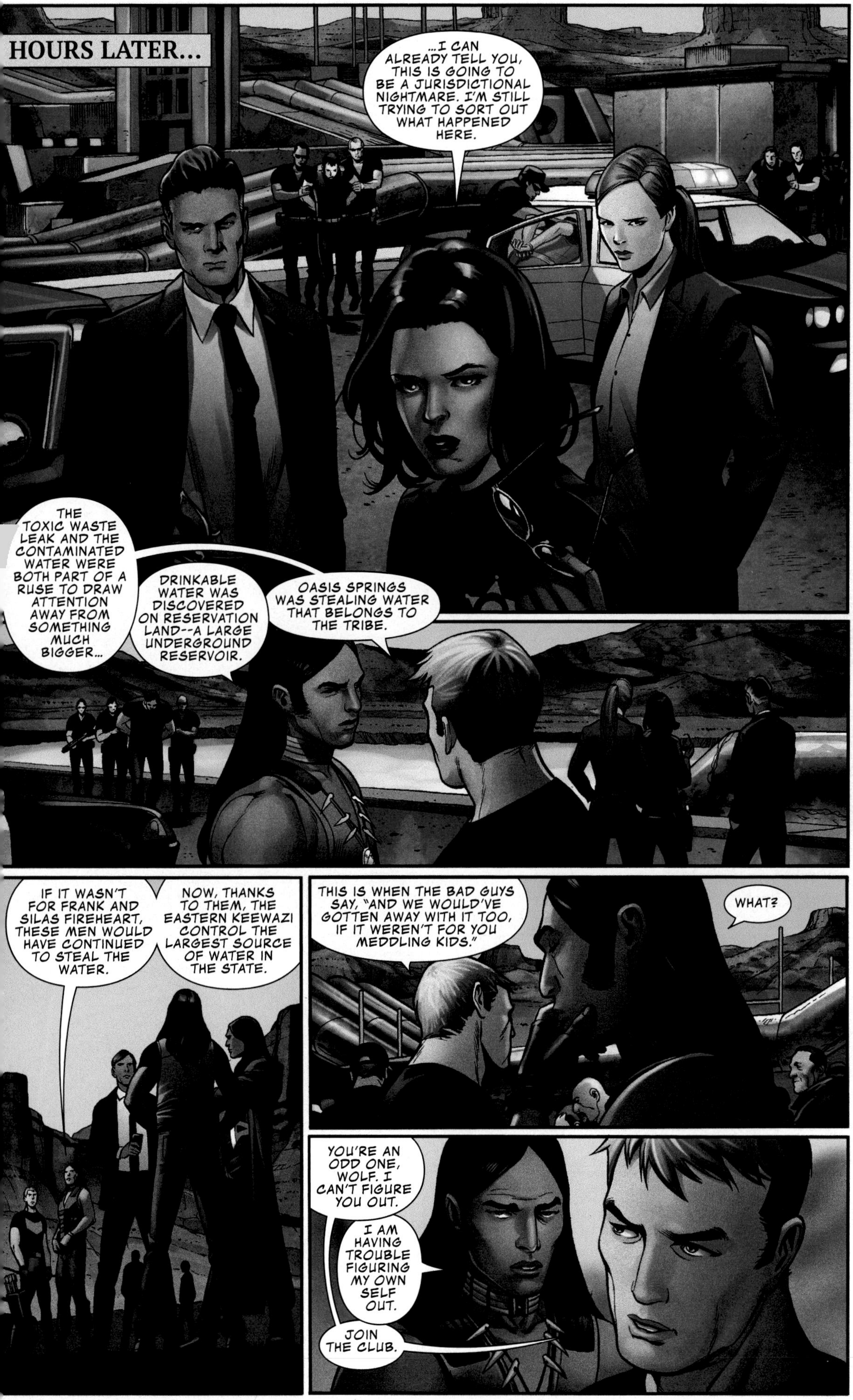
HOURS LATER...
...I CAN ALREADY TELL YOU, THIS IS GOING TO BE A JURISDICTIONAL NIGHTMARE. I'M STILL TRYING TO SORT OUT WHAT HAPPENED HERE.
THE TOXIC WASTE LEAK AND THE CONTAMINATED WATER WERE BOTH PART OF A RUSE TO DRAW ATTENTION AWAY FROM SOMETHING MUCH BIGGER...
DRINKABLE WATER WAS DISCOVERED ON RESERVATION LAND--A LARGE UNDERGROUND RESERVOIR.
OASIS SPRINGS WAS STEALING WATER THAT BELONGS TO THE TRIBE.
IF IT WASN'T FOR FRANK AND SILAS FIREHEART, THESE MEN WOULD HAVE CONTINUED TO STEAL THE WATER.
NOW, THANKS TO THEM, THE EASTERN KEEWAZI CONTROL THE LARGEST SOURCE OF WATER IN THE STATE.
THIS IS WHEN THE BAD GUYS SAY, "AND WE WOULD'VE GOTTEN AWAY WITH IT TOO, IF IT WEREN'T FOR YOU MEDDLING KIDS."
WHAT?
YOU'RE AN ODD ONE, WOLF. I CAN'T FIGURE YOU OUT.
I AM HAVING TROUBLE FIGURING MY OWN SELF OUT.
JOIN THE CLUB.

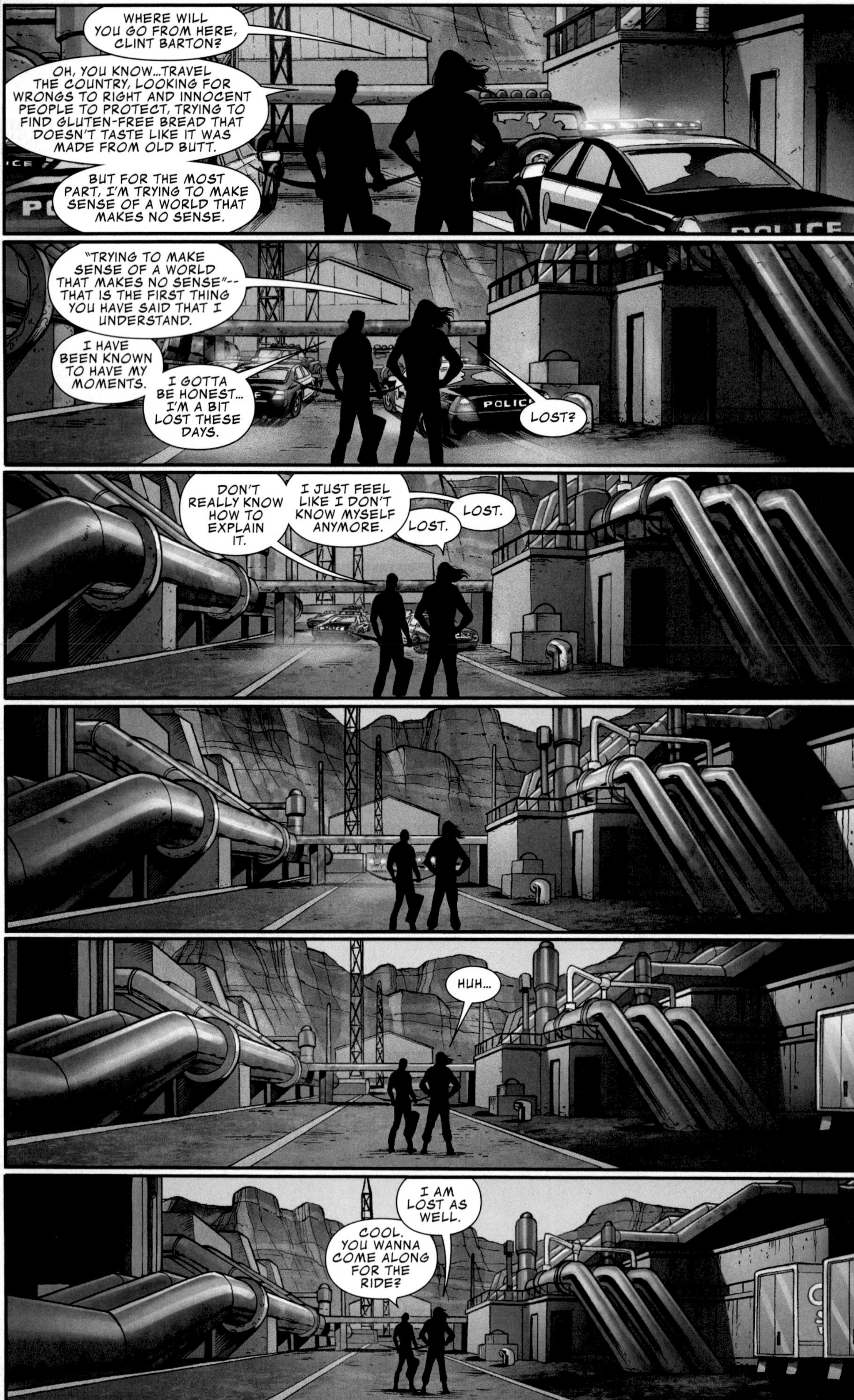

WHERE WILL YOU GO FROM HERE, CLINT BARTON?
OH, YOU KNOW...TRAVEL THE COUNTRY, LOOKING FOR WRONGS TO RIGHT AND INNOCENT PEOPLE TO PROTECT, TRYING TO FIND GLUTEN-FREE BREAD THAT DOESN'T TASTE LIKE IT WAS MADE FROM OLD BUTT.
BUT FOR THE MOST PART, I'M TRYING TO MAKE SENSE OF A WORLD THAT MAKES NO SENSE.
POLICE
"TRYING TO MAKE SENSE OF A WORLD THAT MAKES NO SENSE"--THAT IS THE FIRST THING YOU HAVE SAID THAT I UNDERSTAND.
I HAVE BEEN KNOWN TO HAVE MY MOMENTS.
I GOTTA BE HONEST... I'M A BIT LOST THESE DAYS.
LOST?
POLICE
DON'T REALLY KNOW HOW TO EXPLAIN IT.
I JUST FEEL LIKE I DON'T KNOW MYSELF ANYMORE.
LOST.
LOST.
HUH...
I AM LOST AS WELL.
COOL. YOU WANNA COME ALONG FOR THE RIDE?

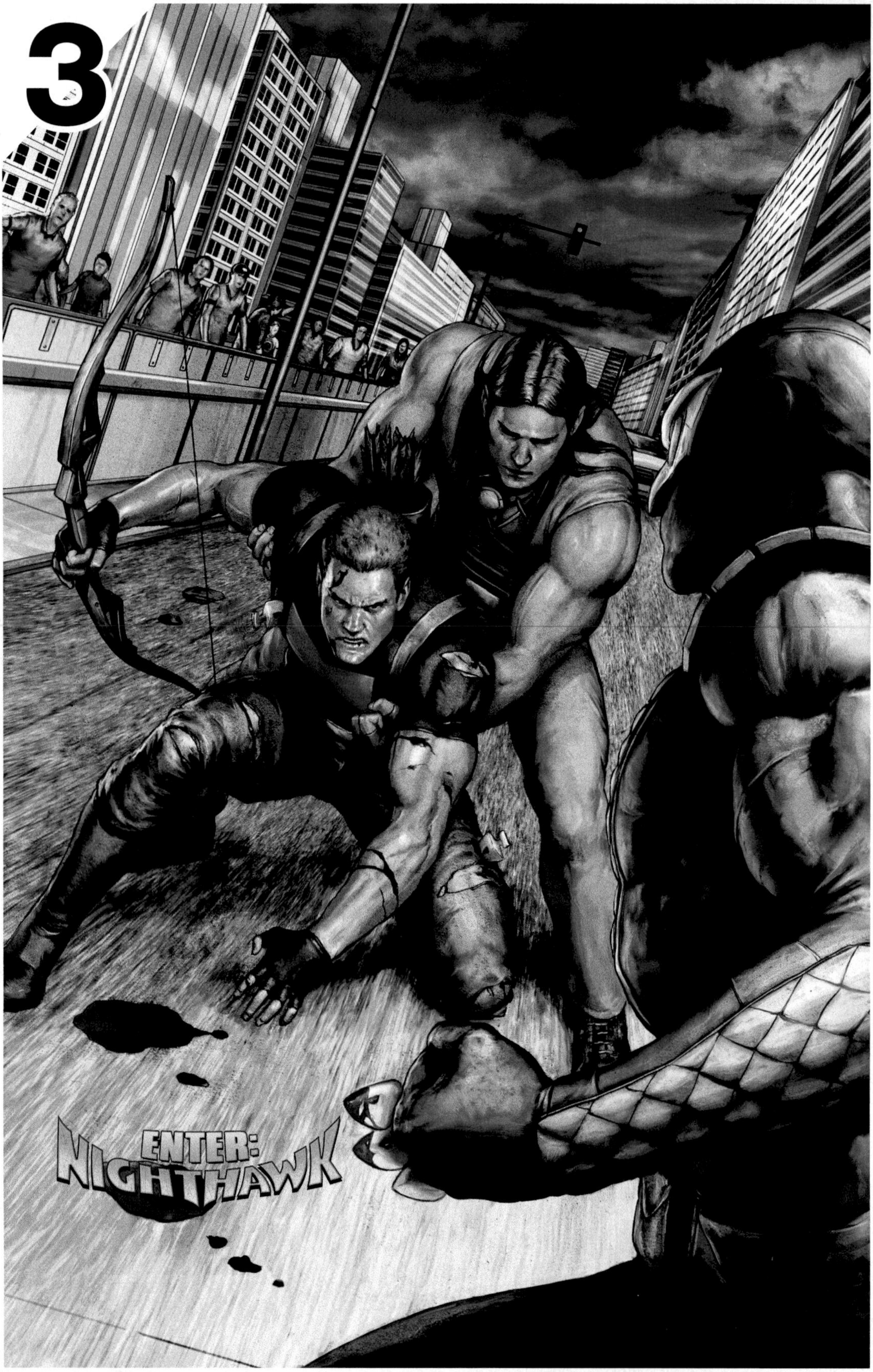
3
ENTER:
NIGHTHAWK

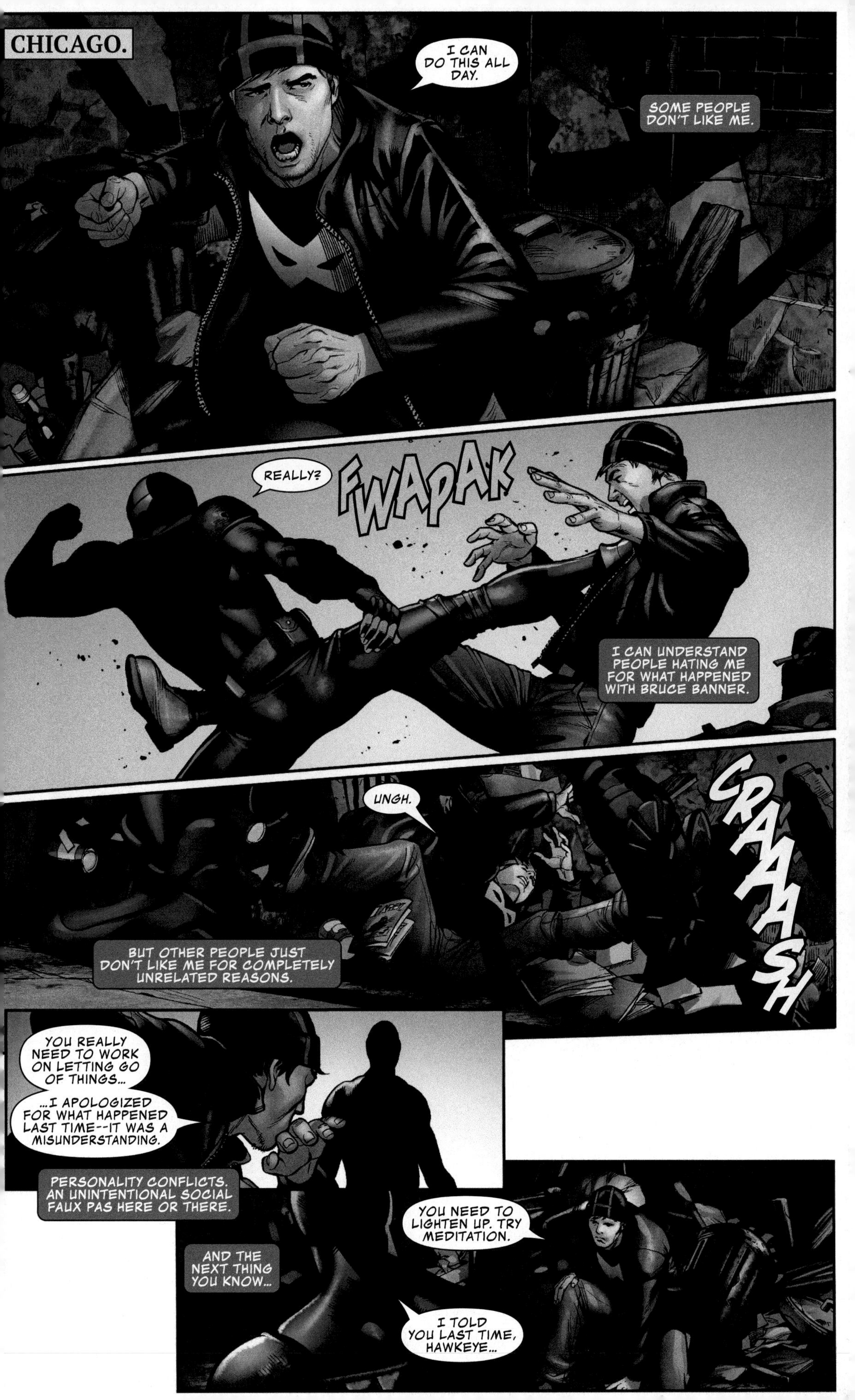
CHICAGO.
I CAN DO THIS ALL DAY.
SOME PEOPLE DON'T LIKE ME.
REALLY?
FWAPAK
I CAN UNDERSTAND PEOPLE HATING ME FOR WHAT HAPPENED WITH BRUCE BANNER.
UNGH.
CRAAASH
BUT OTHER PEOPLE JUST DON'T LIKE ME FOR COMPLETELY UNRELATED REASONS.
YOU REALLY NEED TO WORK ON LETTING GO OF THINGS...
...I APOLOGIZED FOR WHAT HAPPENED LAST TIME--IT WAS A MISUNDERSTANDING.
PERSONALITY CONFLICTS. AN UNINTENTIONAL SOCIAL FAUX PAS HERE OR THERE.
YOU NEED TO LIGHTEN UP. TRY MEDITATION.
AND THE NEXT THING YOU KNOW...
I TOLD YOU LAST TIME, HAWKEYE...

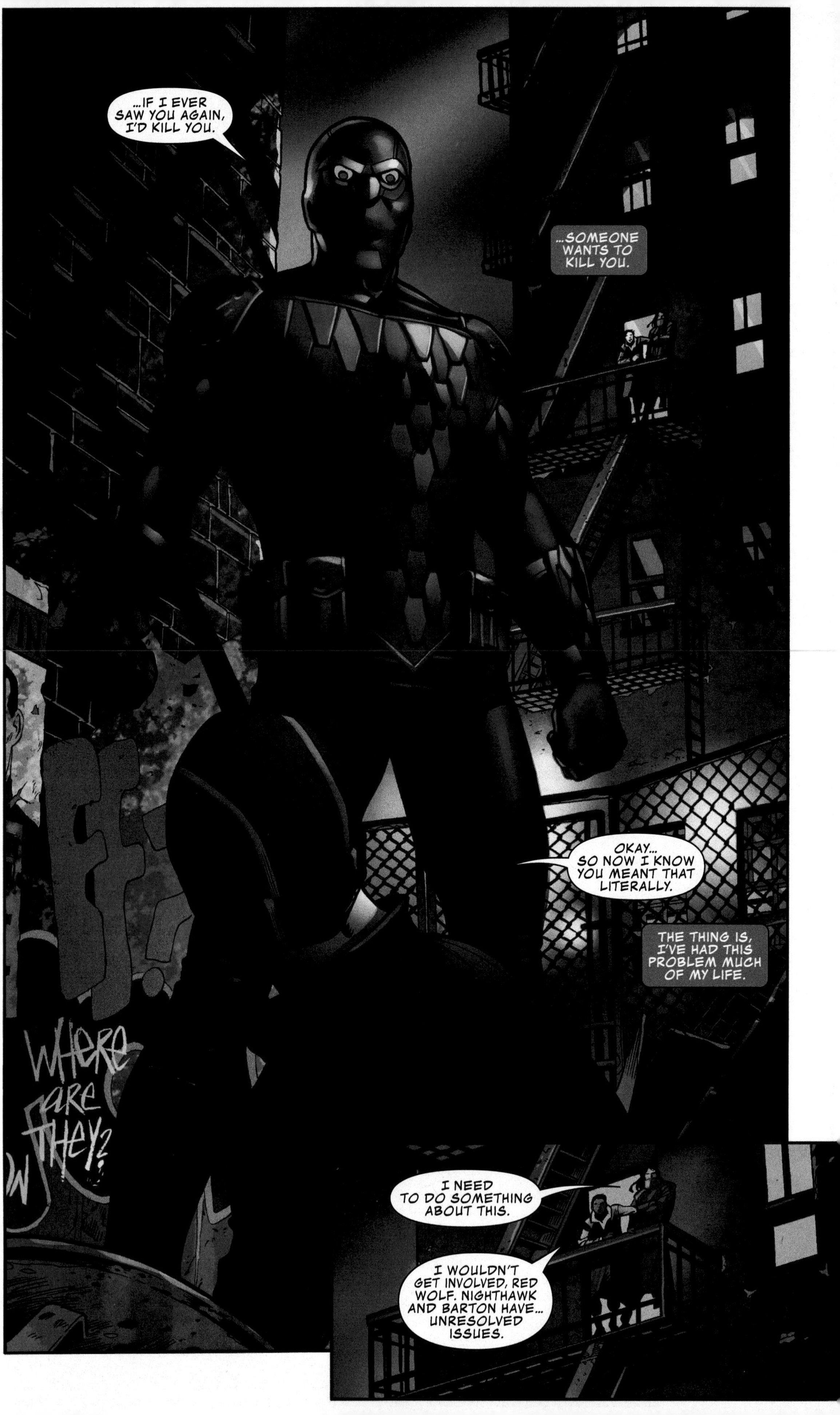
...IF I EVER SAW YOU AGAIN, I'D KILL YOU.
...SOMEONE WANTS TO KILL YOU.
OKAY... SO NOW I KNOW YOU MEANT THAT LITERALLY.
THE THING IS, I'VE HAD THIS PROBLEM MUCH OF MY LIFE.
Where are they?
I NEED TO DO SOMETHING ABOUT THIS.
I WOULDN'T GET INVOLVED, RED WOLF. NIGHTHAWK AND BARTON HAVE... UNRESOLVED ISSUES.

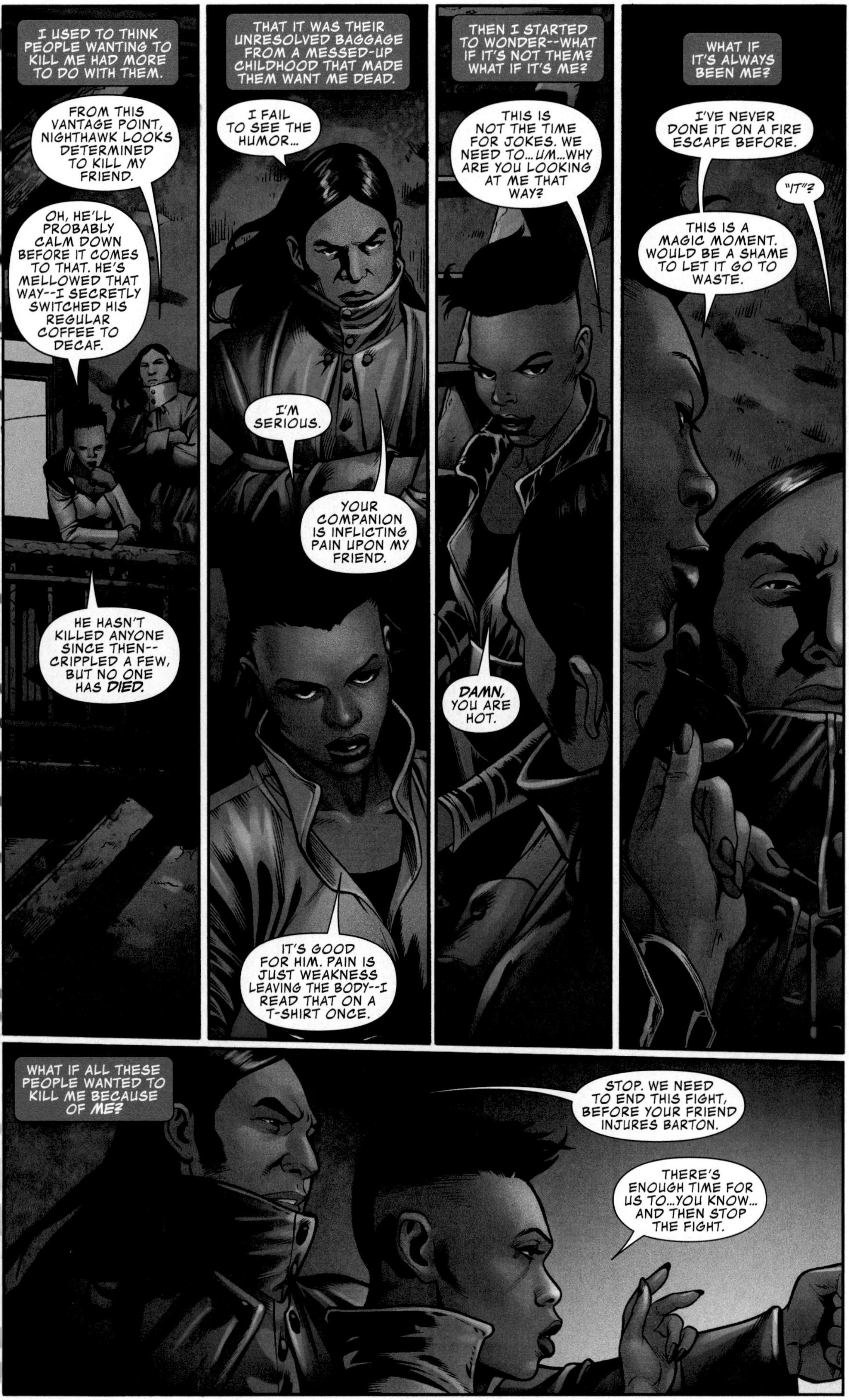
I USED TO THINK PEOPLE WANTING TO KILL ME HAD MORE TO DO WITH THEM.
FROM THIS VANTAGE POINT, NIGHTHAWK LOOKS DETERMINED TO KILL MY FRIEND.
OH, HE'LL PROBABLY CALM DOWN BEFORE IT COMES TO THAT. HE'S MELLOWED THAT WAY--I SECRETLY SWITCHED HIS REGULAR COFFEE TO DECAF.
HE HASN'T KILLED ANYONE SINCE THEN--CRIPPLED A FEW, BUT NO ONE HAS *DIED.*
THAT IT WAS THEIR UNRESOLVED BAGGAGE FROM A MESSED-UP CHILDHOOD THAT MADE THEM WANT ME DEAD.
I FAIL TO SEE THE HUMOR...
I'M SERIOUS.
YOUR COMPANION IS INFLICTING PAIN UPON MY FRIEND.
IT'S GOOD FOR HIM. PAIN IS JUST WEAKNESS LEAVING THE BODY--I READ THAT ON A T-SHIRT ONCE.
THEN I STARTED TO WONDER--WHAT IF IT'S NOT THEM? WHAT IF IT'S ME?
THIS IS NOT THE TIME FOR JOKES. WE NEED TO...UM...WHY ARE YOU LOOKING AT ME THAT WAY?
DAMN, YOU ARE HOT.
WHAT IF IT'S ALWAYS BEEN ME?
I'VE NEVER DONE IT ON A FIRE ESCAPE BEFORE.
"IT"?
THIS IS A MAGIC MOMENT. WOULD BE A SHAME TO LET IT GO TO WASTE.
WHAT IF ALL THESE PEOPLE WANTED TO KILL ME BECAUSE OF *ME?*
STOP. WE NEED TO END THIS FIGHT, BEFORE YOUR FRIEND INJURES BARTON.
THERE'S ENOUGH TIME FOR US TO...YOU KNOW... AND THEN STOP THE FIGHT.

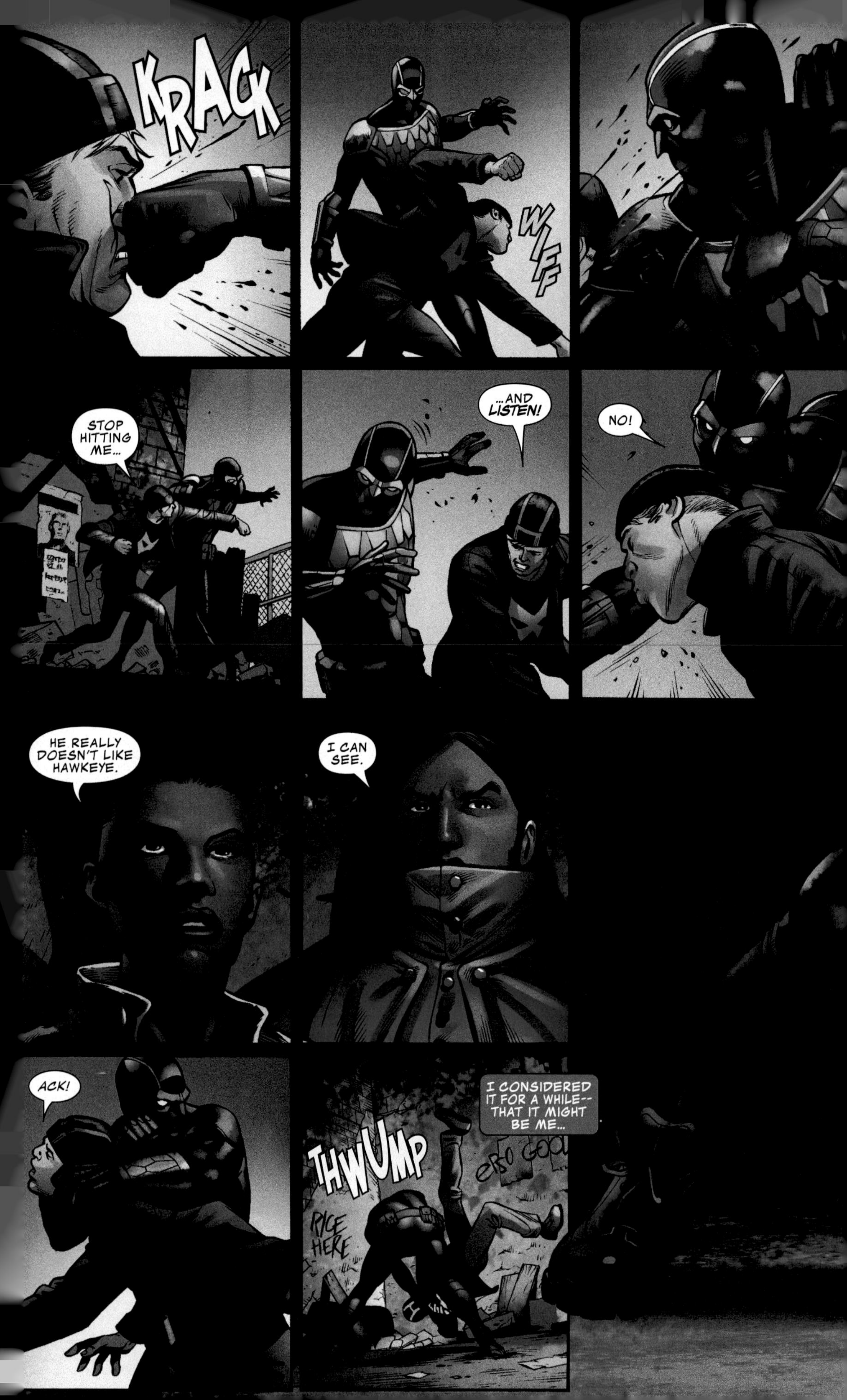
KRACK
WIFF
STOP HITTING ME...
...AND LISTEN!
NO!
HE REALLY DOESN'T LIKE HAWKEYE.
I CAN SEE.
ACK!
THWUMP
I CONSIDERED IT FOR A WHILE-- THAT IT MIGHT BE ME...

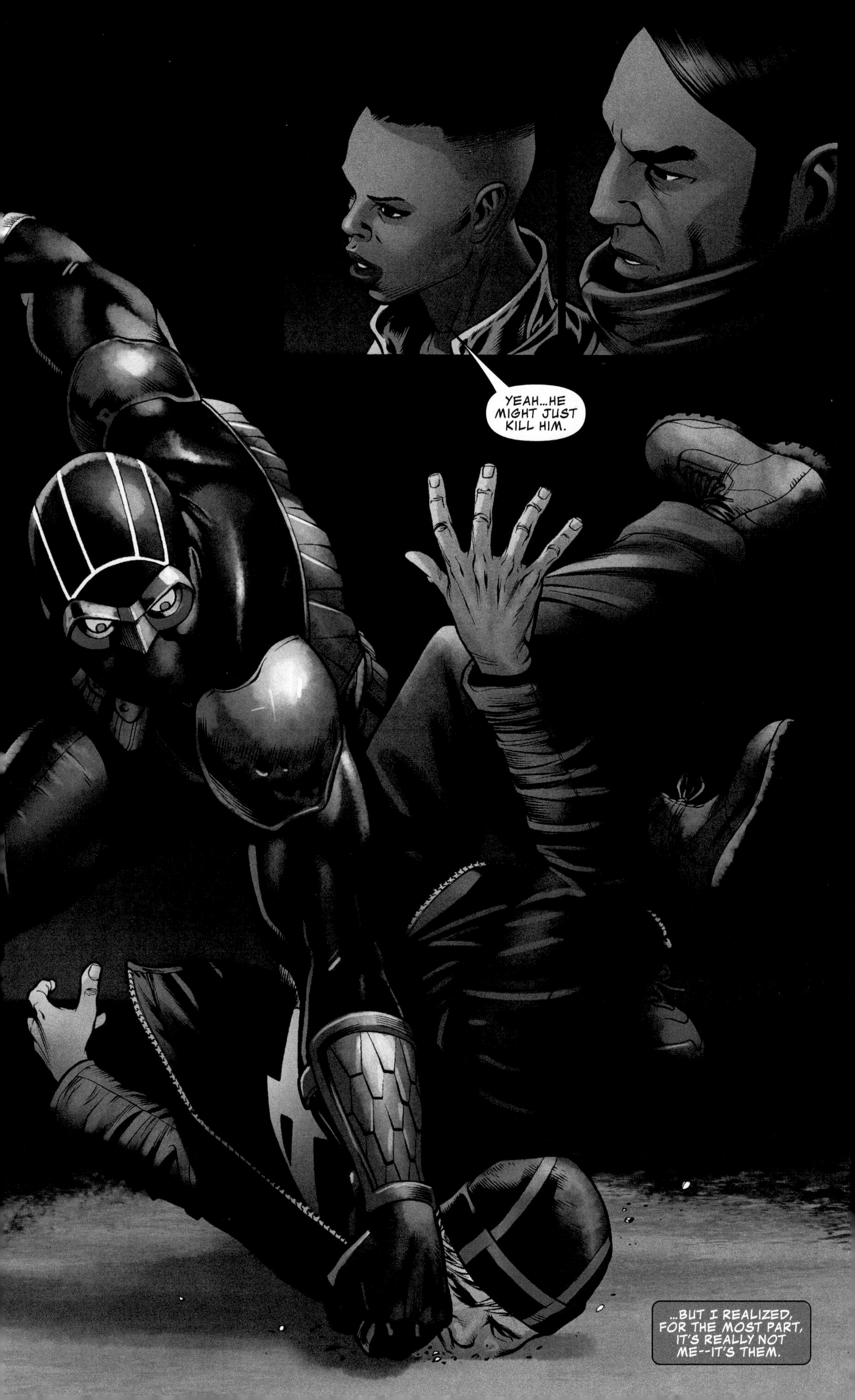
YEAH...HE MIGHT JUST KILL HIM.
...BUT I REALIZED, FOR THE MOST PART, IT'S REALLY NOT ME--IT'S THEM.

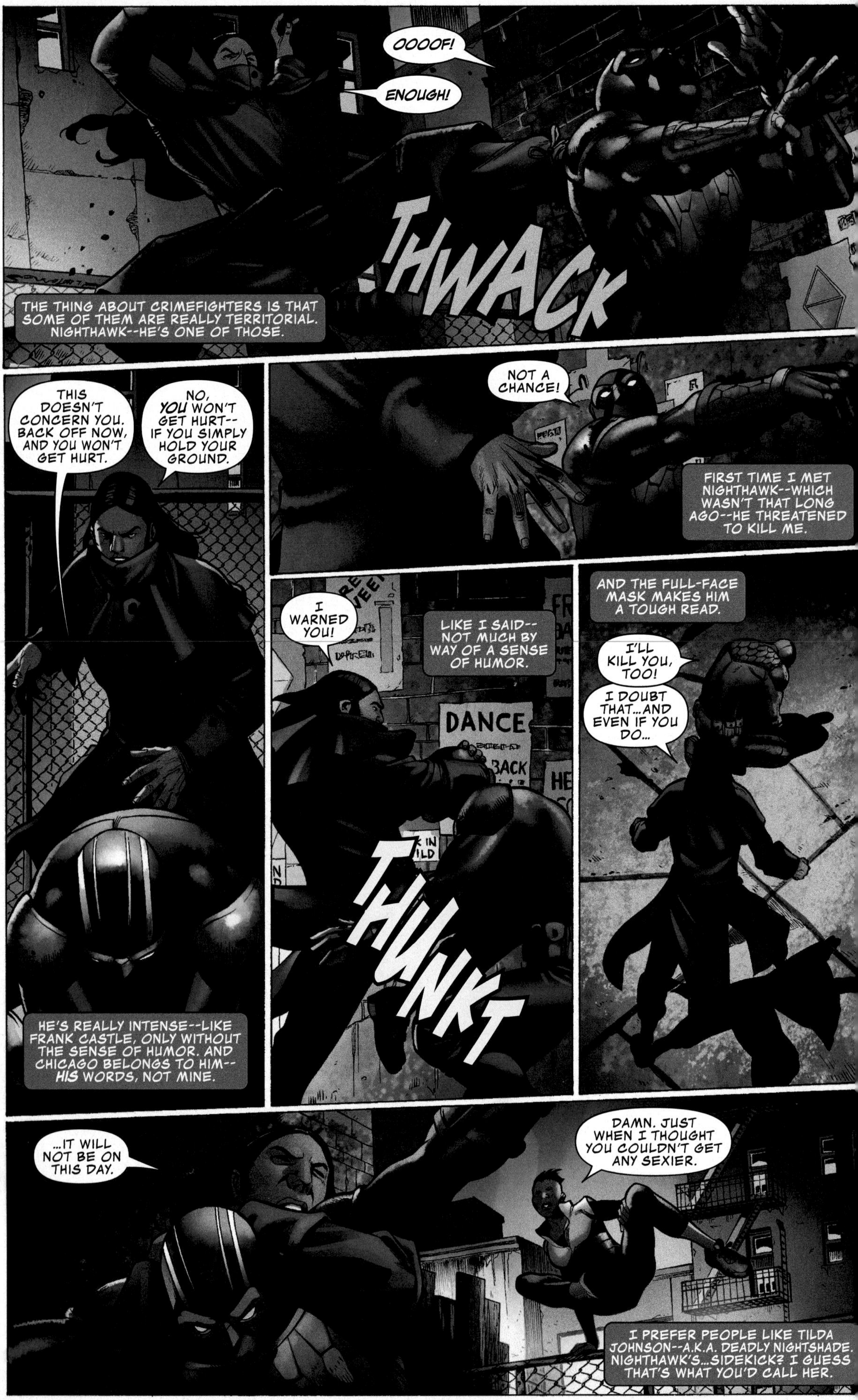

OOOOF!
ENOUGH!
THWACK
THE THING ABOUT CRIMEFIGHTERS IS THAT SOME OF THEM ARE REALLY TERRITORIAL. NIGHTHAWK--HE'S ONE OF THOSE.
THIS DOESN'T CONCERN YOU. BACK OFF NOW, AND YOU WON'T GET HURT.
NO, YOU WON'T GET HURT-- IF YOU SIMPLY HOLD YOUR GROUND.
HE'S REALLY INTENSE--LIKE FRANK CASTLE, ONLY WITHOUT THE SENSE OF HUMOR. AND CHICAGO BELONGS TO HIM-- HIS WORDS, NOT MINE.
NOT A CHANCE!
FIRST TIME I MET NIGHTHAWK--WHICH WASN'T THAT LONG AGO--HE THREATENED TO KILL ME.
I WARNED YOU!
LIKE I SAID-- NOT MUCH BY WAY OF A SENSE OF HUMOR.
DANCE
BACK
THUNKT
AND THE FULL-FACE MASK MAKES HIM A TOUGH READ.
I'LL KILL YOU, TOO!
I DOUBT THAT...AND EVEN IF YOU DO...
...IT WILL NOT BE ON THIS DAY.
DAMN. JUST WHEN I THOUGHT YOU COULDN'T GET ANY SEXIER.
I PREFER PEOPLE LIKE TILDA JOHNSON--A.K.A. DEADLY NIGHTSHADE. NIGHTHAWK'S...SIDEKICK? I GUESS THAT'S WHAT YOU'D CALL HER.

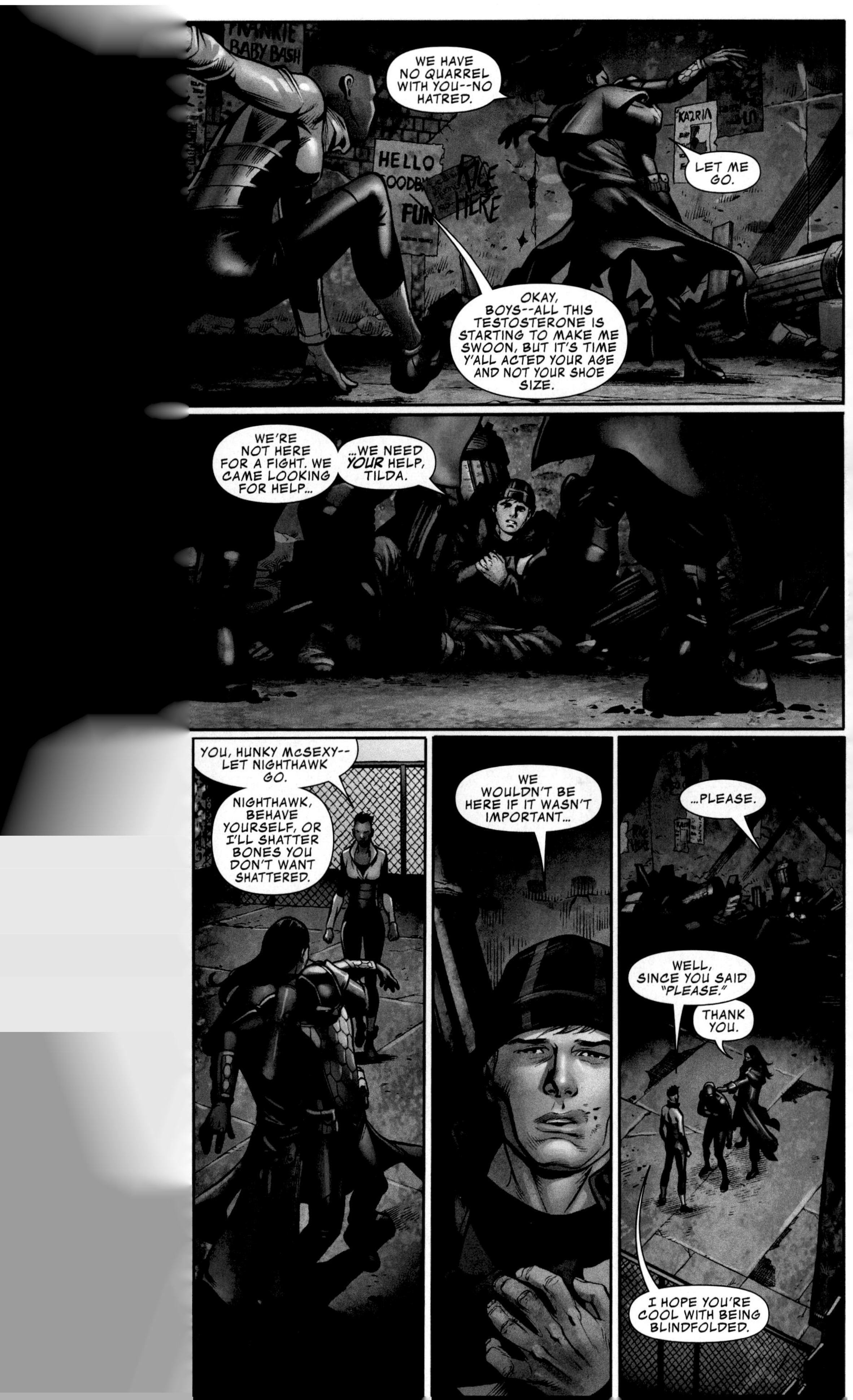
WE HAVE NO QUARREL WITH YOU--NO HATRED.
LET ME GO.
OKAY, BOYS--ALL THIS TESTOSTERONE IS STARTING TO MAKE ME SWOON, BUT IT'S TIME Y'ALL ACTED YOUR AGE AND NOT YOUR SHOE SIZE.
WE'RE NOT HERE FOR A FIGHT. WE CAME LOOKING FOR HELP...
...WE NEED *YOUR* HELP, TILDA.
YOU, HUNKY McSEXY-- LET NIGHTHAWK GO.
NIGHTHAWK, BEHAVE YOURSELF, OR I'LL SHATTER BONES YOU DON'T WANT SHATTERED.
WE WOULDN'T BE HERE IF IT WASN'T IMPORTANT...
...PLEASE.
WELL, SINCE YOU SAID "*PLEASE.*"
THANK YOU.
I HOPE YOU'RE COOL WITH BEING BLINDFOLDED.

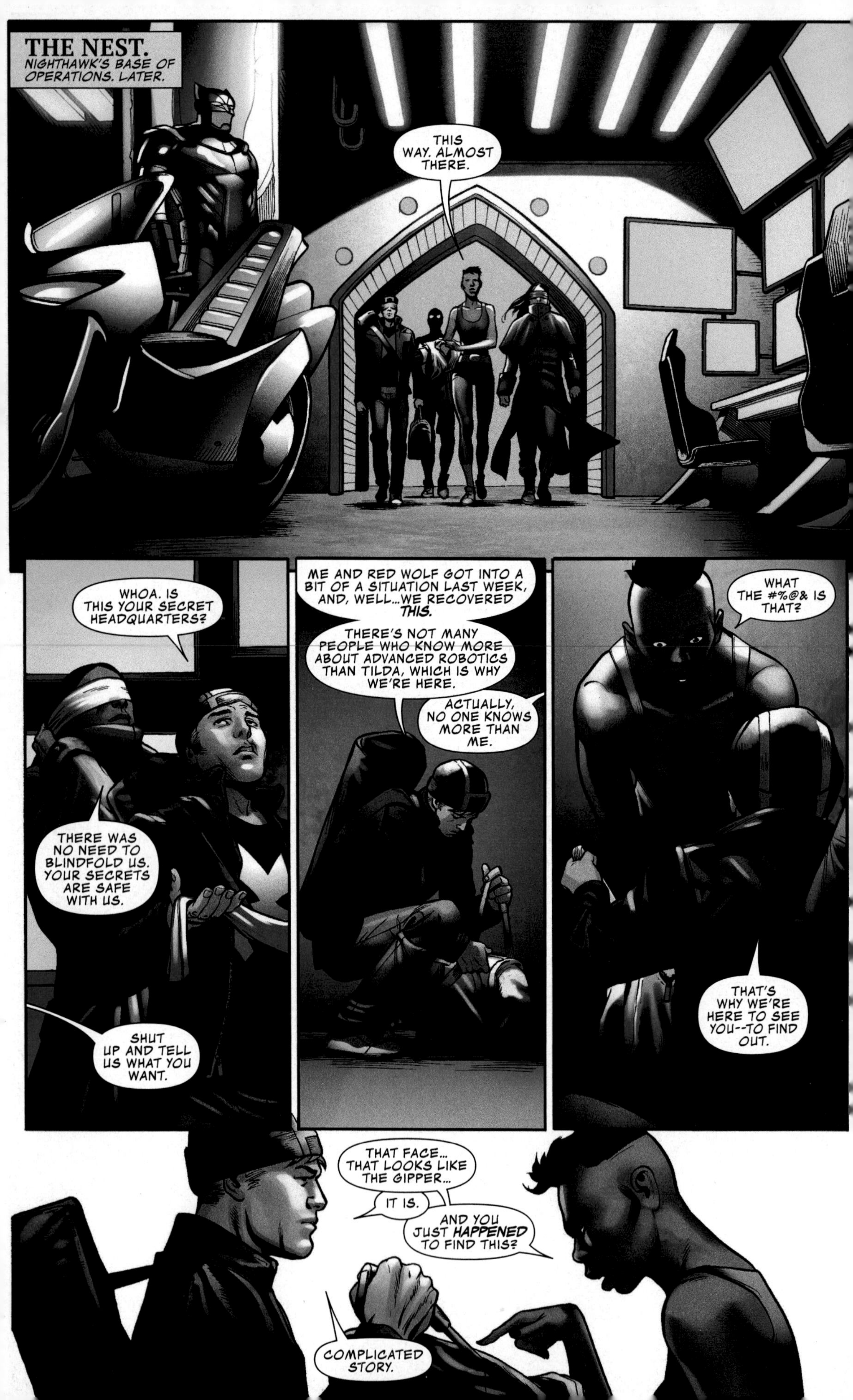
THE NEST.
NIGHTHAWK'S BASE OF OPERATIONS. LATER.
THIS WAY. ALMOST THERE.
WHOA. IS THIS YOUR SECRET HEADQUARTERS?
THERE WAS NO NEED TO BLINDFOLD US. YOUR SECRETS ARE SAFE WITH US.
SHUT UP AND TELL US WHAT YOU WANT.
ME AND RED WOLF GOT INTO A BIT OF A SITUATION LAST WEEK, AND, WELL...WE RECOVERED *THIS.*
THERE'S NOT MANY PEOPLE WHO KNOW MORE ABOUT ADVANCED ROBOTICS THAN TILDA, WHICH IS WHY WE'RE HERE.
ACTUALLY, NO ONE KNOWS MORE THAN ME.
WHAT THE #%@& IS THAT?
THAT'S WHY WE'RE HERE TO SEE YOU--TO FIND OUT.
THAT FACE... THAT LOOKS LIKE THE GIPPER...
IT IS.
AND YOU JUST *HAPPENED* TO FIND THIS?
COMPLICATED STORY.

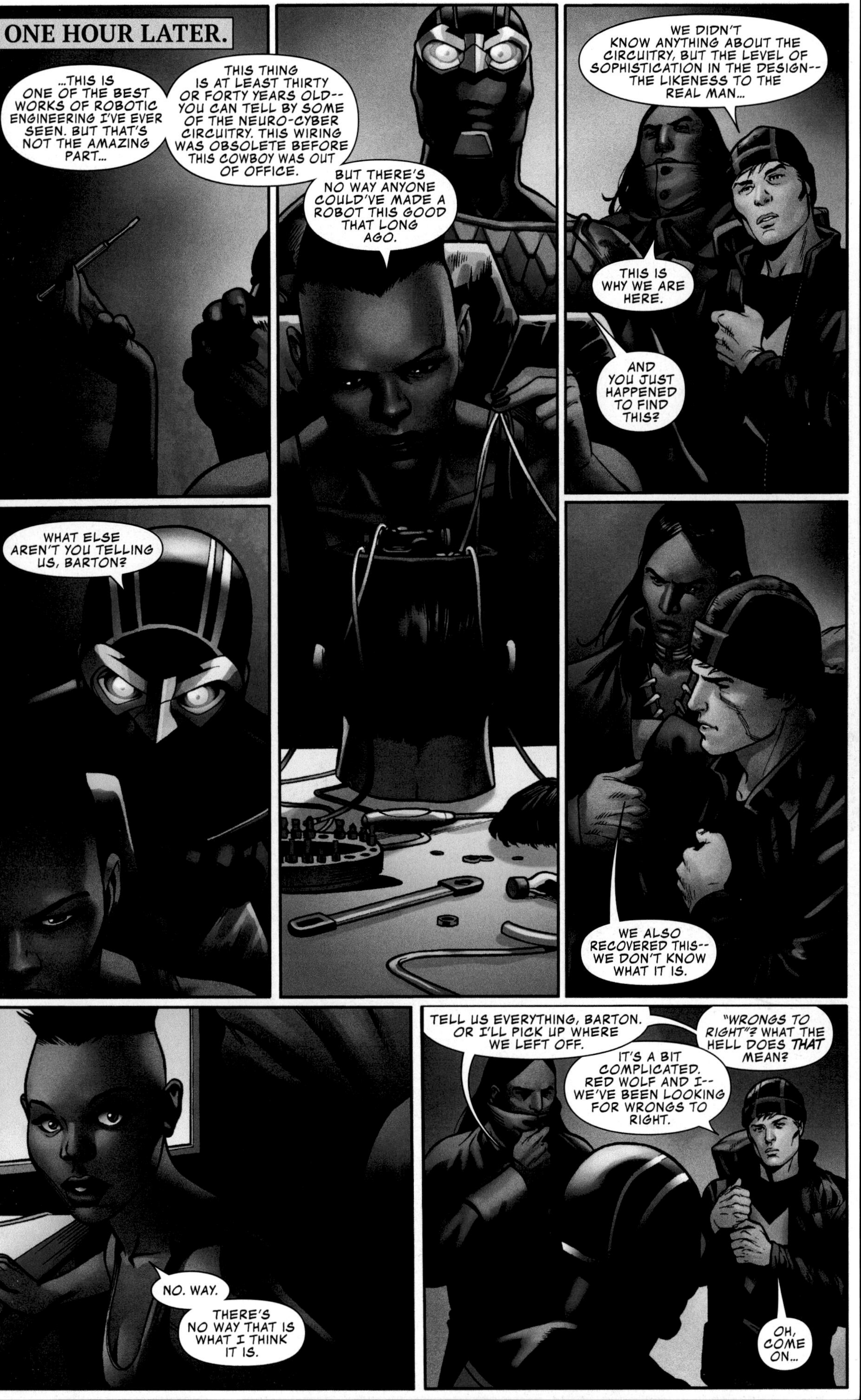
ONE HOUR LATER.
...THIS IS ONE OF THE BEST WORKS OF ROBOTIC ENGINEERING I'VE EVER SEEN. BUT THAT'S NOT THE AMAZING PART...
THIS THING IS AT LEAST THIRTY OR FORTY YEARS OLD-- YOU CAN TELL BY SOME OF THE NEURO-CYBER CIRCUITRY. THIS WIRING WAS OBSOLETE BEFORE THIS COWBOY WAS OUT OF OFFICE.
BUT THERE'S NO WAY ANYONE COULD'VE MADE A ROBOT THIS GOOD THAT LONG AGO.
WE DIDN'T KNOW ANYTHING ABOUT THE CIRCUITRY, BUT THE LEVEL OF SOPHISTICATION IN THE DESIGN-- THE LIKENESS TO THE REAL MAN...
THIS IS WHY WE ARE HERE.
AND YOU JUST HAPPENED TO FIND THIS?
WHAT ELSE AREN'T YOU TELLING US, BARTON?
WE ALSO RECOVERED THIS-- WE DON'T KNOW WHAT IT IS.
NO. WAY.
THERE'S NO WAY THAT IS WHAT I THINK IT IS.
TELL US EVERYTHING, BARTON. OR I'LL PICK UP WHERE WE LEFT OFF.
IT'S A BIT COMPLICATED. RED WOLF AND I-- WE'VE BEEN LOOKING FOR WRONGS TO RIGHT.
"WRONGS TO RIGHT"? WHAT THE HELL DOES *THAT* MEAN?
OH, COME ON...

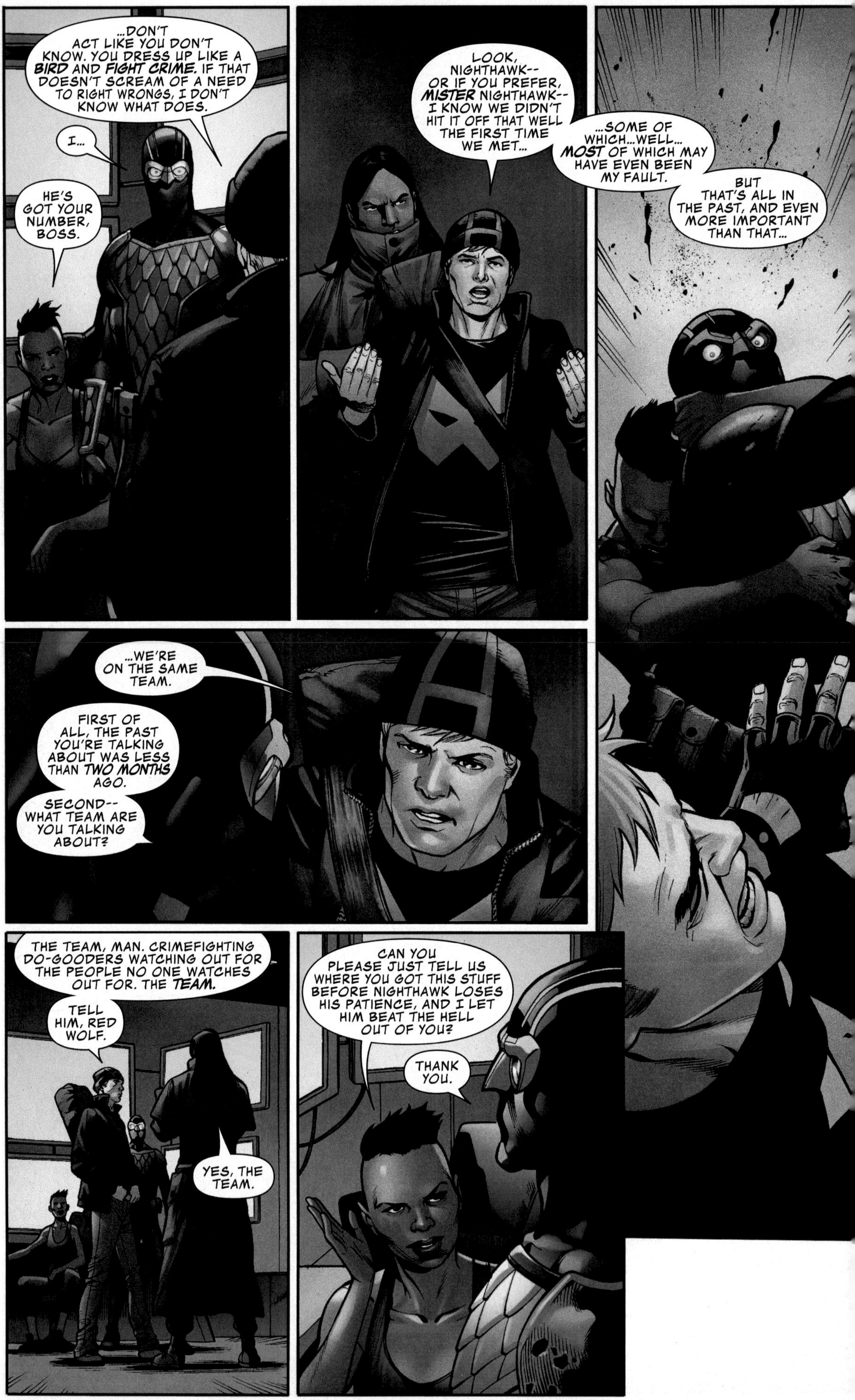
...DON'T ACT LIKE YOU DON'T KNOW. YOU DRESS UP LIKE A BIRD AND FIGHT CRIME. IF THAT DOESN'T SCREAM OF A NEED TO RIGHT WRONGS, I DON'T KNOW WHAT DOES.
I...
HE'S GOT YOUR NUMBER, BOSS.
LOOK, NIGHTHAWK-- OR IF YOU PREFER, MISTER NIGHTHAWK-- I KNOW WE DIDN'T HIT IT OFF THAT WELL THE FIRST TIME WE MET...
...SOME OF WHICH...WELL... MOST OF WHICH MAY HAVE EVEN BEEN MY FAULT.
BUT THAT'S ALL IN THE PAST, AND EVEN MORE IMPORTANT THAN THAT...
...WE'RE ON THE SAME TEAM.
FIRST OF ALL, THE PAST YOU'RE TALKING ABOUT WAS LESS THAN TWO MONTHS AGO.
SECOND-- WHAT TEAM ARE YOU TALKING ABOUT?
THE TEAM, MAN. CRIMEFIGHTING DO-GOODERS WATCHING OUT FOR THE PEOPLE NO ONE WATCHES OUT FOR. THE TEAM.
TELL HIM, RED WOLF.
YES, THE TEAM.
CAN YOU PLEASE JUST TELL US WHERE YOU GOT THIS STUFF BEFORE NIGHTHAWK LOSES HIS PATIENCE, AND I LET HIM BEAT THE HELL OUT OF YOU?
THANK YOU.

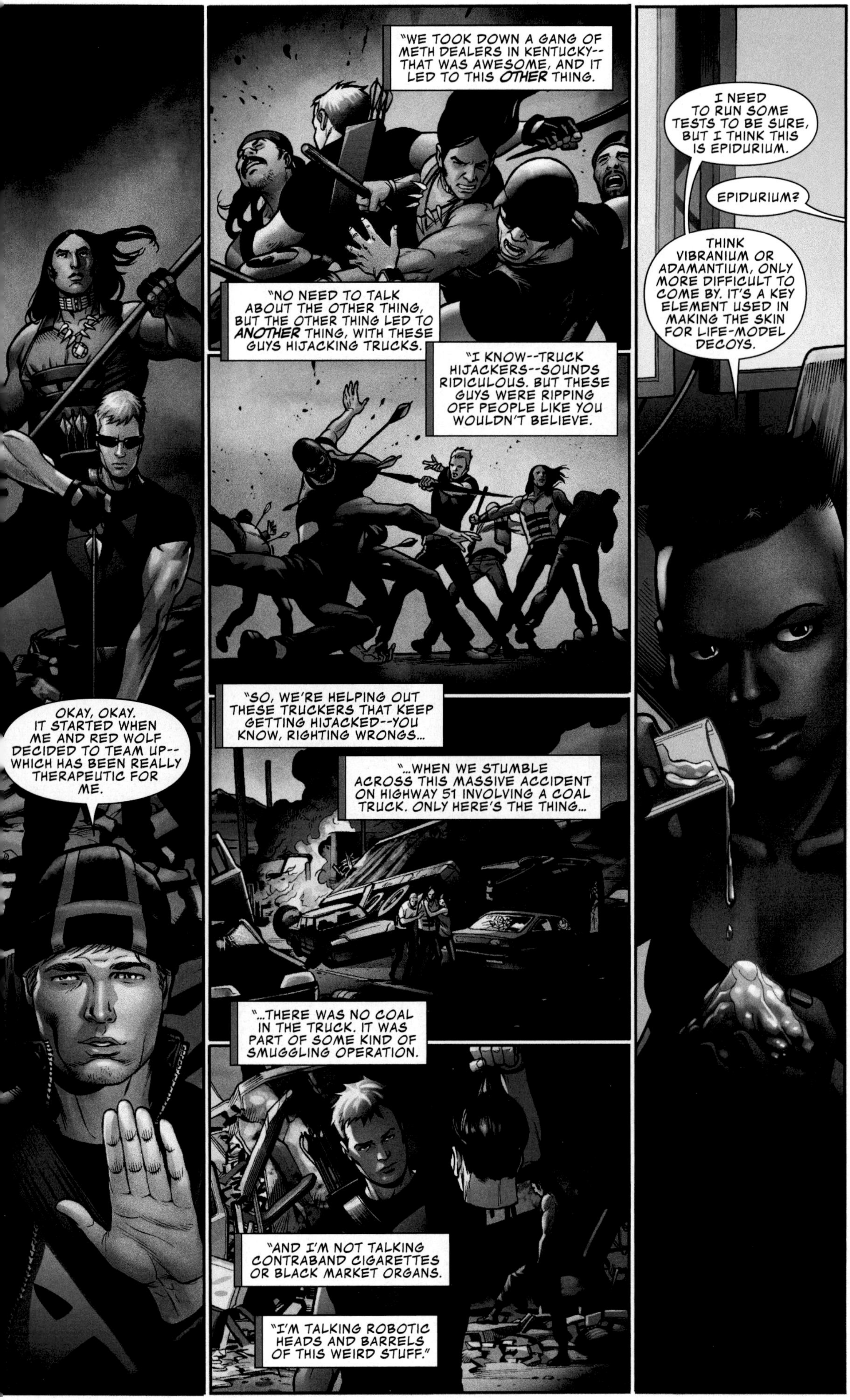
OKAY, OKAY. IT STARTED WHEN ME AND RED WOLF DECIDED TO TEAM UP--WHICH HAS BEEN REALLY THERAPEUTIC FOR ME.
"WE TOOK DOWN A GANG OF METH DEALERS IN KENTUCKY--THAT WAS AWESOME, AND IT LED TO THIS *OTHER* THING.
"NO NEED TO TALK ABOUT THE OTHER THING, BUT THE OTHER THING LED TO *ANOTHER* THING, WITH THESE GUYS HIJACKING TRUCKS.
"I KNOW--TRUCK HIJACKERS--SOUNDS RIDICULOUS. BUT THESE GUYS WERE RIPPING OFF PEOPLE LIKE YOU WOULDN'T BELIEVE.
"SO, WE'RE HELPING OUT THESE TRUCKERS THAT KEEP GETTING HIJACKED--YOU KNOW, RIGHTING WRONGS...
"...WHEN WE STUMBLE ACROSS THIS MASSIVE ACCIDENT ON HIGHWAY 51 INVOLVING A COAL TRUCK. ONLY HERE'S THE THING...
"...THERE WAS NO COAL IN THE TRUCK. IT WAS PART OF SOME KIND OF SMUGGLING OPERATION.
"AND I'M NOT TALKING CONTRABAND CIGARETTES OR BLACK MARKET ORGANS.
"I'M TALKING ROBOTIC HEADS AND BARRELS OF THIS WEIRD STUFF."
I NEED TO RUN SOME TESTS TO BE SURE, BUT I THINK THIS IS EPIDURIUM.
EPIDURIUM?
THINK VIBRANIUM OR ADAMANTIUM, ONLY MORE DIFFICULT TO COME BY. IT'S A KEY ELEMENT USED IN MAKING THE SKIN FOR LIFE-MODEL DECOYS.

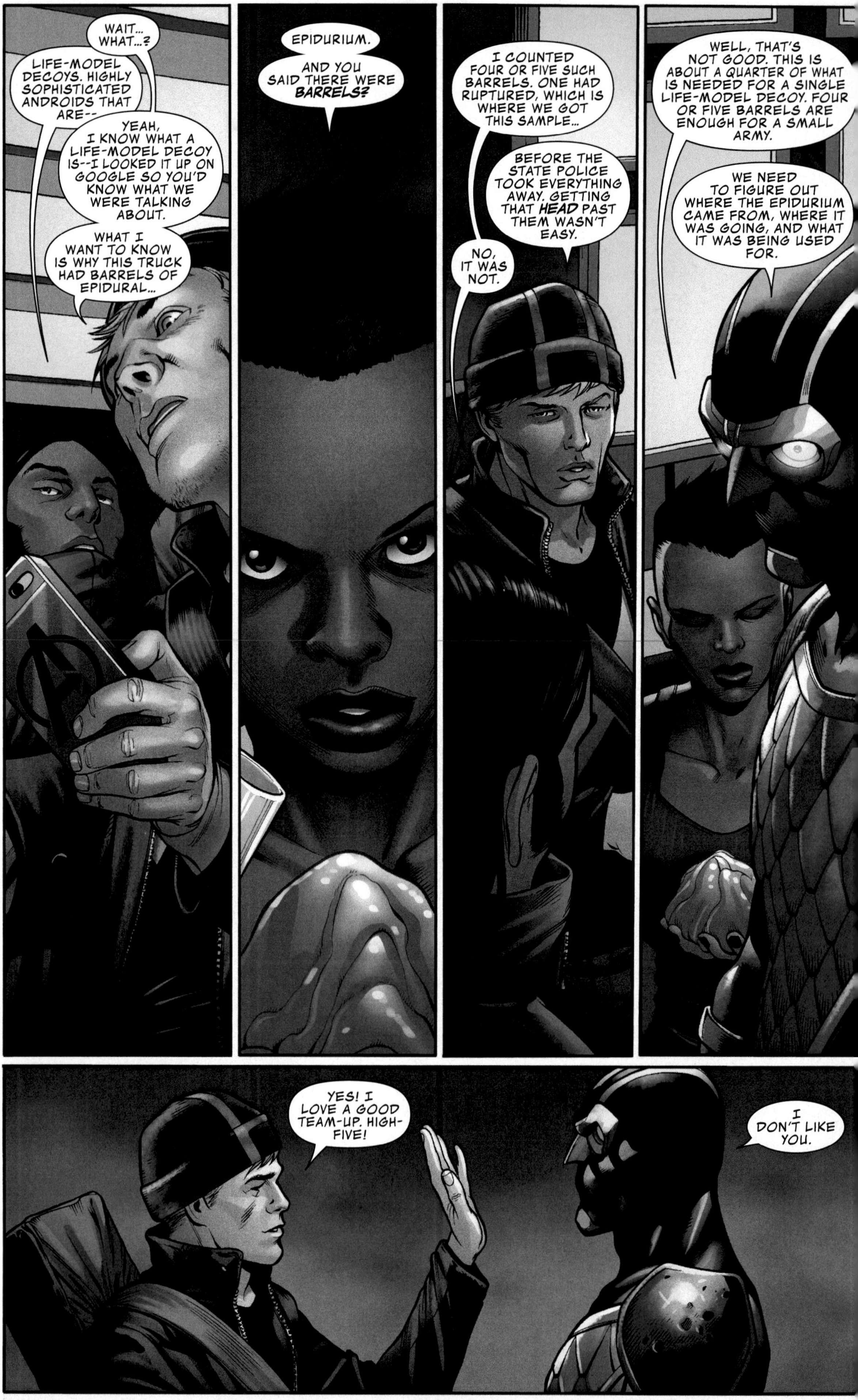
WAIT... WHAT...?
LIFE-MODEL DECOYS. HIGHLY SOPHISTICATED ANDROIDS THAT ARE--
YEAH, I KNOW WHAT A LIFE-MODEL DECOY IS--I LOOKED IT UP ON GOOGLE SO YOU'D KNOW WHAT WE WERE TALKING ABOUT.
WHAT I WANT TO KNOW IS WHY THIS TRUCK HAD BARRELS OF EPIDURAL...
EPIDURIUM.
AND YOU SAID THERE WERE BARRELS?
I COUNTED FOUR OR FIVE SUCH BARRELS. ONE HAD RUPTURED, WHICH IS WHERE WE GOT THIS SAMPLE...
BEFORE THE STATE POLICE TOOK EVERYTHING AWAY. GETTING THAT HEAD PAST THEM WASN'T EASY.
NO, IT WAS NOT.
WELL, THAT'S NOT GOOD. THIS IS ABOUT A QUARTER OF WHAT IS NEEDED FOR A SINGLE LIFE-MODEL DECOY. FOUR OR FIVE BARRELS ARE ENOUGH FOR A SMALL ARMY.
WE NEED TO FIGURE OUT WHERE THE EPIDURIUM CAME FROM, WHERE IT WAS GOING, AND WHAT IT WAS BEING USED FOR.
YES! I LOVE A GOOD TEAM-UP. HIGH-FIVE!
I DON'T LIKE YOU.

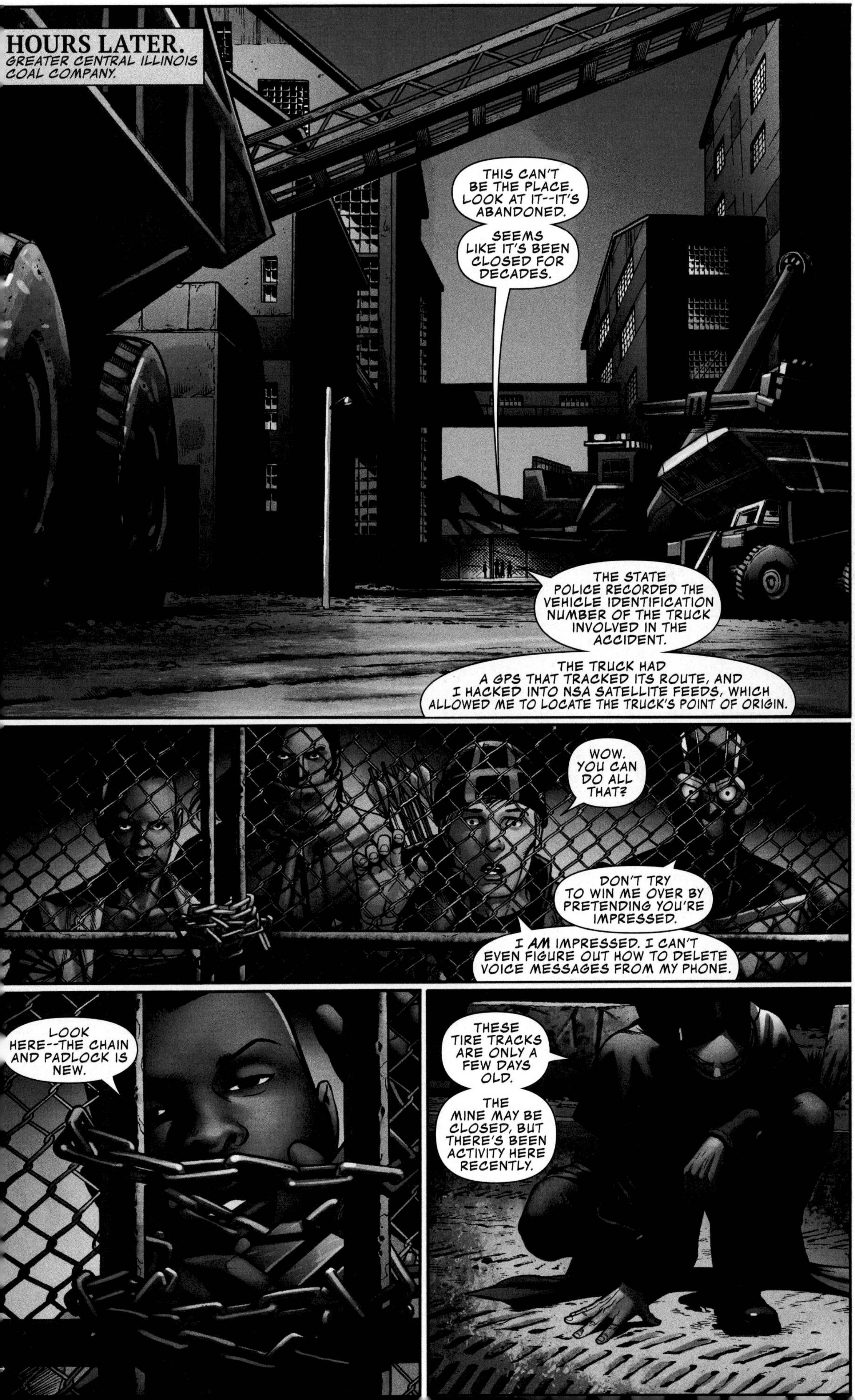
HOURS LATER.
GREATER CENTRAL ILLINOIS COAL COMPANY.
THIS CAN'T BE THE PLACE. LOOK AT IT--IT'S ABANDONED.
SEEMS LIKE IT'S BEEN CLOSED FOR DECADES.
THE STATE POLICE RECORDED THE VEHICLE IDENTIFICATION NUMBER OF THE TRUCK INVOLVED IN THE ACCIDENT.
THE TRUCK HAD A GPS THAT TRACKED ITS ROUTE, AND I HACKED INTO NSA SATELLITE FEEDS, WHICH ALLOWED ME TO LOCATE THE TRUCK'S POINT OF ORIGIN.
WOW. YOU CAN DO ALL THAT?
DON'T TRY TO WIN ME OVER BY PRETENDING YOU'RE IMPRESSED.
I *AM* IMPRESSED. I CAN'T EVEN FIGURE OUT HOW TO DELETE VOICE MESSAGES FROM MY PHONE.
LOOK HERE--THE CHAIN AND PADLOCK IS NEW.
THESE TIRE TRACKS ARE ONLY A FEW DAYS OLD.
THE MINE MAY BE CLOSED, BUT THERE'S BEEN ACTIVITY HERE RECENTLY.

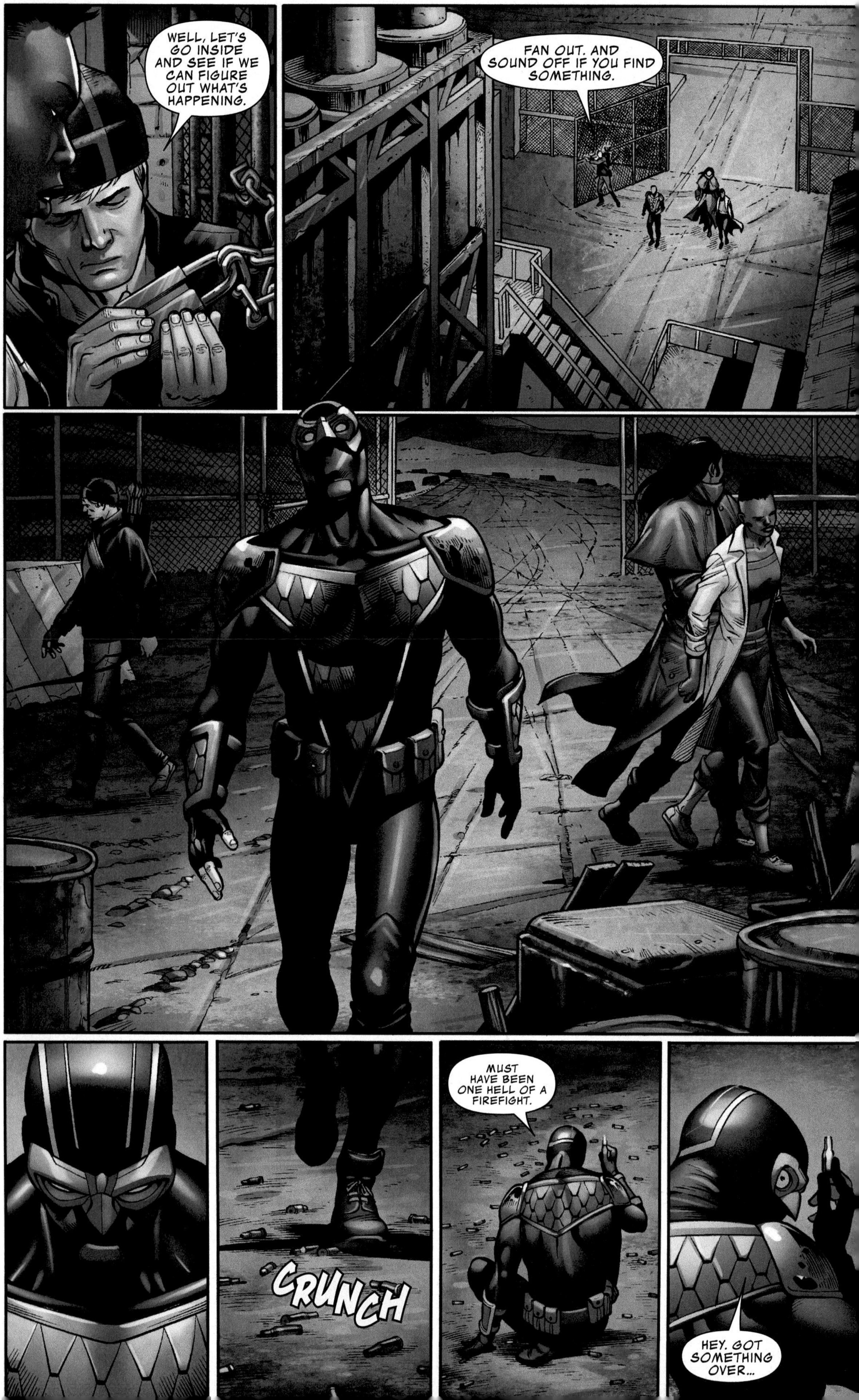
WELL, LET'S GO INSIDE AND SEE IF WE CAN FIGURE OUT WHAT'S HAPPENING.
FAN OUT. AND SOUND OFF IF YOU FIND SOMETHING.
CRUNCH
MUST HAVE BEEN ONE HELL OF A FIREFIGHT.
HEY. GOT SOMETHING OVER...

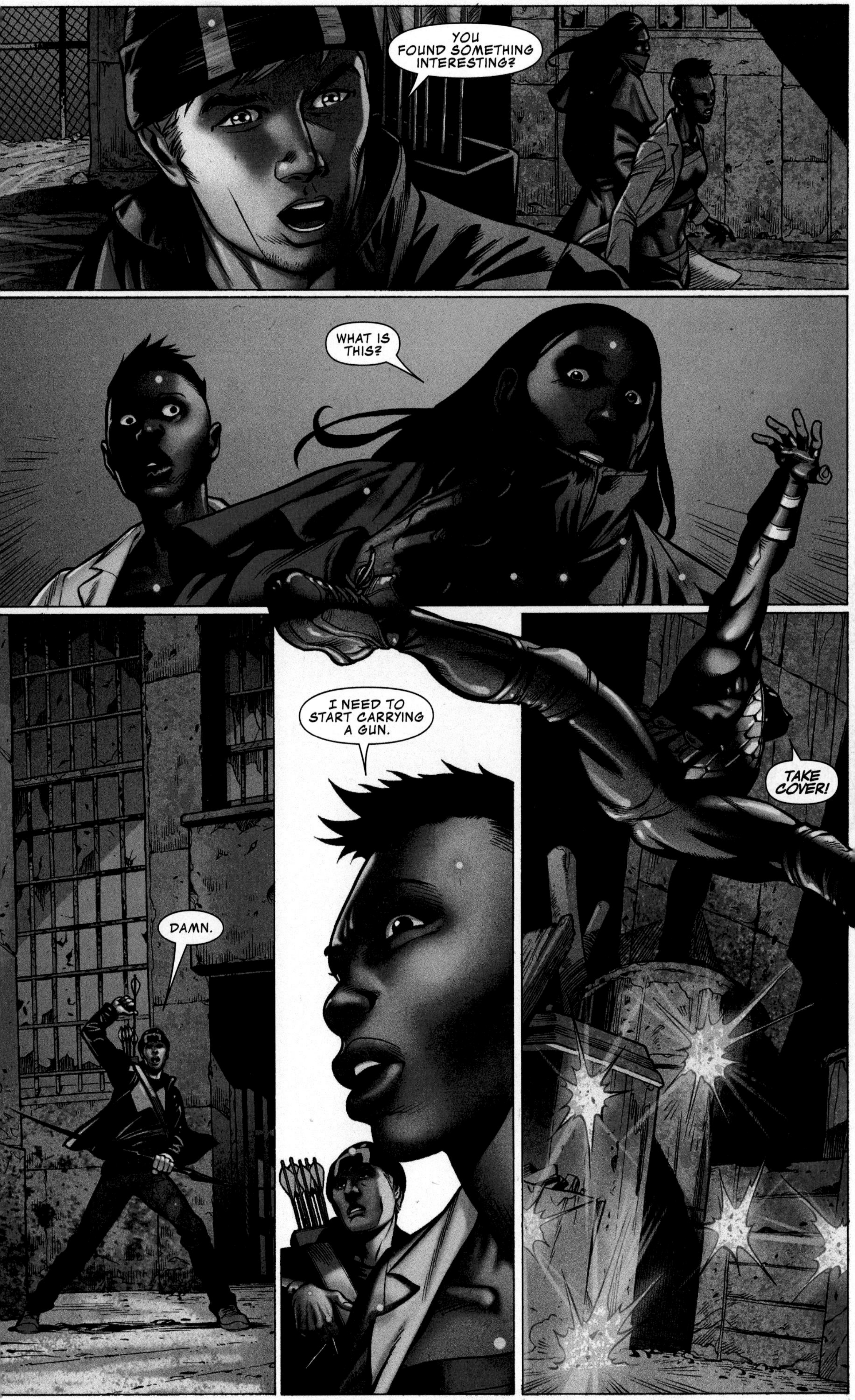
YOU FOUND SOMETHING INTERESTING?
WHAT IS THIS?
DAMN.
I NEED TO START CARRYING A GUN.
TAKE COVER!

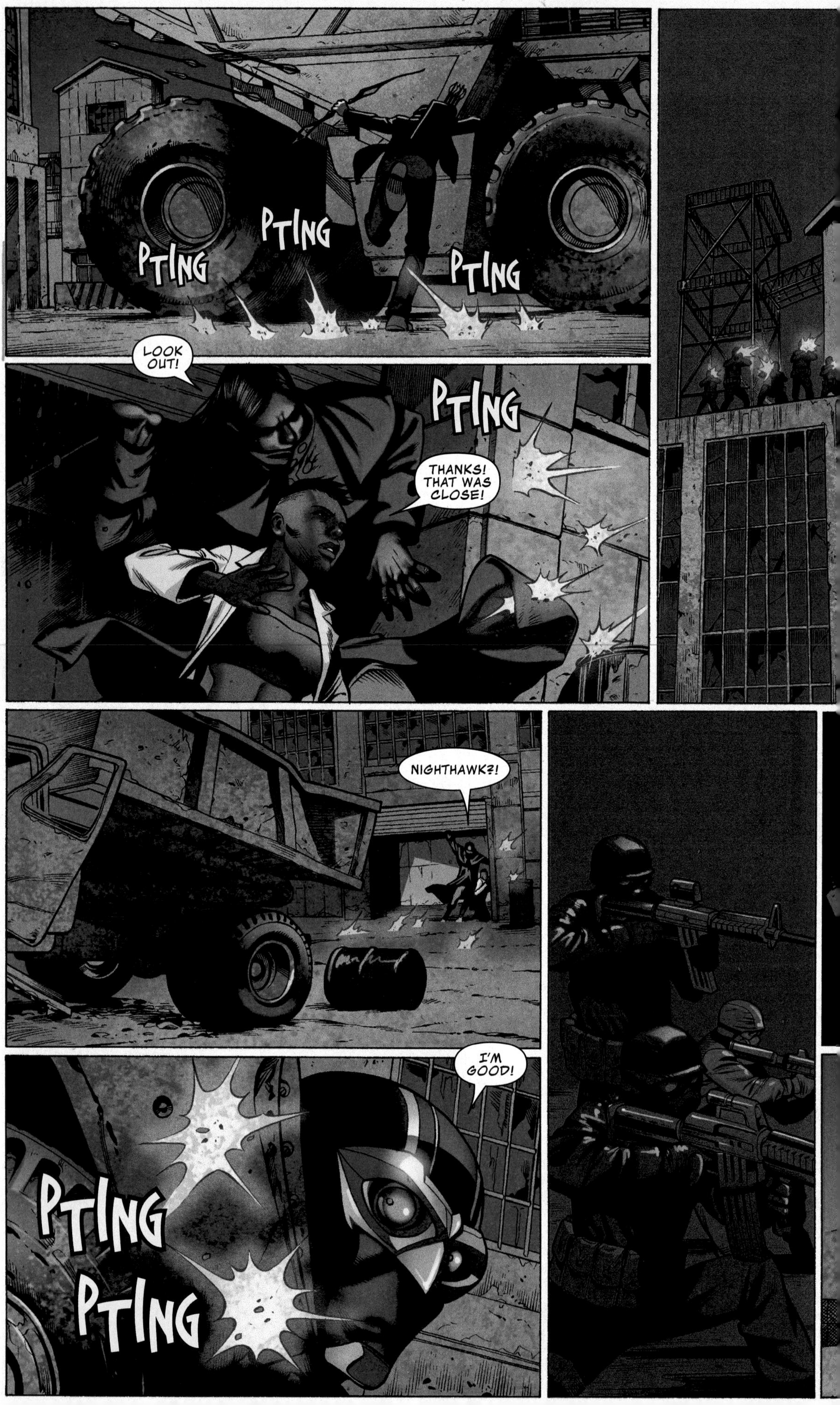
PTING
PTING
PTING
LOOK OUT!
PTING
THANKS! THAT WAS CLOSE!
NIGHTHAWK?!
I'M GOOD!
PTING
PTING

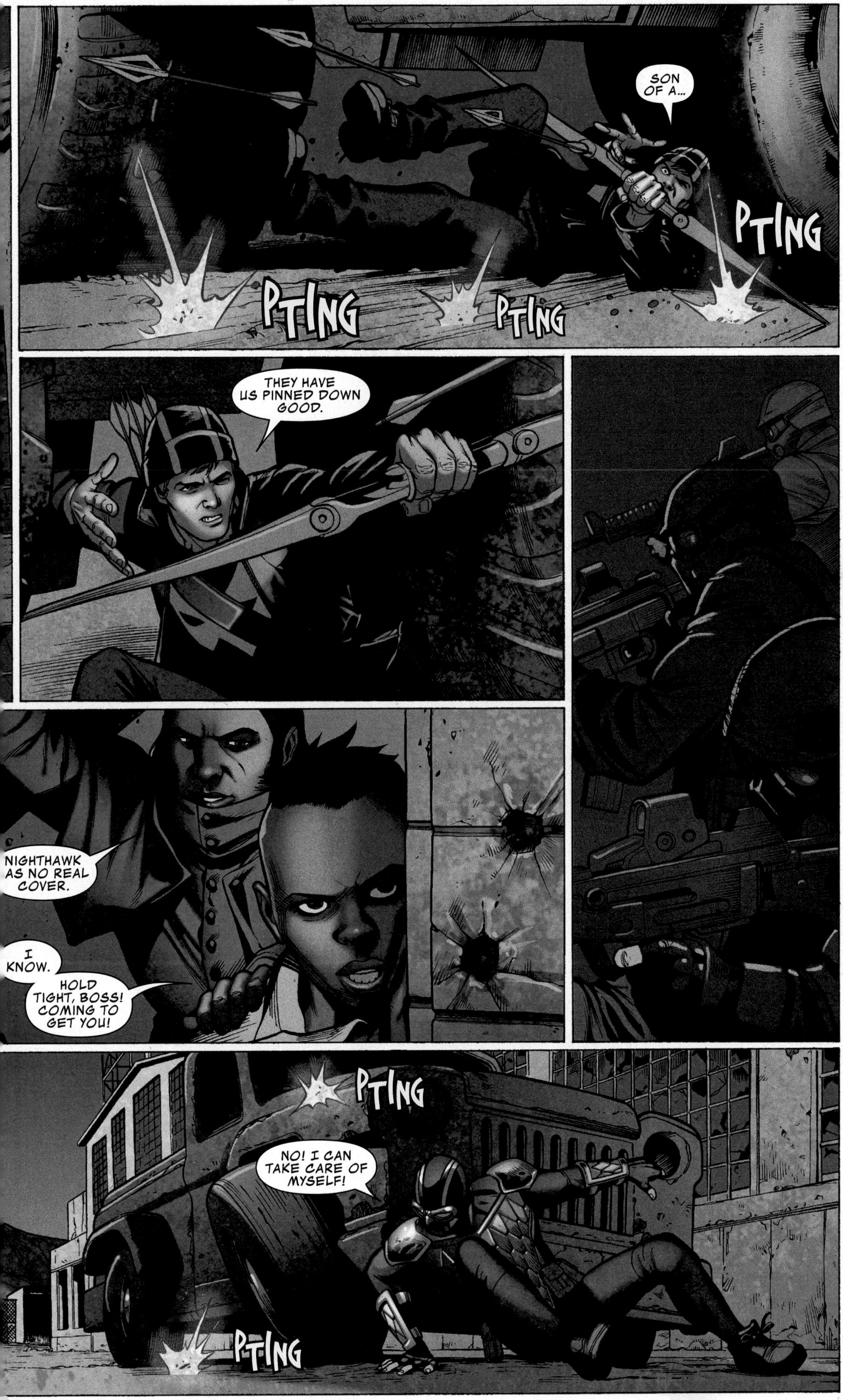
SON OF A...
PTING
PTING
PTING
THEY HAVE US PINNED DOWN GOOD.
NIGHTHAWK AS NO REAL COVER.
I KNOW.
HOLD TIGHT, BOSS! COMING TO GET YOU!
PTING
NO! I CAN TAKE CARE OF MYSELF!
PTING

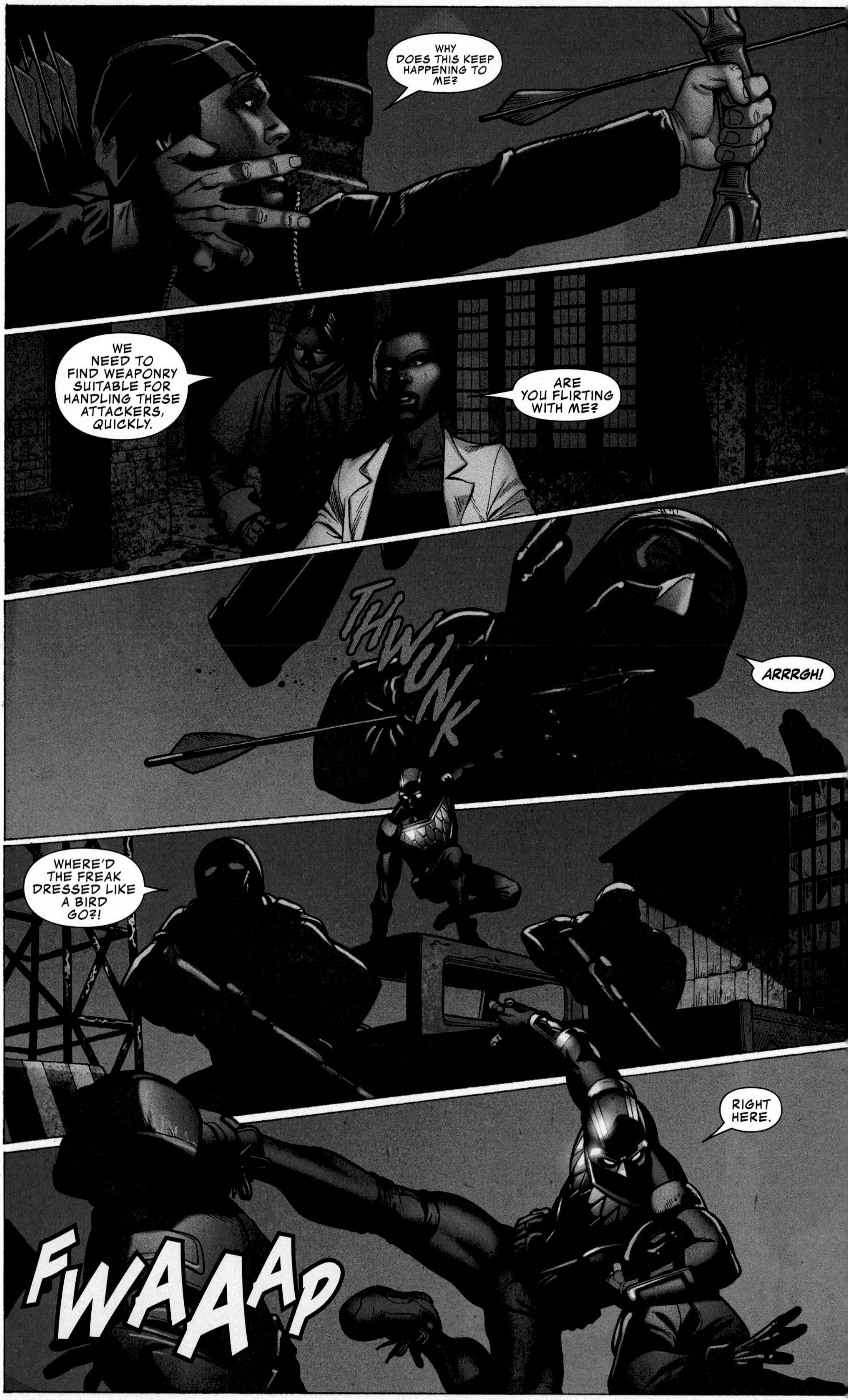
WHY DOES THIS KEEP HAPPENING TO ME?
WE NEED TO FIND WEAPONRY SUITABLE FOR HANDLING THESE ATTACKERS, QUICKLY.
ARE YOU FLIRTING WITH ME?
THWUNK
ARRRGH!
WHERE'D THE FREAK DRESSED LIKE A BIRD GO?!
RIGHT HERE.
FWAAAP

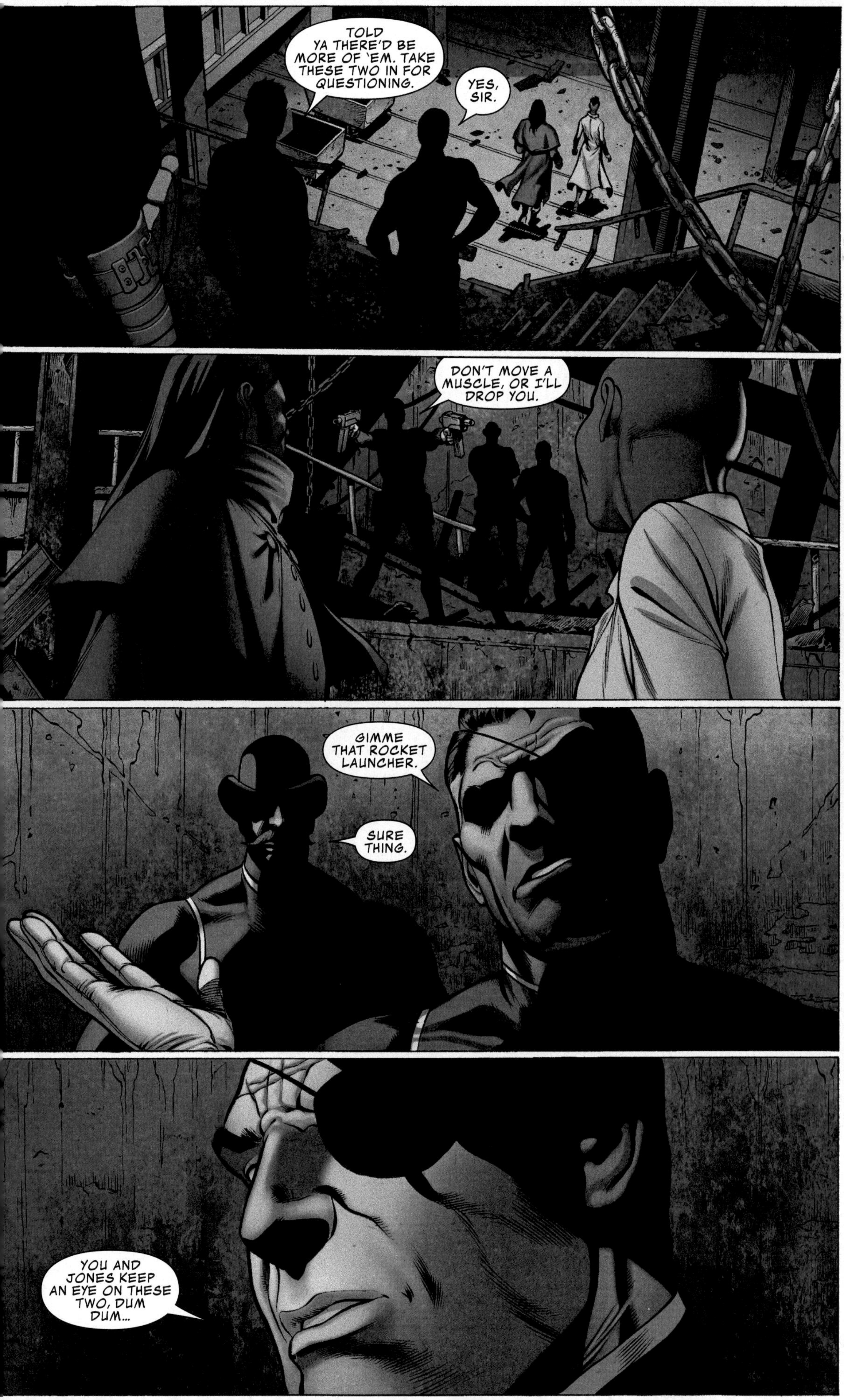
TOLD YA THERE'D BE MORE OF 'EM. TAKE THESE TWO IN FOR QUESTIONING.
YES, SIR.
DON'T MOVE A MUSCLE, OR I'LL DROP YOU.
GIMME THAT ROCKET LAUNCHER.
SURE THING.
YOU AND JONES KEEP AN EYE ON THESE TWO, DUM DUM...

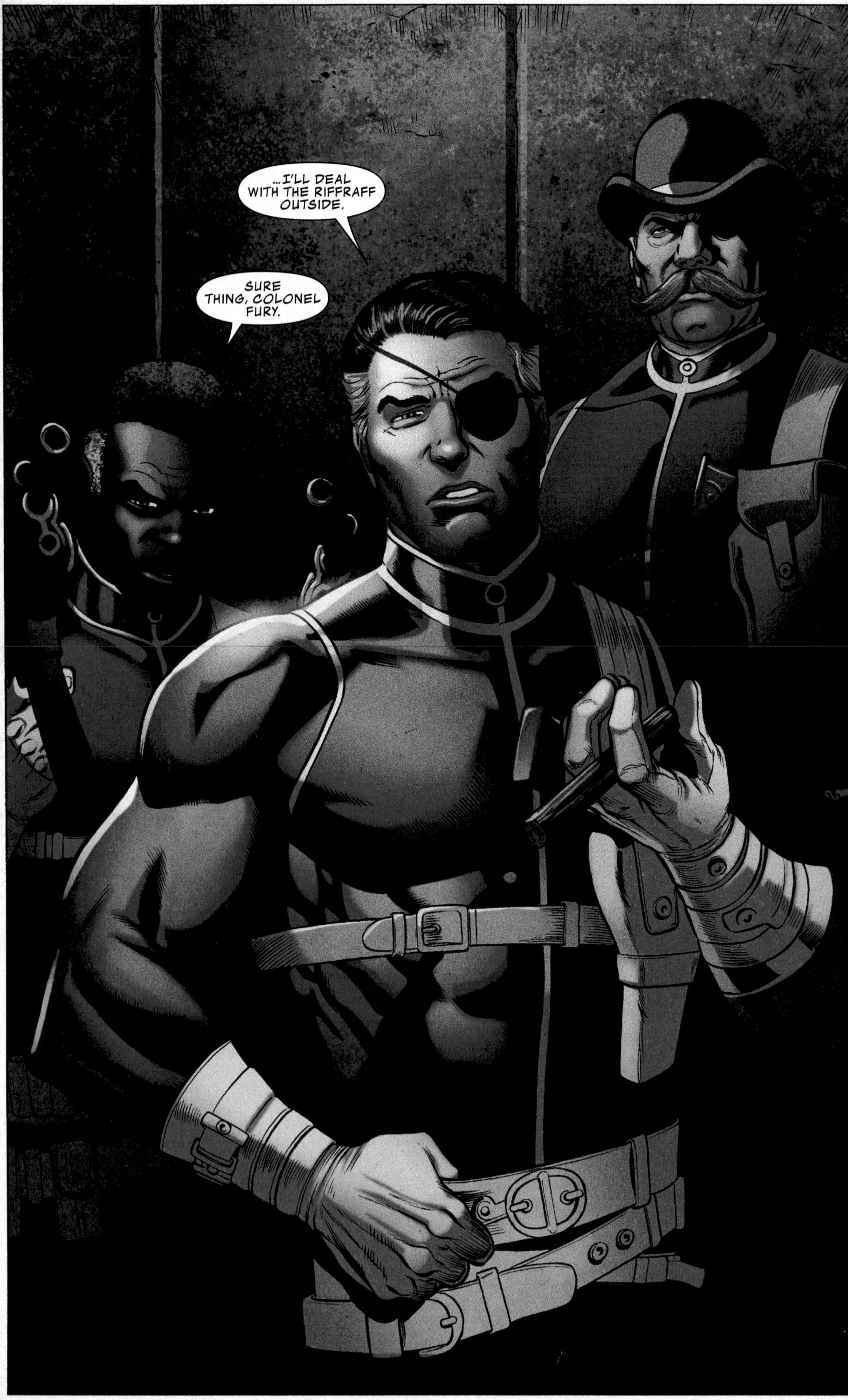
...I'LL DEAL WITH THE RIFFRAFF OUTSIDE.
SURE THING, COLONEL FURY.

4
MIKE DEODATO JR.
HEY! IS THAT
NICK FURY, AGENT OF...
S.H.I.E.L.D.?
ANSWER INSIDE.

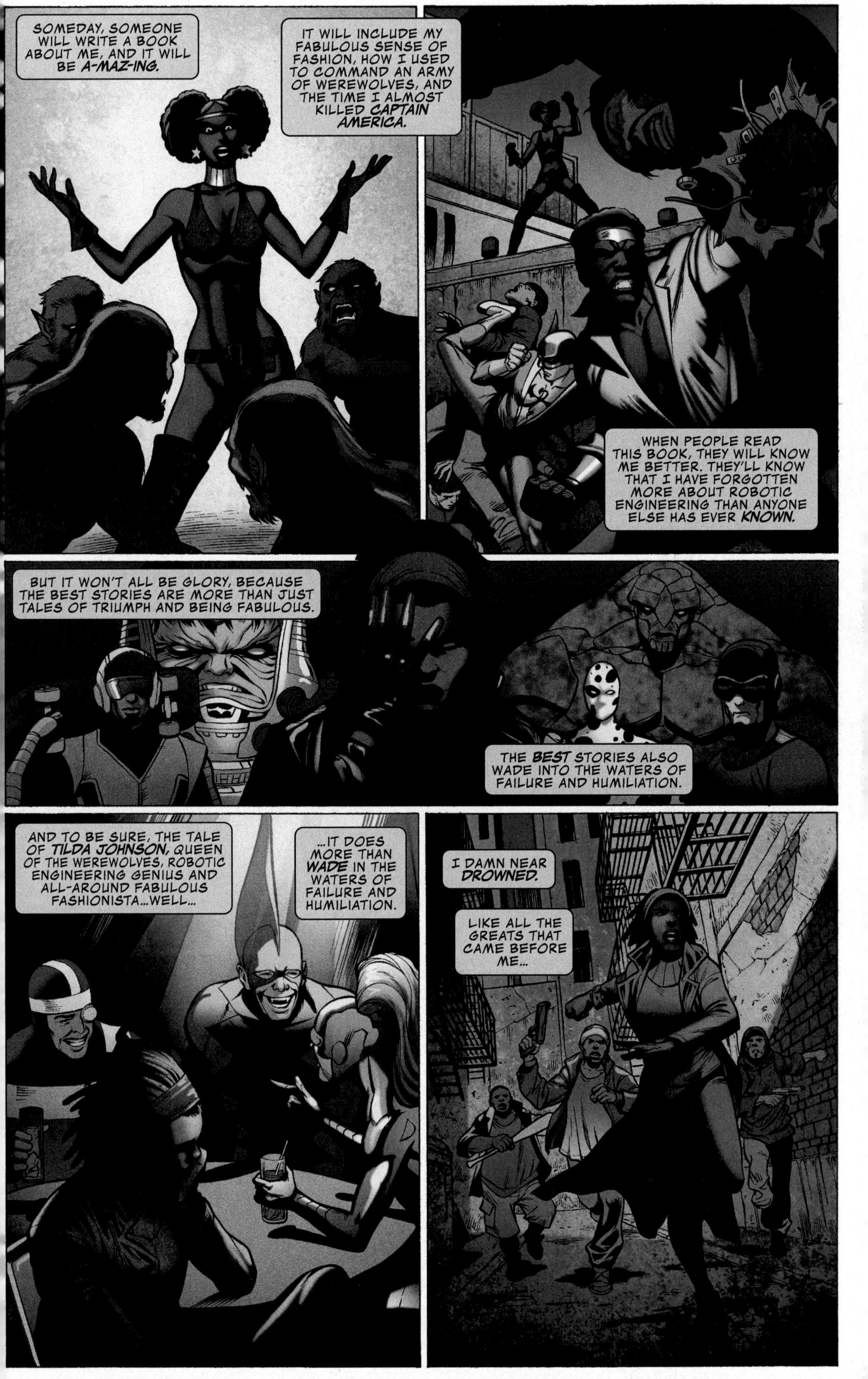
SOMEDAY, SOMEONE WILL WRITE A BOOK ABOUT ME, AND IT WILL BE A-MAZ-ING.
IT WILL INCLUDE MY FABULOUS SENSE OF FASHION, HOW I USED TO COMMAND AN ARMY OF WEREWOLVES, AND THE TIME I ALMOST KILLED CAPTAIN AMERICA.
WHEN PEOPLE READ THIS BOOK, THEY WILL KNOW ME BETTER. THEY'LL KNOW THAT I HAVE FORGOTTEN MORE ABOUT ROBOTIC ENGINEERING THAN ANYONE ELSE HAS EVER KNOWN.
BUT IT WON'T ALL BE GLORY, BECAUSE THE BEST STORIES ARE MORE THAN JUST TALES OF TRIUMPH AND BEING FABULOUS.
THE BEST STORIES ALSO WADE INTO THE WATERS OF FAILURE AND HUMILIATION.
AND TO BE SURE, THE TALE OF TILDA JOHNSON, QUEEN OF THE WEREWOLVES, ROBOTIC ENGINEERING GENIUS AND ALL-AROUND FABULOUS FASHIONISTA...WELL...
...IT DOES MORE THAN WADE IN THE WATERS OF FAILURE AND HUMILIATION.
I DAMN NEAR DROWNED.
LIKE ALL THE GREATS THAT CAME BEFORE ME...

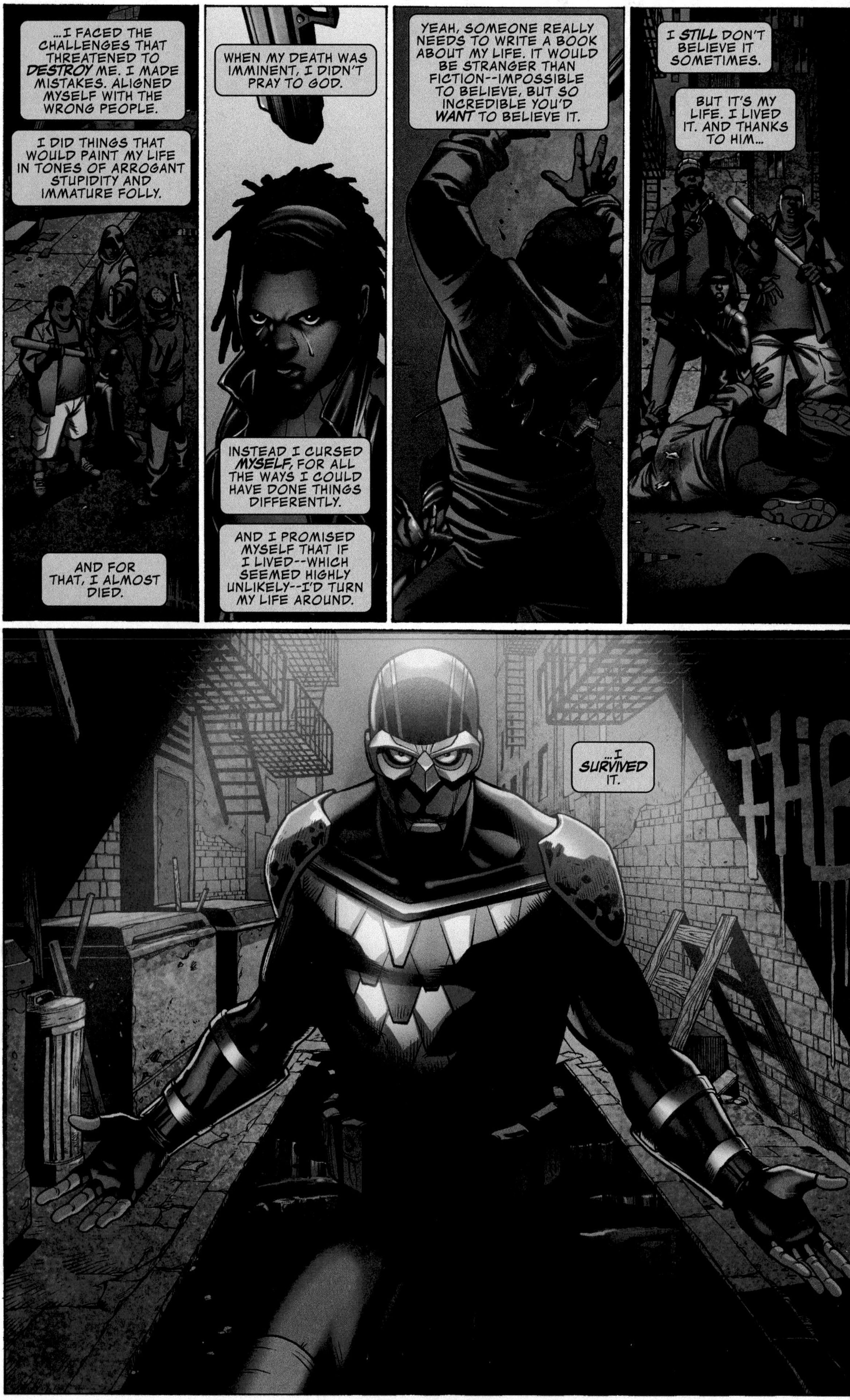
...I FACED THE CHALLENGES THAT THREATENED TO DESTROY ME. I MADE MISTAKES. ALIGNED MYSELF WITH THE WRONG PEOPLE.
I DID THINGS THAT WOULD PAINT MY LIFE IN TONES OF ARROGANT STUPIDITY AND IMMATURE FOLLY.
AND FOR THAT, I ALMOST DIED.
WHEN MY DEATH WAS IMMINENT, I DIDN'T PRAY TO GOD.
INSTEAD I CURSED MYSELF, FOR ALL THE WAYS I COULD HAVE DONE THINGS DIFFERENTLY.
AND I PROMISED MYSELF THAT IF I LIVED--WHICH SEEMED HIGHLY UNLIKELY--I'D TURN MY LIFE AROUND.
YEAH, SOMEONE REALLY NEEDS TO WRITE A BOOK ABOUT MY LIFE. IT WOULD BE STRANGER THAN FICTION--IMPOSSIBLE TO BELIEVE, BUT SO INCREDIBLE YOU'D WANT TO BELIEVE IT.
I STILL DON'T BELIEVE IT SOMETIMES.
BUT IT'S MY LIFE. I LIVED IT. AND THANKS TO HIM...
...I SURVIVED IT.

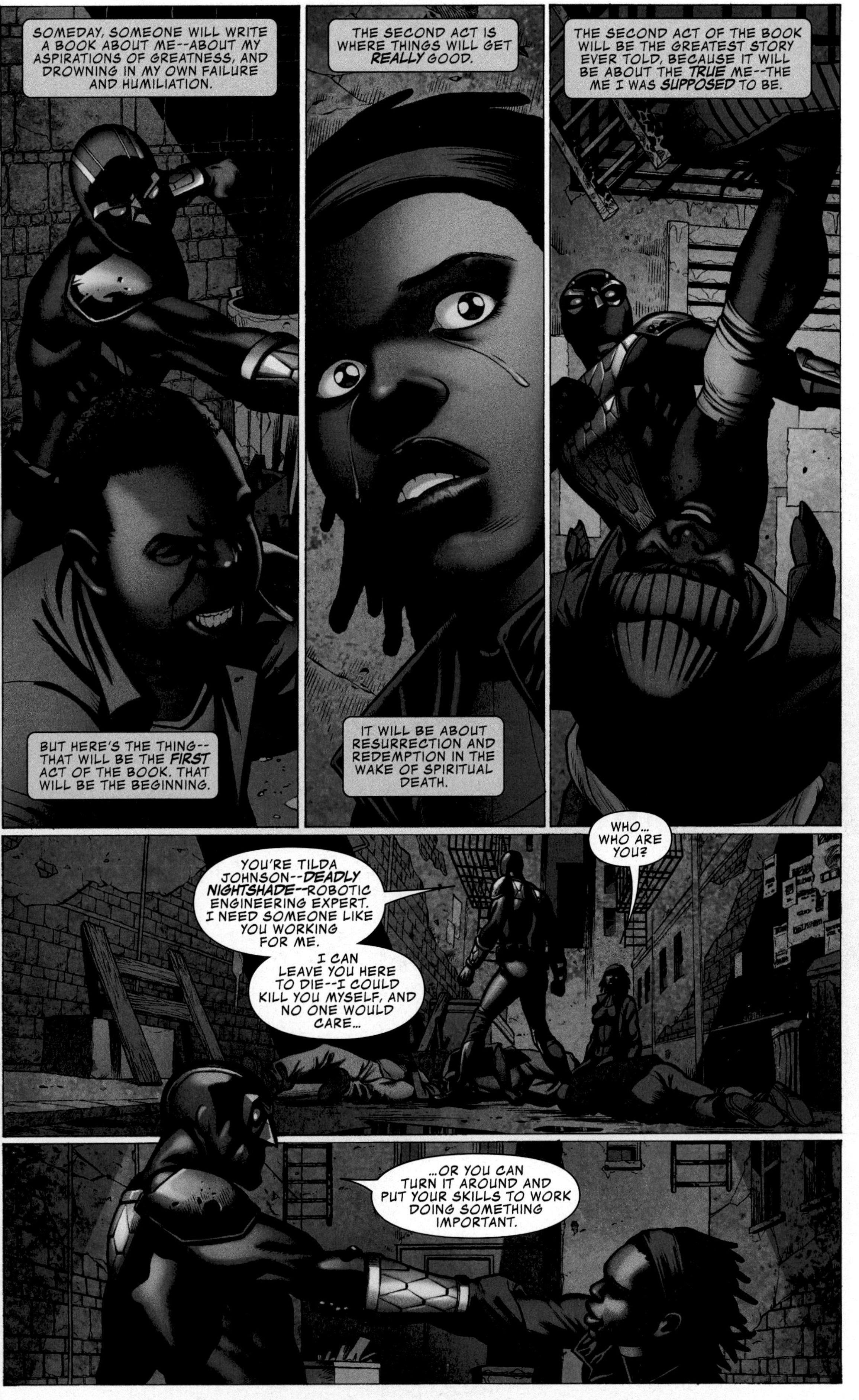
SOMEDAY, SOMEONE WILL WRITE A BOOK ABOUT ME--ABOUT MY ASPIRATIONS OF GREATNESS, AND DROWNING IN MY OWN FAILURE AND HUMILIATION.
BUT HERE'S THE THING--THAT WILL BE THE FIRST ACT OF THE BOOK. THAT WILL BE THE BEGINNING.
THE SECOND ACT IS WHERE THINGS WILL GET REALLY GOOD.
IT WILL BE ABOUT RESURRECTION AND REDEMPTION IN THE WAKE OF SPIRITUAL DEATH.
THE SECOND ACT OF THE BOOK WILL BE THE GREATEST STORY EVER TOLD, BECAUSE IT WILL BE ABOUT THE TRUE ME--THE ME I WAS SUPPOSED TO BE.
WHO... WHO ARE YOU?
YOU'RE TILDA JOHNSON--DEADLY NIGHTSHADE--ROBOTIC ENGINEERING EXPERT. I NEED SOMEONE LIKE YOU WORKING FOR ME.
I CAN LEAVE YOU HERE TO DIE--I COULD KILL YOU MYSELF, AND NO ONE WOULD CARE...
...OR YOU CAN TURN IT AROUND AND PUT YOUR SKILLS TO WORK DOING SOMETHING IMPORTANT.

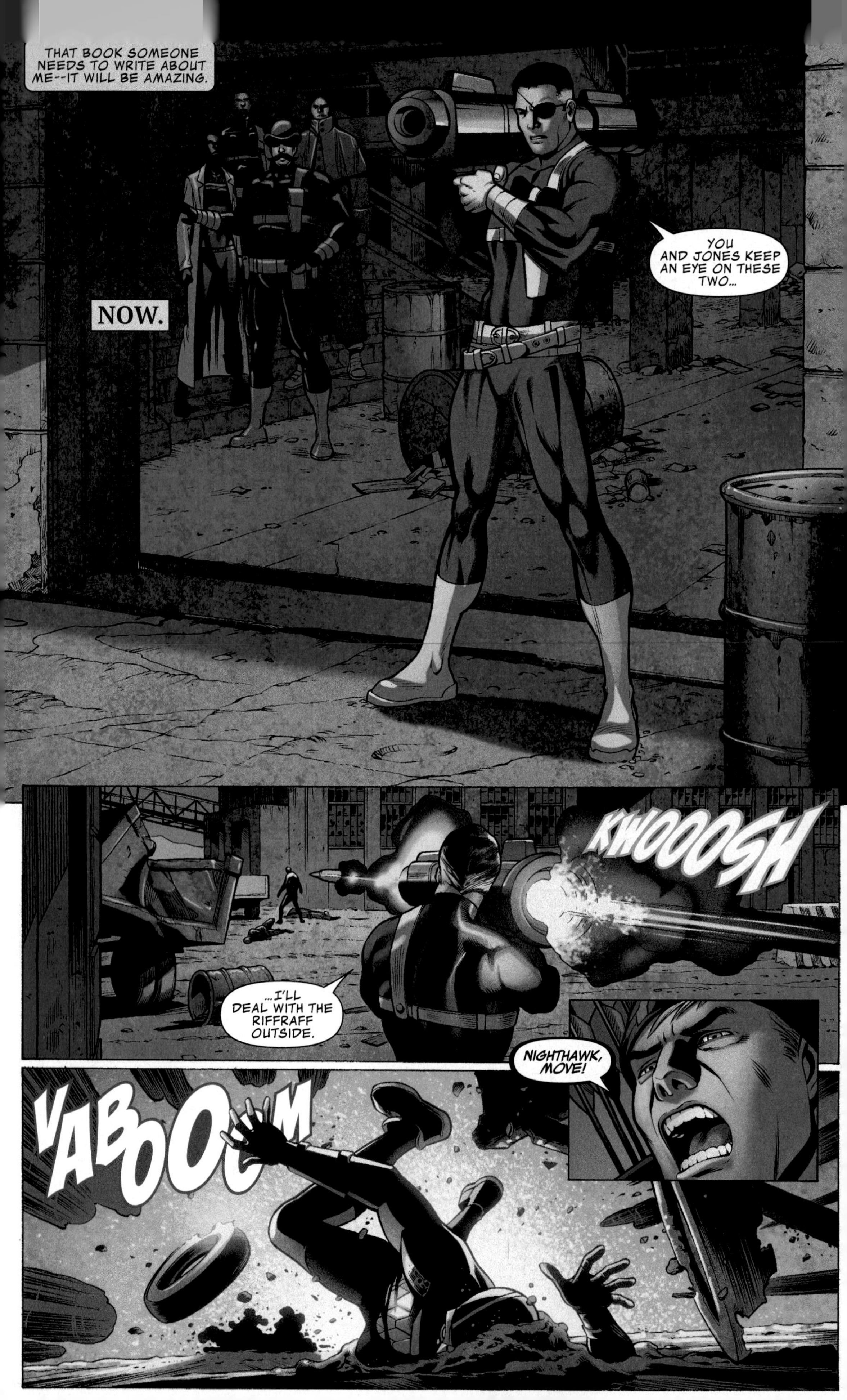

THAT BOOK SOMEONE NEEDS TO WRITE ABOUT ME--IT WILL BE AMAZING.
NOW.
YOU AND JONES KEEP AN EYE ON THESE TWO...
KWOOOSH
...I'LL DEAL WITH THE RIFFRAFF OUTSIDE.
NIGHTHAWK, MOVE!
VABOOOM

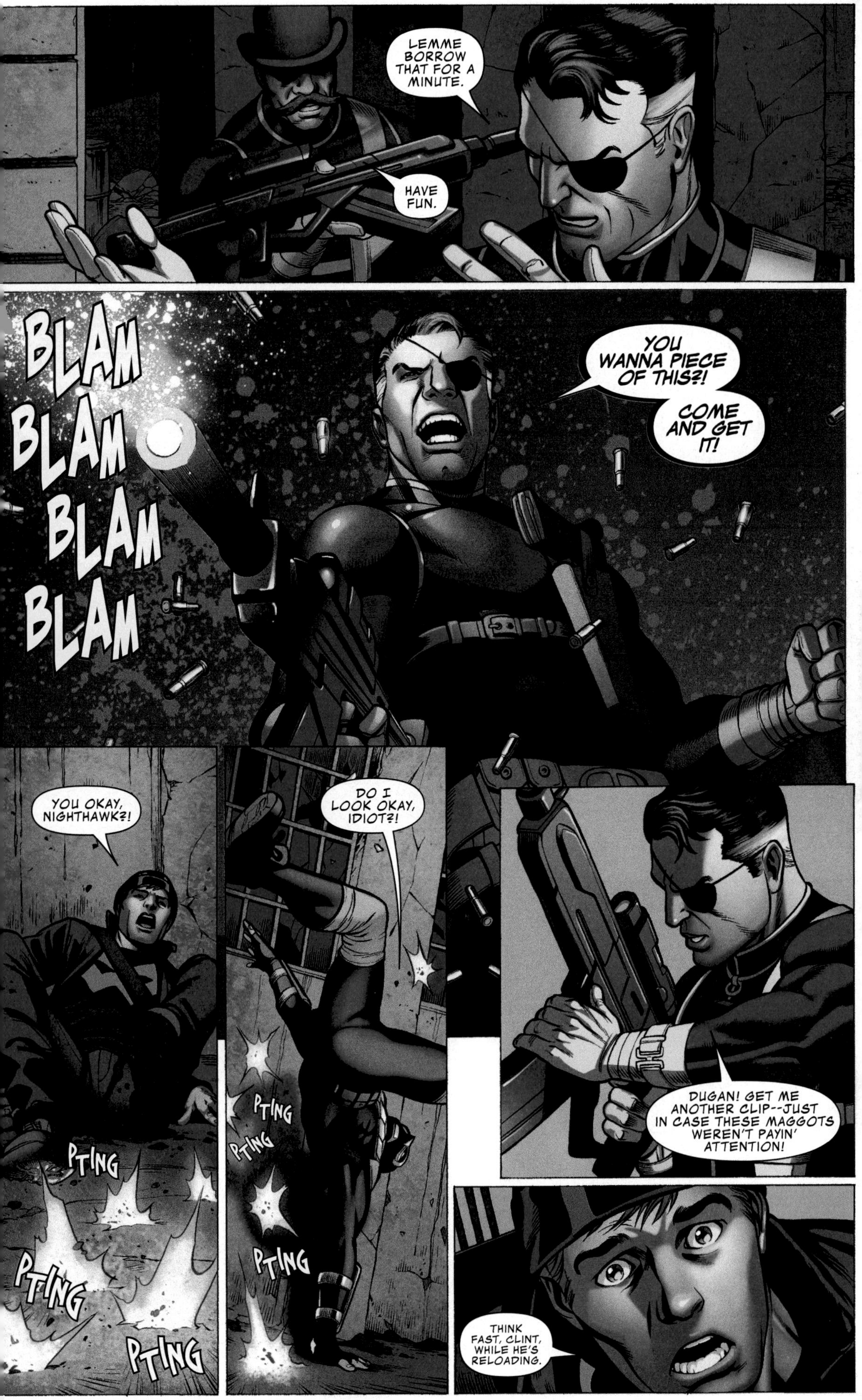
LEMME BORROW THAT FOR A MINUTE.
HAVE FUN.
BLAM BLAM BLAM BLAM
YOU WANNA PIECE OF THIS?!
COME AND GET IT!
YOU OKAY, NIGHTHAWK?!
DO I LOOK OKAY, IDIOT?!
PTING
PTING
PTING
PTING
PTING
PTING
PTING
DUGAN! GET ME ANOTHER CLIP--JUST IN CASE THESE MAGGOTS WEREN'T PAYIN' ATTENTION!
THINK FAST, CLINT, WHILE HE'S RELOADING.

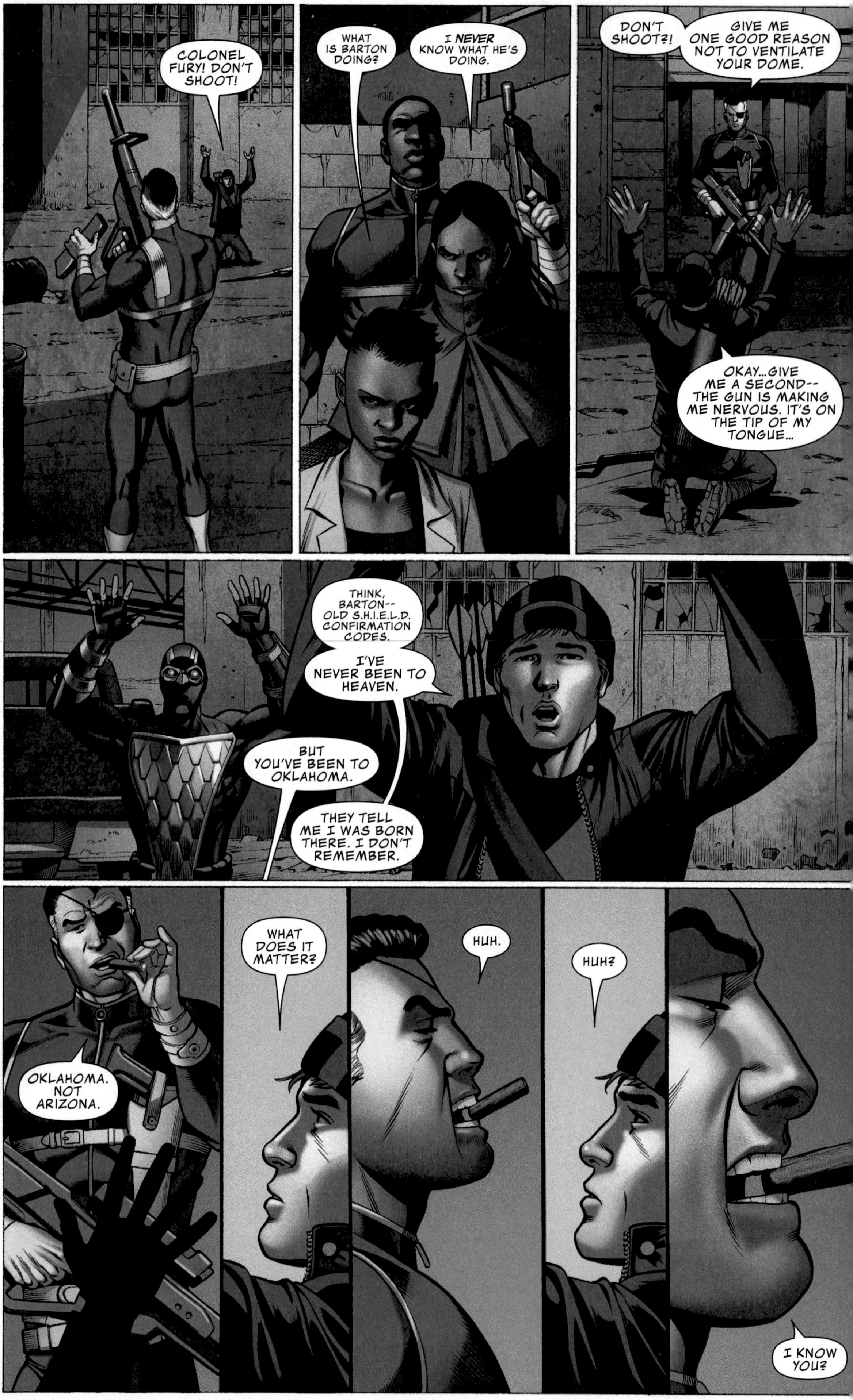
COLONEL FURY! DON'T SHOOT!
WHAT IS BARTON DOING?
I NEVER KNOW WHAT HE'S DOING.
DON'T SHOOT?!
GIVE ME ONE GOOD REASON NOT TO VENTILATE YOUR DOME.
OKAY...GIVE ME A SECOND--THE GUN IS MAKING ME NERVOUS. IT'S ON THE TIP OF MY TONGUE...
THINK, BARTON--OLD S.H.I.E.L.D. CONFIRMATION CODES.
I'VE NEVER BEEN TO HEAVEN.
BUT YOU'VE BEEN TO OKLAHOMA.
THEY TELL ME I WAS BORN THERE. I DON'T REMEMBER.
OKLAHOMA. NOT ARIZONA.
WHAT DOES IT MATTER?
HUH.
HUH?
I KNOW YOU?

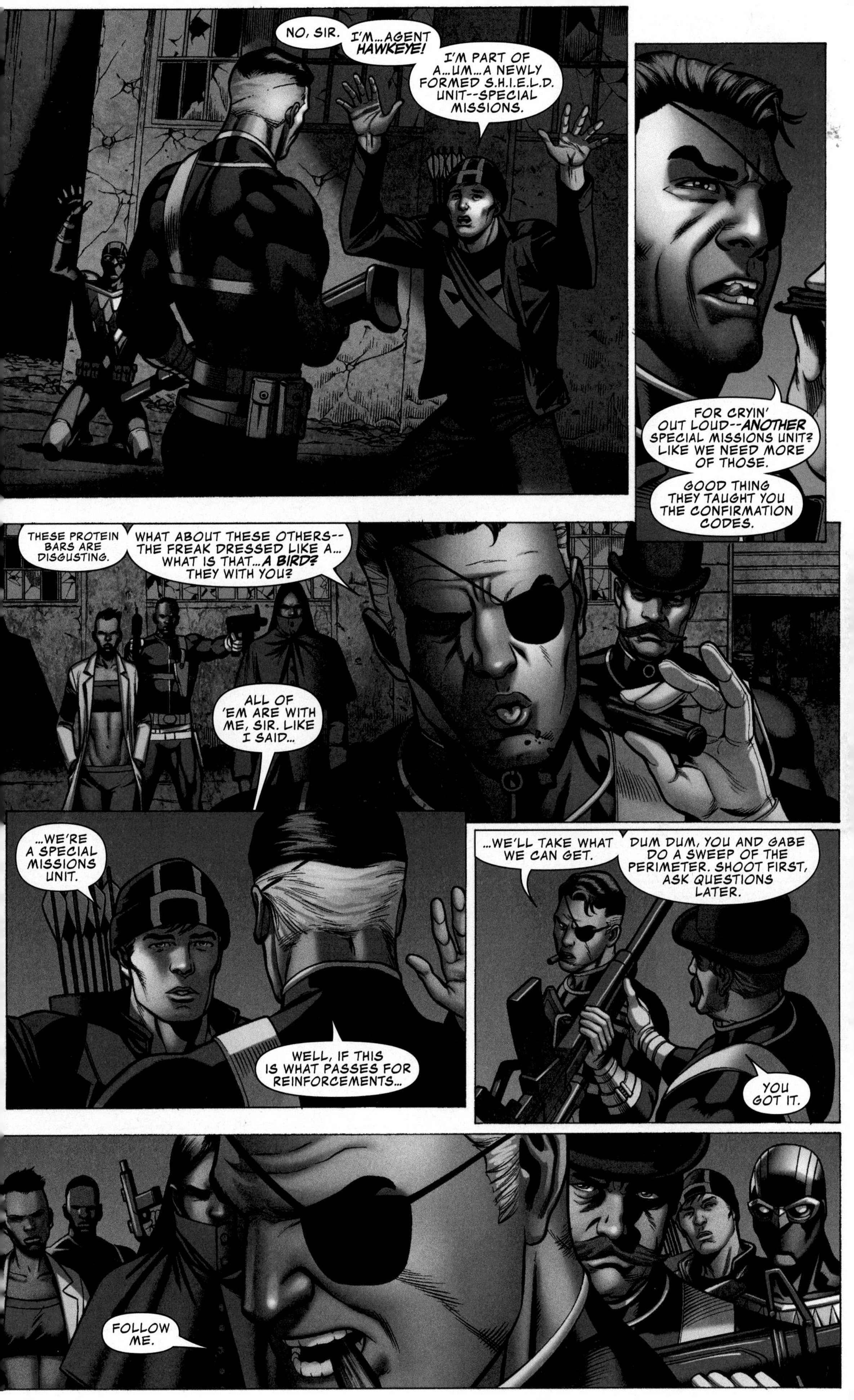

NO, SIR.
I'M...AGENT HAWKEYE!
I'M PART OF A...UM...A NEWLY FORMED S.H.I.E.L.D. UNIT--SPECIAL MISSIONS.
FOR CRYIN' OUT LOUD--ANOTHER SPECIAL MISSIONS UNIT? LIKE WE NEED MORE OF THOSE.
GOOD THING THEY TAUGHT YOU THE CONFIRMATION CODES.
THESE PROTEIN BARS ARE DISGUSTING.
WHAT ABOUT THESE OTHERS--THE FREAK DRESSED LIKE A... WHAT IS THAT...A BIRD? THEY WITH YOU?
ALL OF 'EM ARE WITH ME, SIR. LIKE I SAID...
...WE'RE A SPECIAL MISSIONS UNIT.
WELL, IF THIS IS WHAT PASSES FOR REINFORCEMENTS...
...WE'LL TAKE WHAT WE CAN GET.
DUM DUM, YOU AND GABE DO A SWEEP OF THE PERIMETER. SHOOT FIRST, ASK QUESTIONS LATER.
YOU GOT IT.
FOLLOW ME.

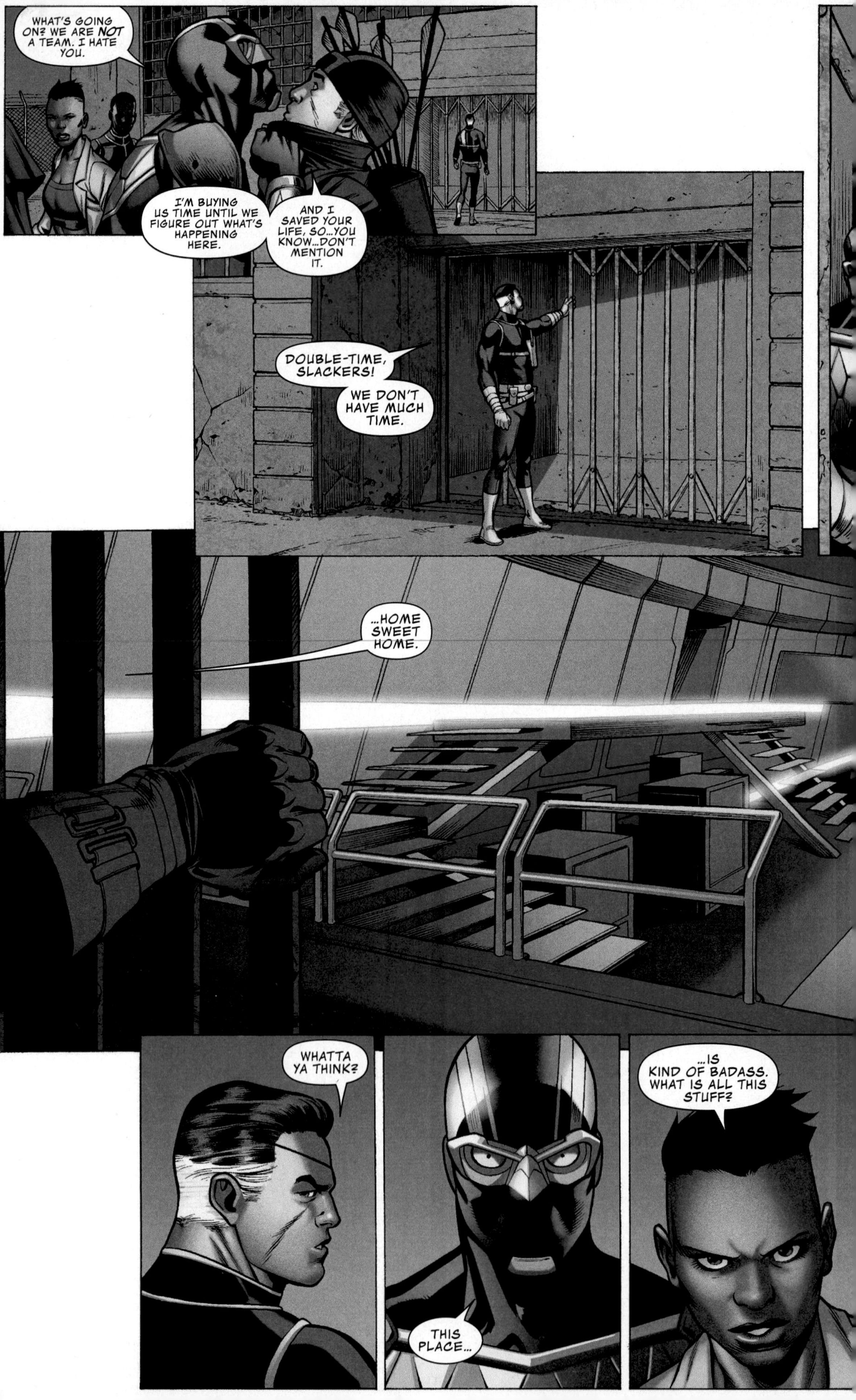
WHAT'S GOING ON? WE ARE NOT A TEAM. I HATE YOU.
I'M BUYING US TIME UNTIL WE FIGURE OUT WHAT'S HAPPENING HERE.
AND I SAVED YOUR LIFE, SO...YOU KNOW...DON'T MENTION IT.
DOUBLE-TIME, SLACKERS!
WE DON'T HAVE MUCH TIME.
...HOME SWEET HOME.
WHATTA YA THINK?
THIS PLACE...
...IS KIND OF BADASS. WHAT IS ALL THIS STUFF?

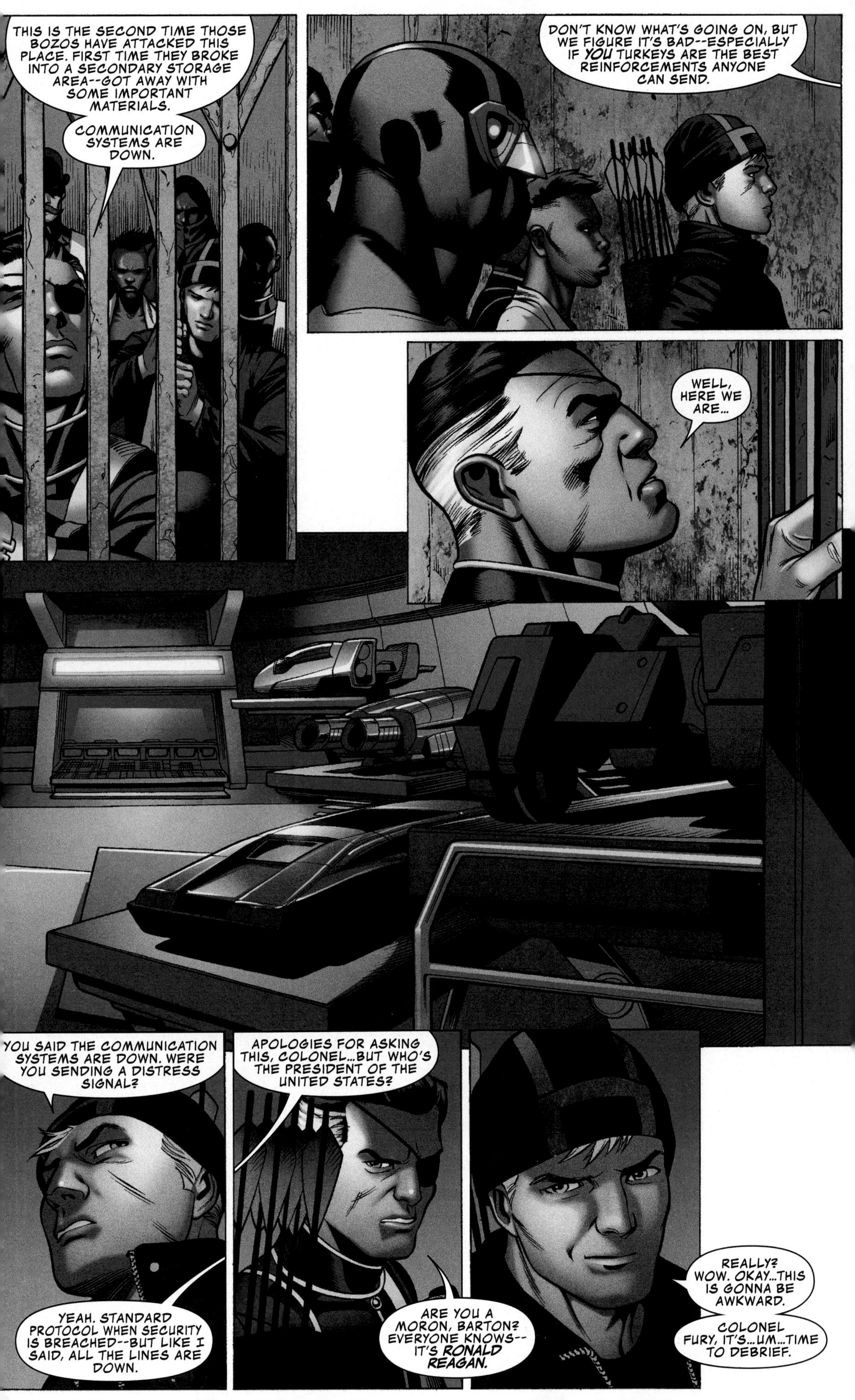
THIS IS THE SECOND TIME THOSE BOZOS HAVE ATTACKED THIS PLACE. FIRST TIME THEY BROKE INTO A SECONDARY STORAGE AREA--GOT AWAY WITH SOME IMPORTANT MATERIALS.
COMMUNICATION SYSTEMS ARE DOWN.
DON'T KNOW WHAT'S GOING ON, BUT WE FIGURE IT'S BAD--ESPECIALLY IF *YOU* TURKEYS ARE THE BEST REINFORCEMENTS ANYONE CAN SEND.
WELL, HERE WE ARE...
YOU SAID THE COMMUNICATION SYSTEMS ARE DOWN. WERE YOU SENDING A DISTRESS SIGNAL?
YEAH. STANDARD PROTOCOL WHEN SECURITY IS BREACHED--BUT LIKE I SAID, ALL THE LINES ARE DOWN.
APOLOGIES FOR ASKING THIS, COLONEL...BUT WHO'S THE PRESIDENT OF THE UNITED STATES?
ARE YOU A MORON, BARTON? EVERYONE KNOWS--IT'S *RONALD REAGAN.*
REALLY? WOW. OKAY...THIS IS GONNA BE AWKWARD.
COLONEL FURY, IT'S...UM...TIME TO DEBRIEF.

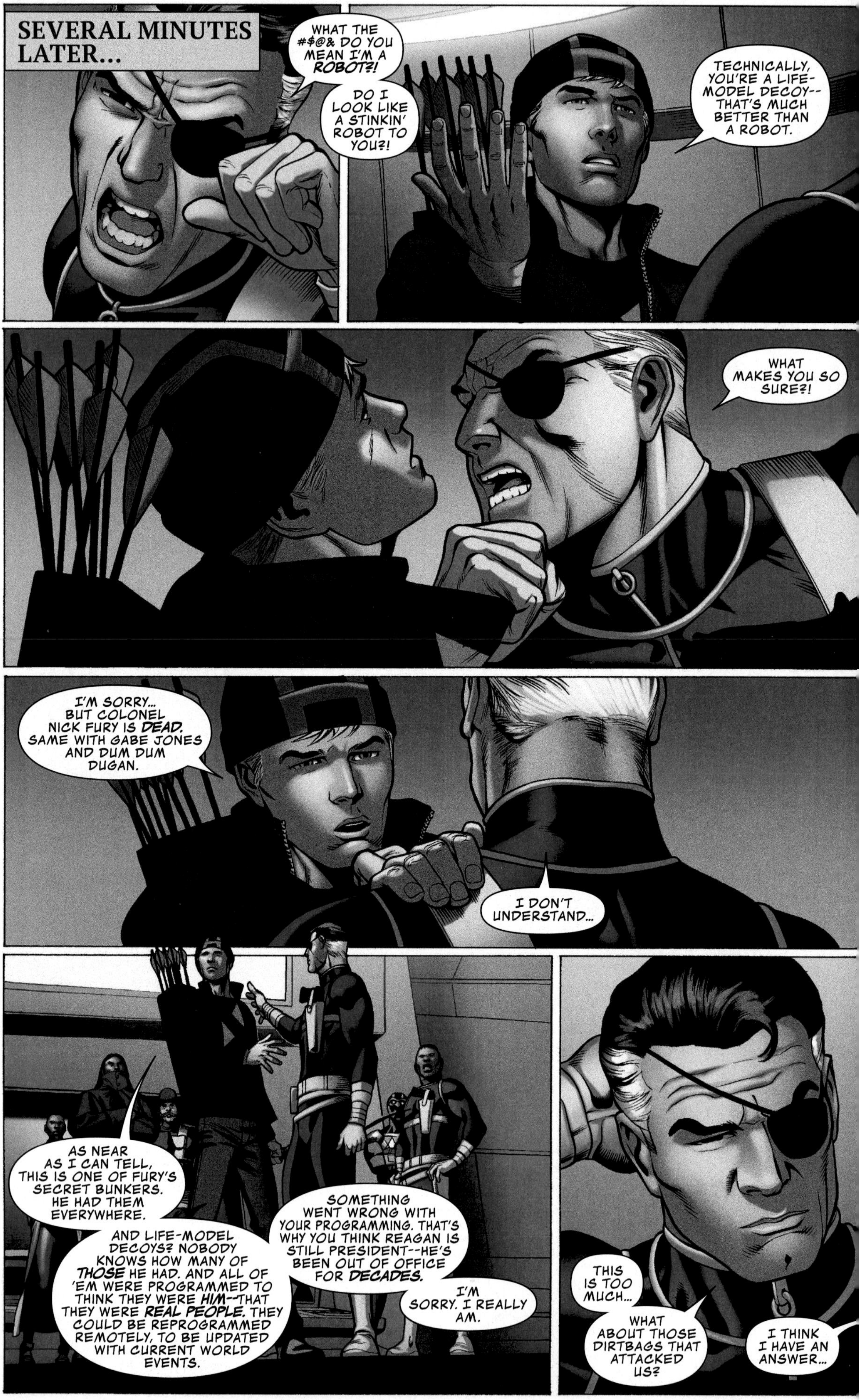
SEVERAL MINUTES LATER...
WHAT THE #$@& DO YOU MEAN I'M A ROBOT?!
DO I LOOK LIKE A STINKIN' ROBOT TO YOU?!
TECHNICALLY, YOU'RE A LIFE-MODEL DECOY--THAT'S MUCH BETTER THAN A ROBOT.
WHAT MAKES YOU SO SURE?!
I'M SORRY... BUT COLONEL NICK FURY IS DEAD. SAME WITH GABE JONES AND DUM DUM DUGAN.
I DON'T UNDERSTAND...
AS NEAR AS I CAN TELL, THIS IS ONE OF FURY'S SECRET BUNKERS. HE HAD THEM EVERYWHERE.
AND LIFE-MODEL DECOYS? NOBODY KNOWS HOW MANY OF THOSE HE HAD. AND ALL OF 'EM WERE PROGRAMMED TO THINK THEY WERE HIM--THAT THEY WERE REAL PEOPLE. THEY COULD BE REPROGRAMMED REMOTELY, TO BE UPDATED WITH CURRENT WORLD EVENTS.
SOMETHING WENT WRONG WITH YOUR PROGRAMMING. THAT'S WHY YOU THINK REAGAN IS STILL PRESIDENT--HE'S BEEN OUT OF OFFICE FOR DECADES.
I'M SORRY. I REALLY AM.
THIS IS TOO MUCH...
WHAT ABOUT THOSE DIRTBAGS THAT ATTACKED US?
I THINK I HAVE AN ANSWER...

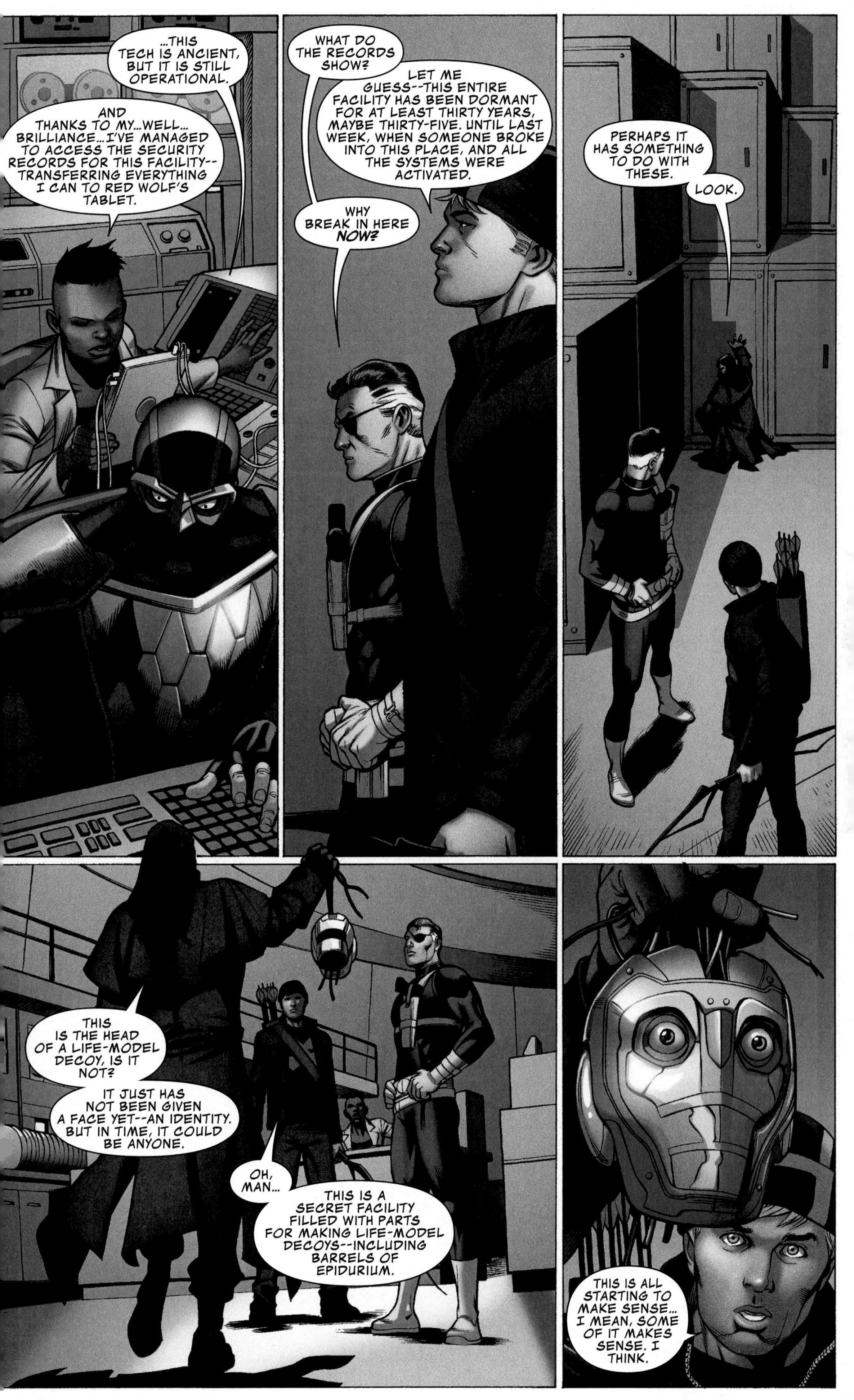
...THIS TECH IS ANCIENT, BUT IT IS STILL OPERATIONAL.
AND THANKS TO MY...WELL... BRILLIANCE...I'VE MANAGED TO ACCESS THE SECURITY RECORDS FOR THIS FACILITY--TRANSFERRING EVERYTHING I CAN TO RED WOLF'S TABLET.
WHAT DO THE RECORDS SHOW?
LET ME GUESS--THIS ENTIRE FACILITY HAS BEEN DORMANT FOR AT LEAST THIRTY YEARS, MAYBE THIRTY-FIVE. UNTIL LAST WEEK, WHEN SOMEONE BROKE INTO THIS PLACE, AND ALL THE SYSTEMS WERE ACTIVATED.
WHY BREAK IN HERE *NOW?*
PERHAPS IT HAS SOMETHING TO DO WITH THESE.
LOOK.
THIS IS THE HEAD OF A LIFE-MODEL DECOY, IS IT NOT?
IT JUST HAS NOT BEEN GIVEN A FACE YET--AN IDENTITY. BUT IN TIME, IT COULD BE ANYONE.
OH, MAN...
THIS IS A SECRET FACILITY FILLED WITH PARTS FOR MAKING LIFE-MODEL DECOYS--INCLUDING BARRELS OF EPIDURIUM.
THIS IS ALL STARTING TO MAKE SENSE... I MEAN, SOME OF IT MAKES SENSE. I THINK.

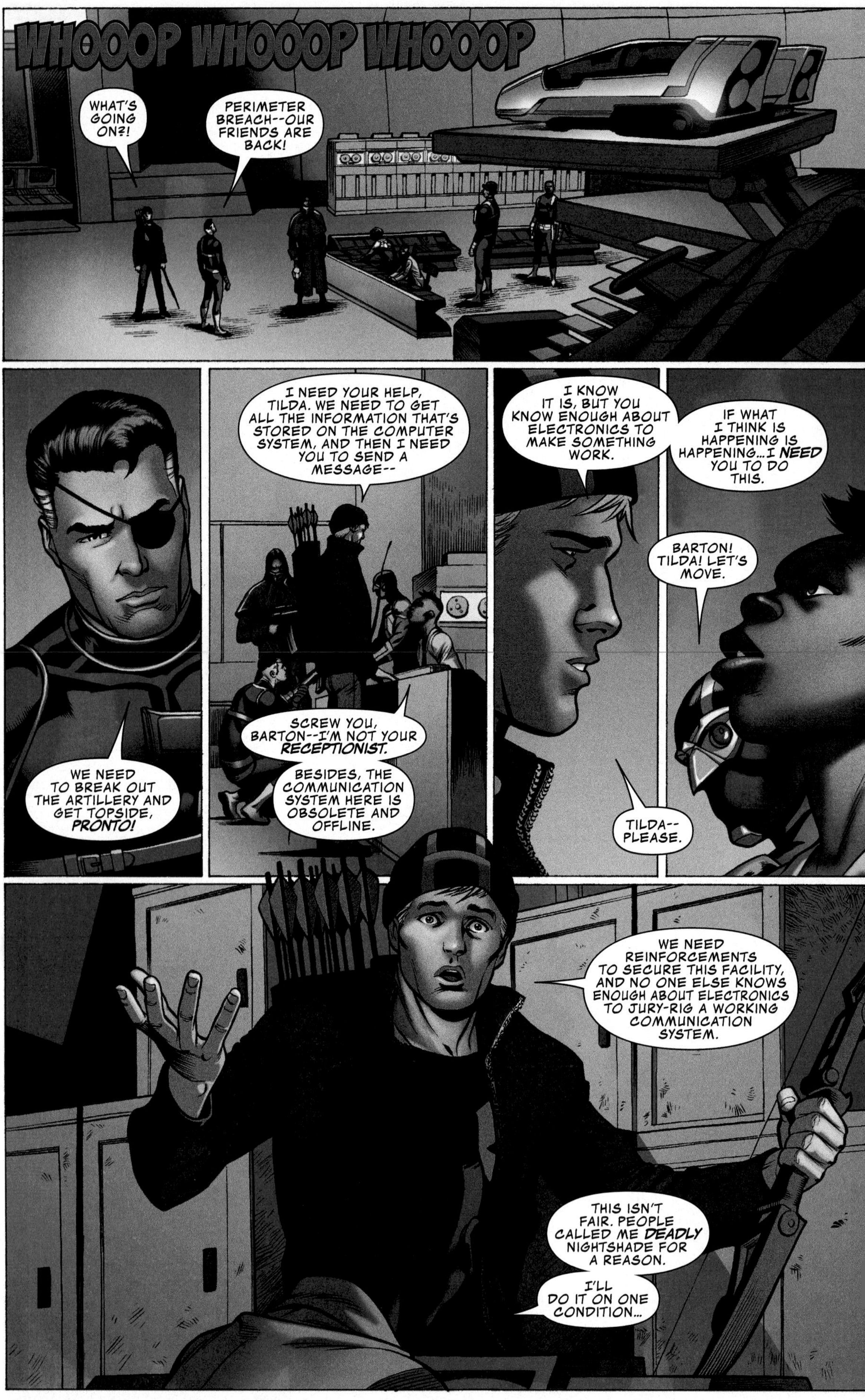
WHOOOP WHOOOP WHOOOP
WHAT'S GOING ON?!
PERIMETER BREACH--OUR FRIENDS ARE BACK!
WE NEED TO BREAK OUT THE ARTILLERY AND GET TOPSIDE, PRONTO!
I NEED YOUR HELP, TILDA. WE NEED TO GET ALL THE INFORMATION THAT'S STORED ON THE COMPUTER SYSTEM, AND THEN I NEED YOU TO SEND A MESSAGE--
SCREW YOU, BARTON--I'M NOT YOUR RECEPTIONIST.
BESIDES, THE COMMUNICATION SYSTEM HERE IS OBSOLETE AND OFFLINE.
I KNOW IT IS, BUT YOU KNOW ENOUGH ABOUT ELECTRONICS TO MAKE SOMETHING WORK.
TILDA--PLEASE.
IF WHAT I THINK IS HAPPENING IS HAPPENING...I NEED YOU TO DO THIS.
BARTON! TILDA! LET'S MOVE.
WE NEED REINFORCEMENTS TO SECURE THIS FACILITY, AND NO ONE ELSE KNOWS ENOUGH ABOUT ELECTRONICS TO JURY-RIG A WORKING COMMUNICATION SYSTEM.
THIS ISN'T FAIR. PEOPLE CALLED ME DEADLY NIGHTSHADE FOR A REASON.
I'LL DO IT ON ONE CONDITION...

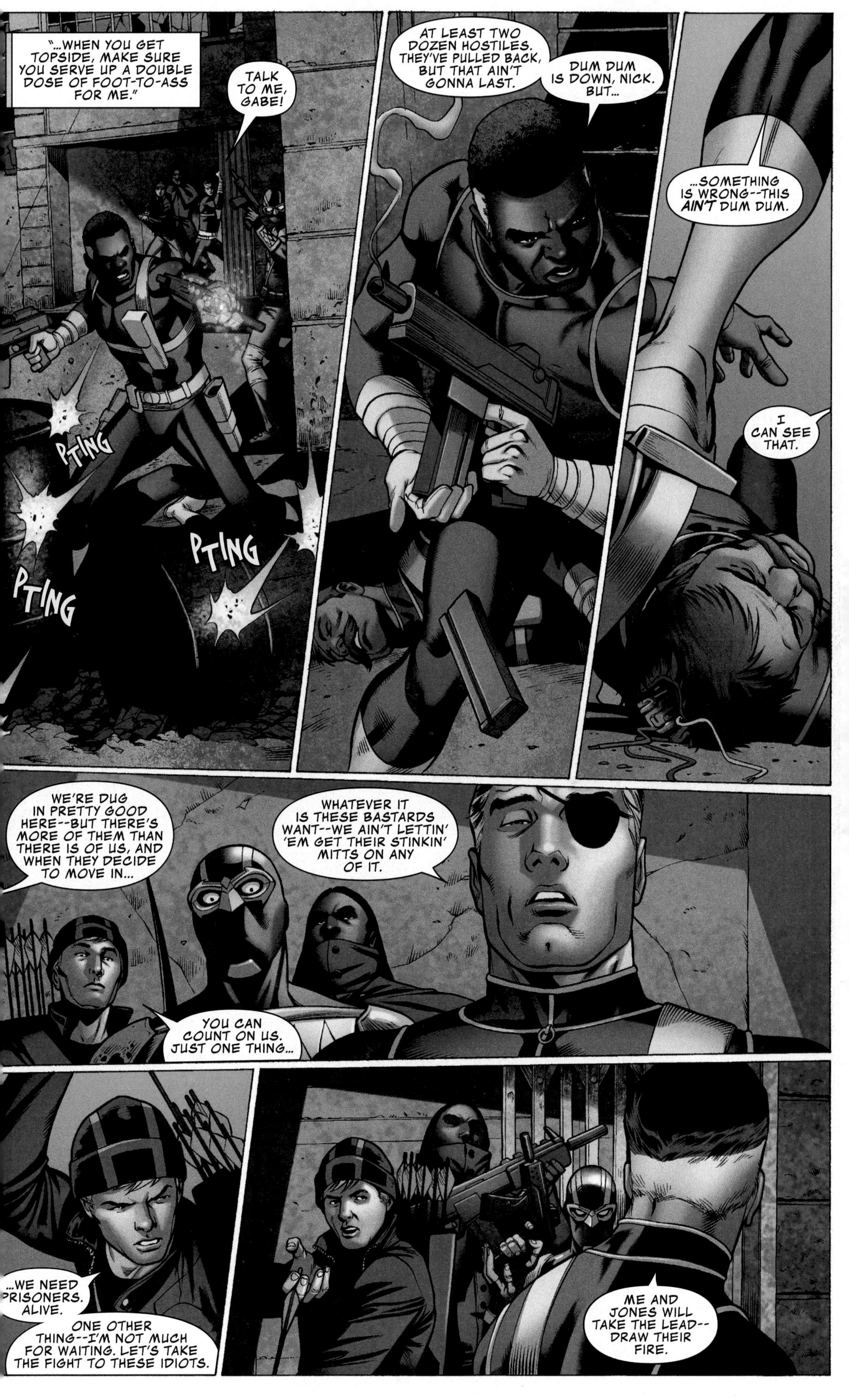
"...WHEN YOU GET TOPSIDE, MAKE SURE YOU SERVE UP A DOUBLE DOSE OF FOOT-TO-ASS FOR ME."
TALK TO ME, GABE!
PTING
PTING
PTING
AT LEAST TWO DOZEN HOSTILES. THEY'VE PULLED BACK, BUT THAT AIN'T GONNA LAST.
DUM DUM IS DOWN, NICK. BUT...
...SOMETHING IS WRONG--THIS AIN'T DUM DUM.
I CAN SEE THAT.
WE'RE DUG IN PRETTY GOOD HERE--BUT THERE'S MORE OF THEM THAN THERE IS OF US, AND WHEN THEY DECIDE TO MOVE IN...
WHATEVER IT IS THESE BASTARDS WANT--WE AIN'T LETTIN' 'EM GET THEIR STINKIN' MITTS ON ANY OF IT.
YOU CAN COUNT ON US. JUST ONE THING...
...WE NEED PRISONERS. ALIVE.
ONE OTHER THING--I'M NOT MUCH FOR WAITING. LET'S TAKE THE FIGHT TO THESE IDIOTS.
ME AND JONES WILL TAKE THE LEAD-- DRAW THEIR FIRE.

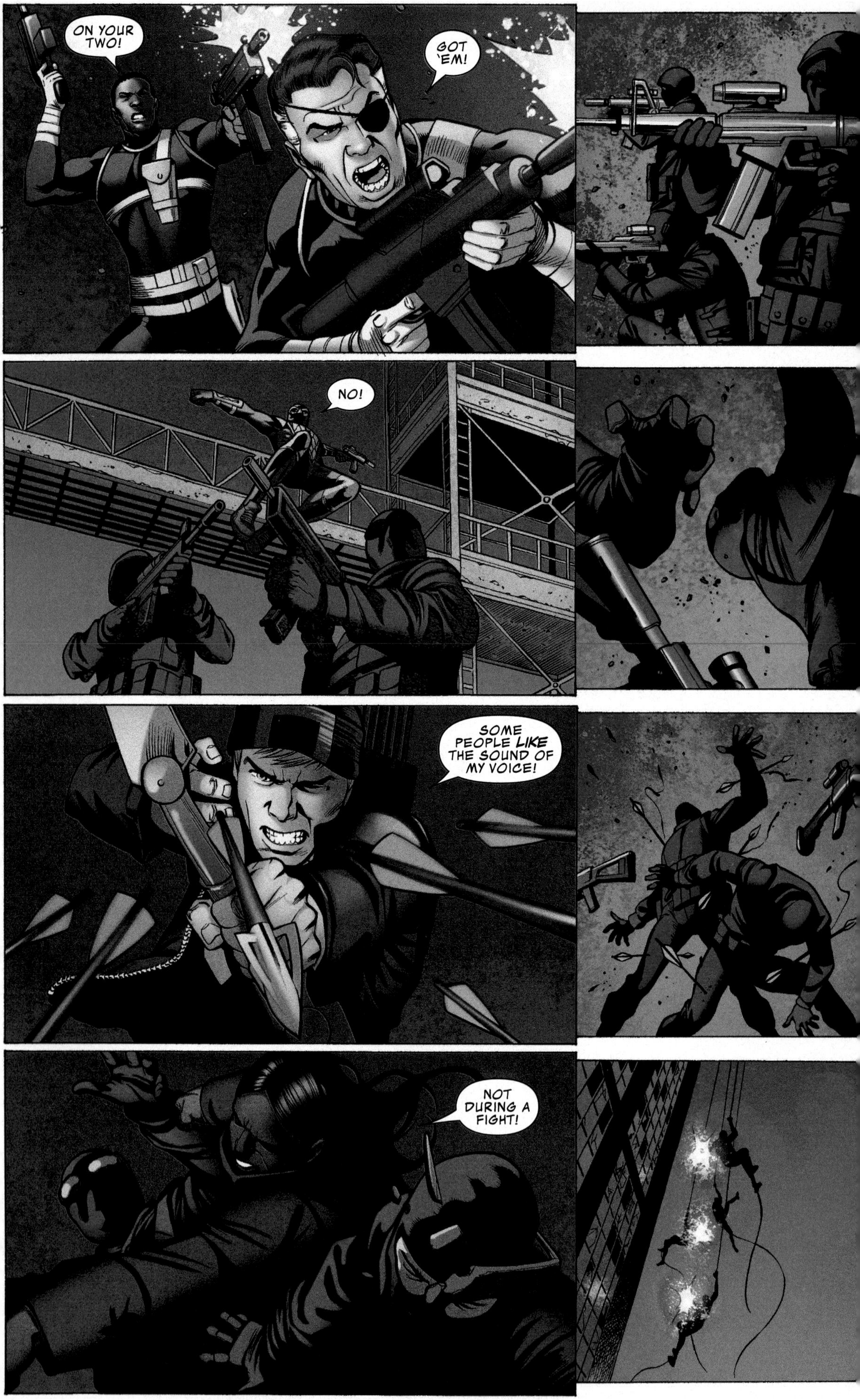
ON YOUR TWO!
GOT 'EM!
NO!
SOME PEOPLE LIKE THE SOUND OF MY VOICE!
NOT DURING A FIGHT!

SOMEDAY, SOMEONE WILL WRITE A BOOK ABOUT ME, TILDA JOHNSON.

HEY, NIGHTHAWK-- AREN'T YOU GLAD WE TEAMED UP?!

ALSO KNOWN AS NIGHTSHADE.

MUST YOU TALK SO MUCH, BARTON?!

ALSO KNOWN AS *DEADLY* NIGHTSHADE.

NOT ME!

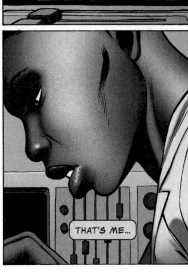

LESS TALK, MORE REVENGE!

THAT'S ME...

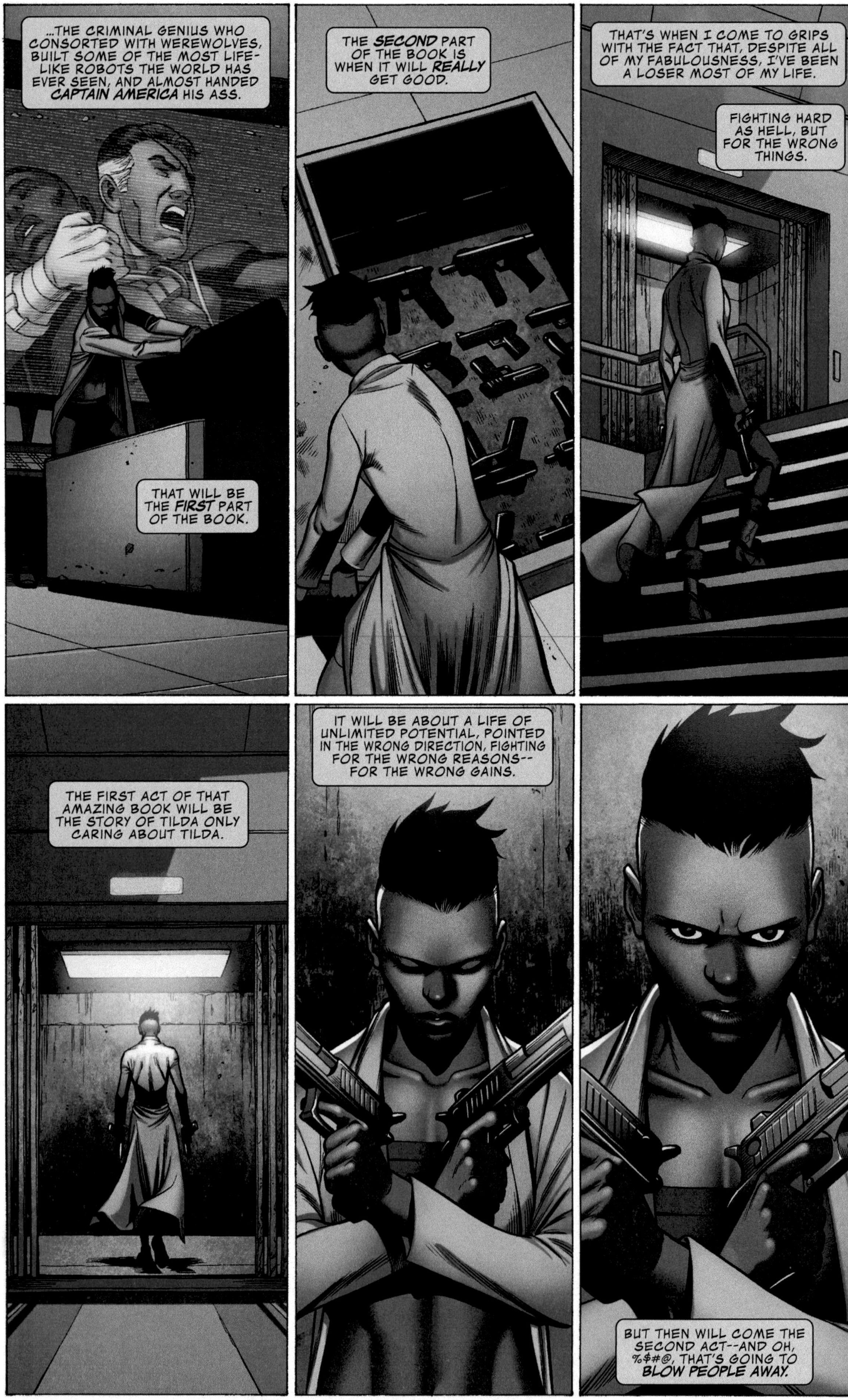
...THE CRIMINAL GENIUS WHO CONSORTED WITH WEREWOLVES, BUILT SOME OF THE MOST LIFE-LIKE ROBOTS THE WORLD HAS EVER SEEN, AND ALMOST HANDED CAPTAIN AMERICA HIS ASS.
THAT WILL BE THE FIRST PART OF THE BOOK.
THE SECOND PART OF THE BOOK IS WHEN IT WILL REALLY GET GOOD.
THAT'S WHEN I COME TO GRIPS WITH THE FACT THAT, DESPITE ALL OF MY FABULOUSNESS, I'VE BEEN A LOSER MOST OF MY LIFE.
FIGHTING HARD AS HELL, BUT FOR THE WRONG THINGS.
THE FIRST ACT OF THAT AMAZING BOOK WILL BE THE STORY OF TILDA ONLY CARING ABOUT TILDA.
IT WILL BE ABOUT A LIFE OF UNLIMITED POTENTIAL, POINTED IN THE WRONG DIRECTION, FIGHTING FOR THE WRONG REASONS-- FOR THE WRONG GAINS.
BUT THEN WILL COME THE SECOND ACT--AND OH, %$#@, THAT'S GOING TO BLOW PEOPLE AWAY.

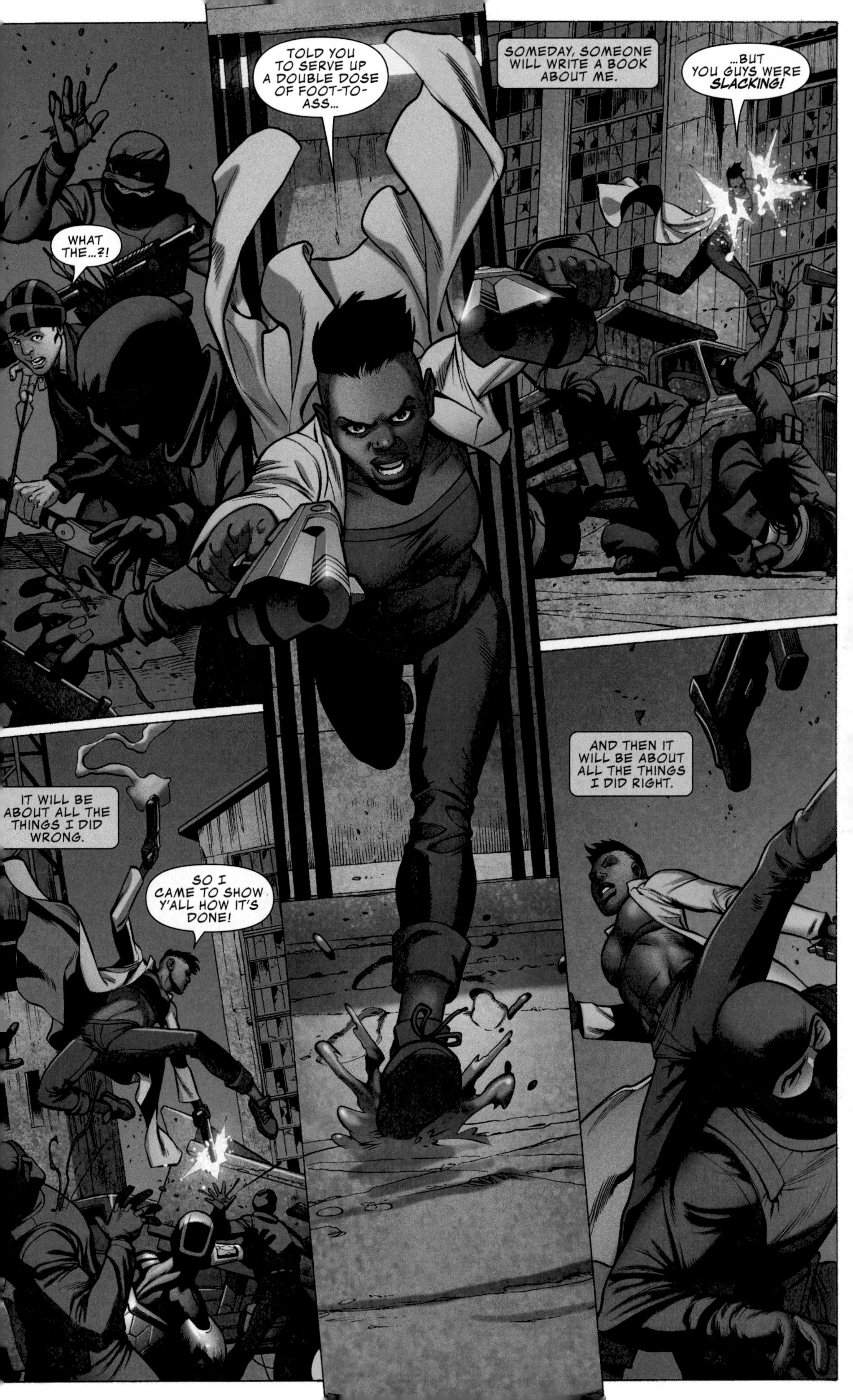
WHAT THE...?!
TOLD YOU TO SERVE UP A DOUBLE DOSE OF FOOT-TO-ASS...
SOMEDAY, SOMEONE WILL WRITE A BOOK ABOUT ME.
...BUT YOU GUYS WERE SLACKING!
IT WILL BE ABOUT ALL THE THINGS I DID WRONG.
SO I CAME TO SHOW Y'ALL HOW IT'S DONE!
AND THEN IT WILL BE ABOUT ALL THE THINGS I DID RIGHT.

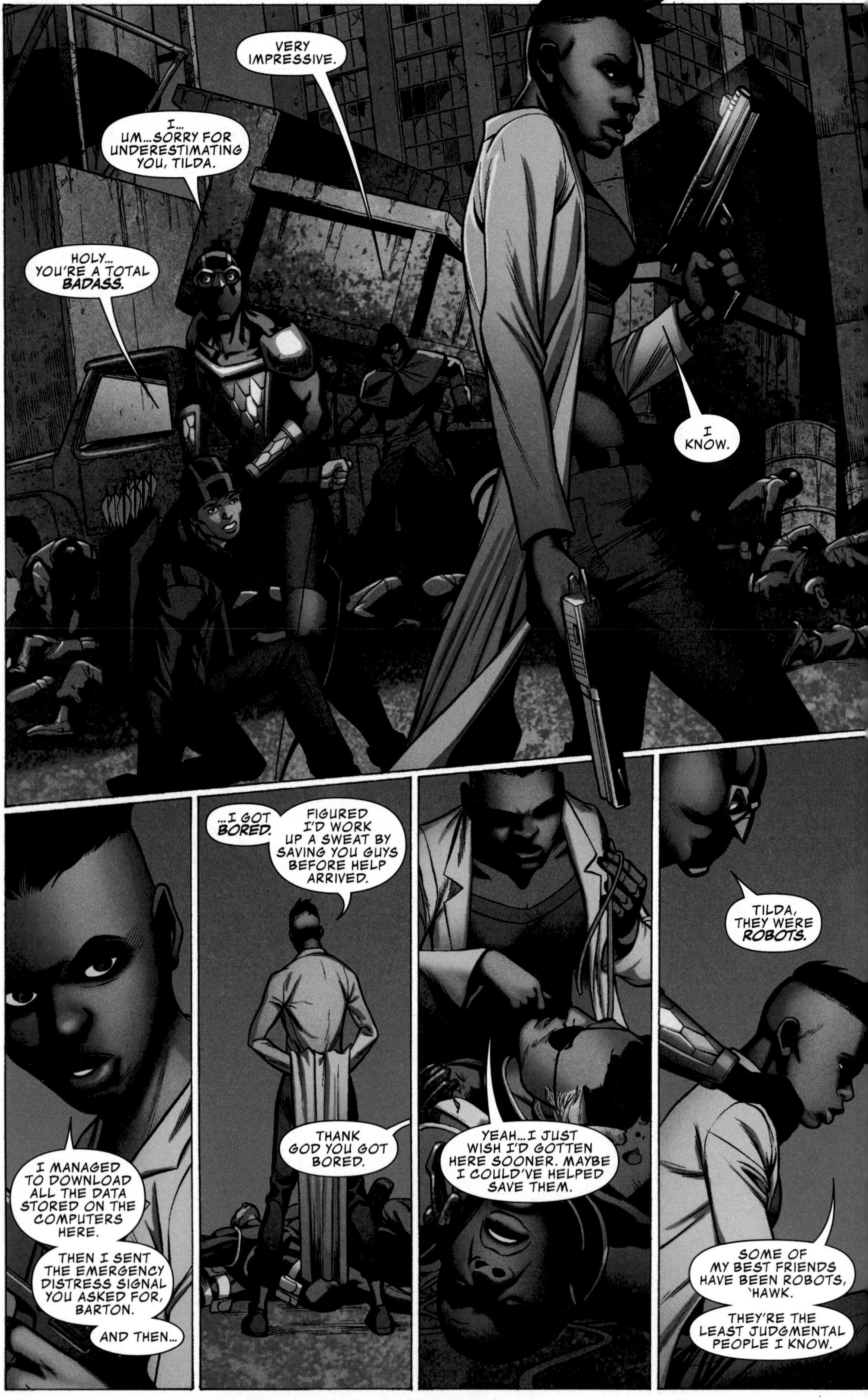
VERY IMPRESSIVE.
I... UM...SORRY FOR UNDERESTIMATING YOU, TILDA.
HOLY... YOU'RE A TOTAL BADASS.
I KNOW.
...I GOT BORED.
FIGURED I'D WORK UP A SWEAT BY SAVING YOU GUYS BEFORE HELP ARRIVED.
I MANAGED TO DOWNLOAD ALL THE DATA STORED ON THE COMPUTERS HERE.
THEN I SENT THE EMERGENCY DISTRESS SIGNAL YOU ASKED FOR, BARTON.
AND THEN...
THANK GOD YOU GOT BORED.
YEAH...I JUST WISH I'D GOTTEN HERE SOONER. MAYBE I COULD'VE HELPED SAVE THEM.
TILDA, THEY WERE ROBOTS.
SOME OF MY BEST FRIENDS HAVE BEEN ROBOTS, 'HAWK.
THEY'RE THE LEAST JUDGMENTAL PEOPLE I KNOW.

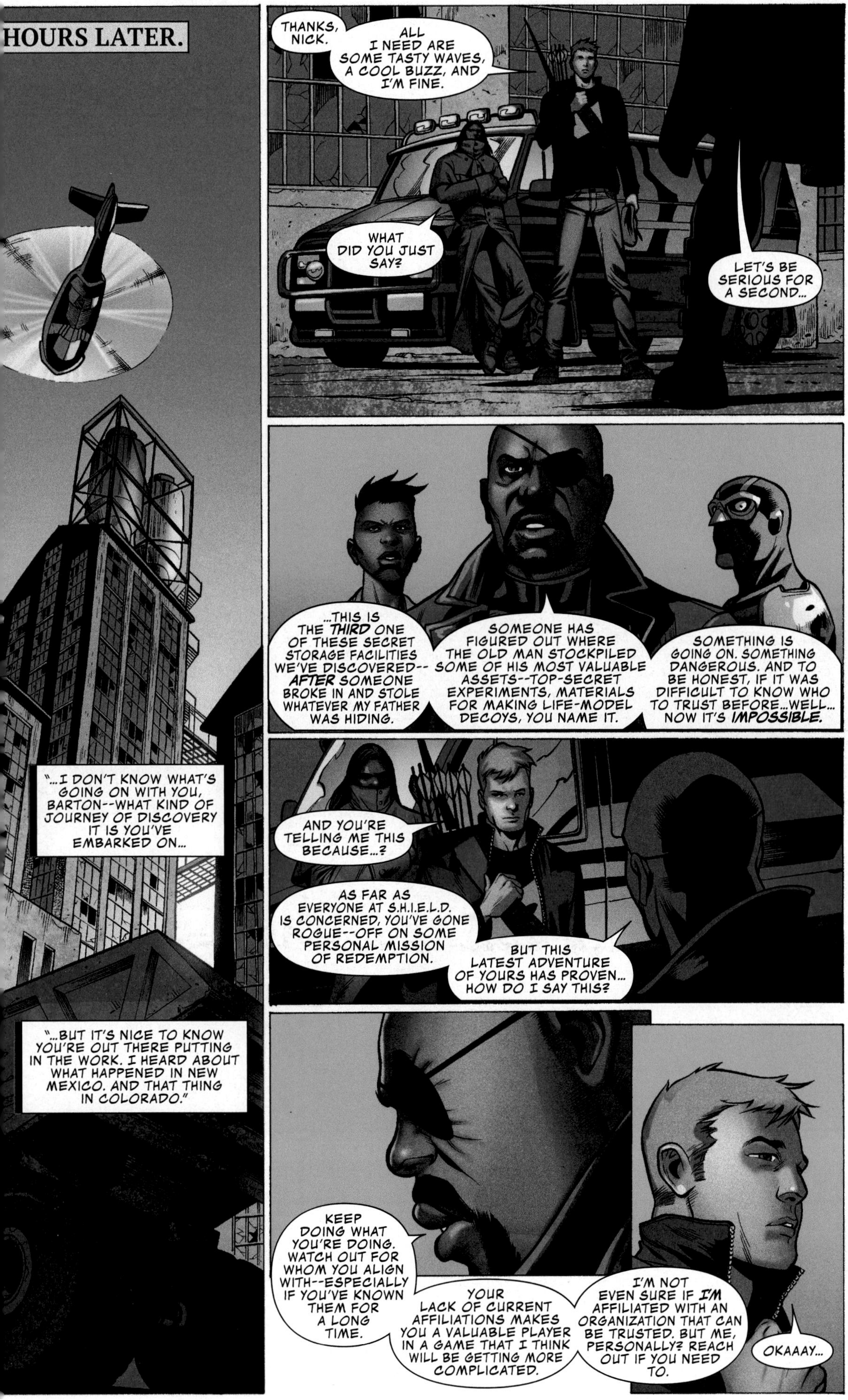
HOURS LATER.
THANKS, NICK.
ALL I NEED ARE SOME TASTY WAVES, A COOL BUZZ, AND I'M FINE.
WHAT DID YOU JUST SAY?
LET'S BE SERIOUS FOR A SECOND...
...THIS IS THE THIRD ONE OF THESE SECRET STORAGE FACILITIES WE'VE DISCOVERED--AFTER SOMEONE BROKE IN AND STOLE WHATEVER MY FATHER WAS HIDING.
SOMEONE HAS FIGURED OUT WHERE THE OLD MAN STOCKPILED SOME OF HIS MOST VALUABLE ASSETS--TOP-SECRET EXPERIMENTS, MATERIALS FOR MAKING LIFE-MODEL DECOYS, YOU NAME IT.
SOMETHING IS GOING ON. SOMETHING DANGEROUS. AND TO BE HONEST, IF IT WAS DIFFICULT TO KNOW WHO TO TRUST BEFORE...WELL... NOW IT'S IMPOSSIBLE.
"...I DON'T KNOW WHAT'S GOING ON WITH YOU, BARTON--WHAT KIND OF JOURNEY OF DISCOVERY IT IS YOU'VE EMBARKED ON...
"...BUT IT'S NICE TO KNOW YOU'RE OUT THERE PUTTING IN THE WORK. I HEARD ABOUT WHAT HAPPENED IN NEW MEXICO. AND THAT THING IN COLORADO."
AND YOU'RE TELLING ME THIS BECAUSE...?
AS FAR AS EVERYONE AT S.H.I.E.L.D. IS CONCERNED, YOU'VE GONE ROGUE--OFF ON SOME PERSONAL MISSION OF REDEMPTION.
BUT THIS LATEST ADVENTURE OF YOURS HAS PROVEN... HOW DO I SAY THIS?
KEEP DOING WHAT YOU'RE DOING. WATCH OUT FOR WHOM YOU ALIGN WITH--ESPECIALLY IF YOU'VE KNOWN THEM FOR A LONG TIME.
YOUR LACK OF CURRENT AFFILIATIONS MAKES YOU A VALUABLE PLAYER IN A GAME THAT I THINK WILL BE GETTING MORE COMPLICATED.
I'M NOT EVEN SURE IF I'M AFFILIATED WITH AN ORGANIZATION THAT CAN BE TRUSTED. BUT ME, PERSONALLY? REACH OUT IF YOU NEED TO.
OKAAAY...

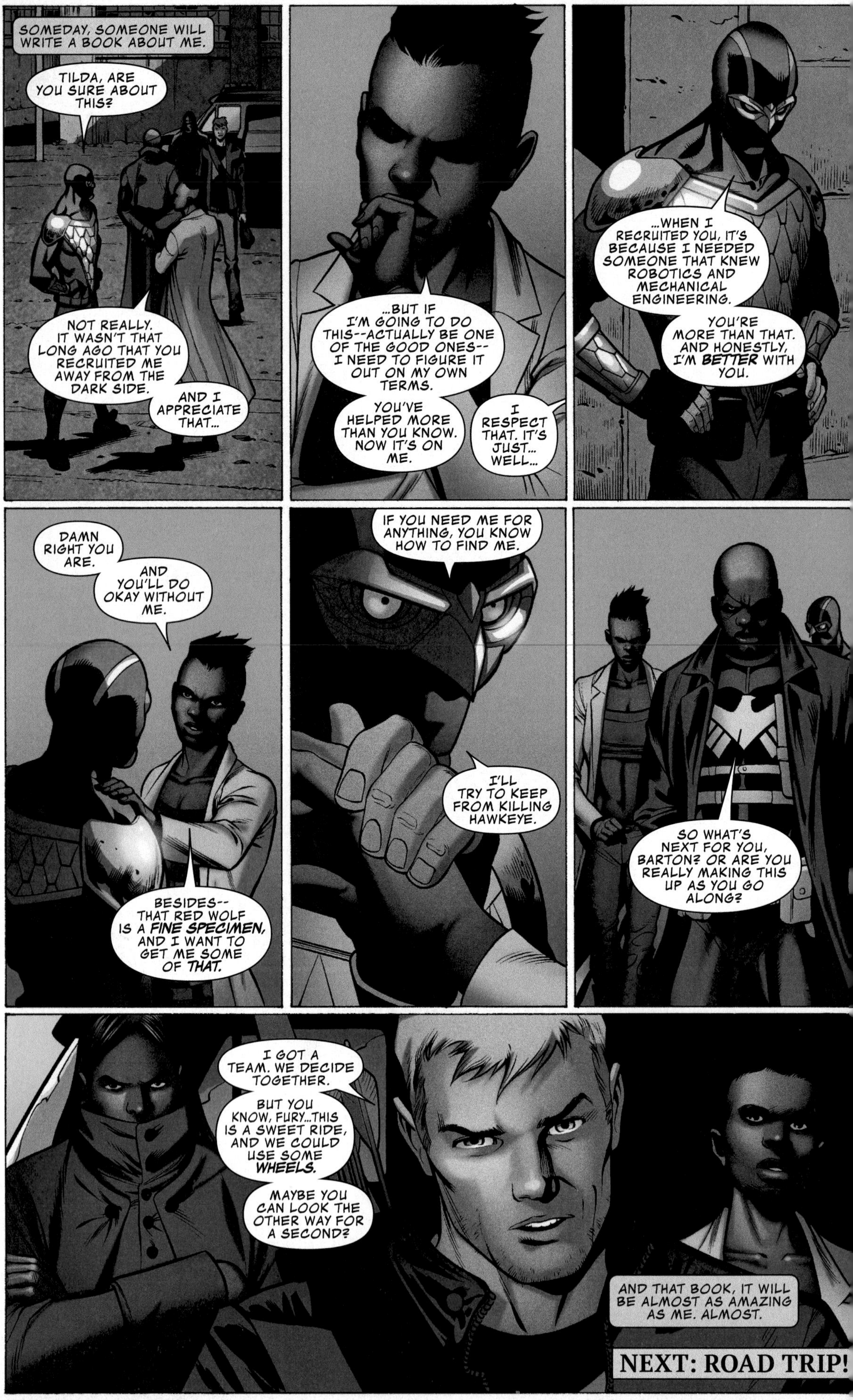

SOMEDAY, SOMEONE WILL WRITE A BOOK ABOUT ME.
TILDA, ARE YOU SURE ABOUT THIS?
NOT REALLY. IT WASN'T THAT LONG AGO THAT YOU RECRUITED ME AWAY FROM THE DARK SIDE.
AND I APPRECIATE THAT...
...BUT IF I'M GOING TO DO THIS--ACTUALLY BE ONE OF THE GOOD ONES--I NEED TO FIGURE IT OUT ON MY OWN TERMS.
YOU'VE HELPED MORE THAN YOU KNOW. NOW IT'S ON ME.
I RESPECT THAT. IT'S JUST... WELL...
...WHEN I RECRUITED YOU, IT'S BECAUSE I NEEDED SOMEONE THAT KNEW ROBOTICS AND MECHANICAL ENGINEERING.
YOU'RE MORE THAN THAT. AND HONESTLY, I'M BETTER WITH YOU.
DAMN RIGHT YOU ARE.
AND YOU'LL DO OKAY WITHOUT ME.
BESIDES--THAT RED WOLF IS A FINE SPECIMEN, AND I WANT TO GET ME SOME OF THAT.
IF YOU NEED ME FOR ANYTHING, YOU KNOW HOW TO FIND ME.
I'LL TRY TO KEEP FROM KILLING HAWKEYE.
SO WHAT'S NEXT FOR YOU, BARTON? OR ARE YOU REALLY MAKING THIS UP AS YOU GO ALONG?
I GOT A TEAM. WE DECIDE TOGETHER.
BUT YOU KNOW, FURY...THIS IS A SWEET RIDE, AND WE COULD USE SOME WHEELS.
MAYBE YOU CAN LOOK THE OTHER WAY FOR A SECOND?
AND THAT BOOK, IT WILL BE ALMOST AS AMAZING AS ME. ALMOST.
NEXT: ROAD TRIP!

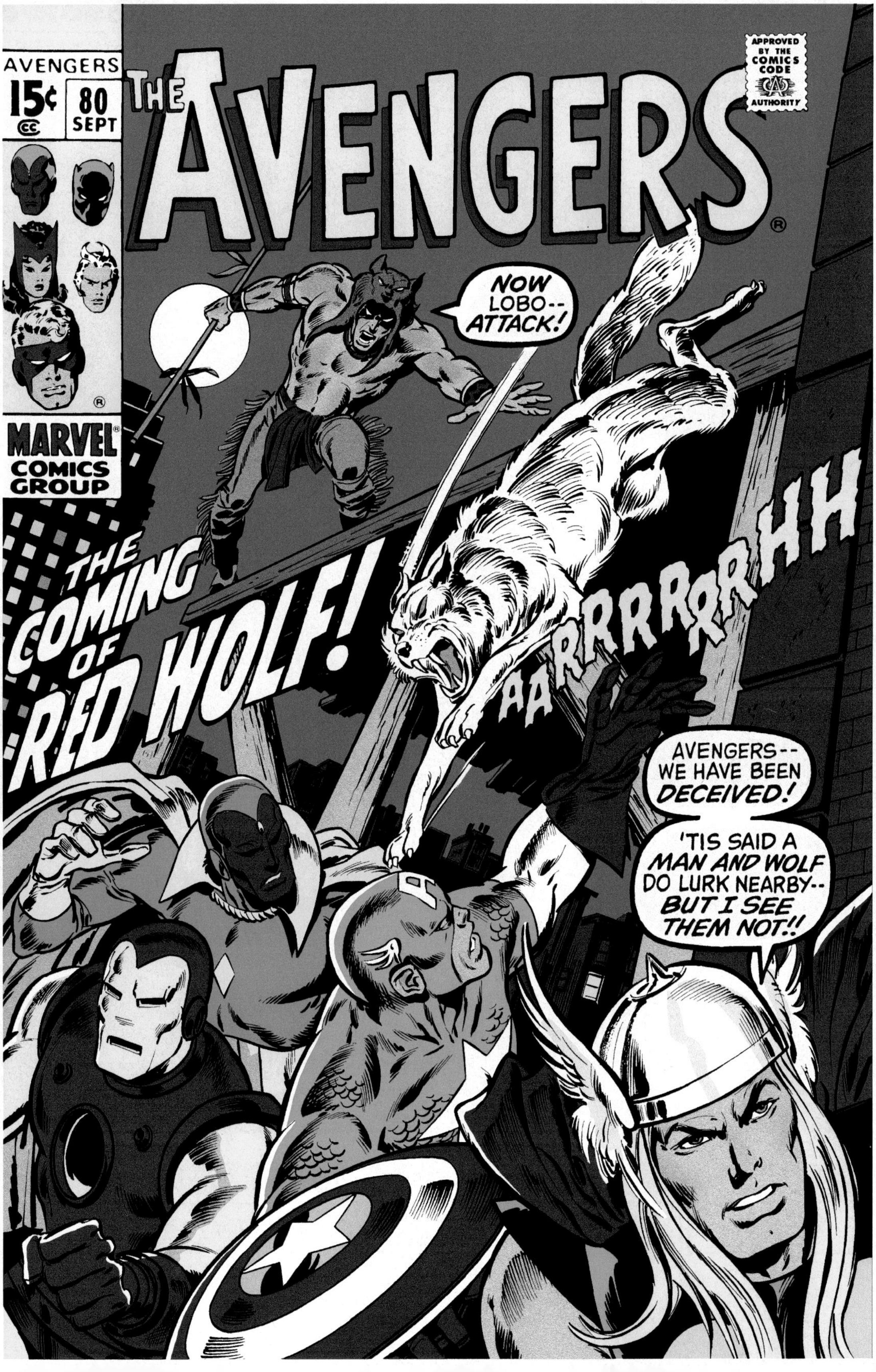
AVENGERS
15¢
80
SEPT
CC
MARVEL
COMICS
GROUP
THE AVENGERS
APPROVED BY THE COMICS CODE AUTHORITY
THE COMING OF RED WOLF!
NOW LOBO-- ATTACK!
AARRRRRRRHH
AVENGERS-- WE HAVE BEEN DECEIVED!
'TIS SAID A MAN AND WOLF DO LURK NEARBY-- BUT I SEE THEM NOT!!

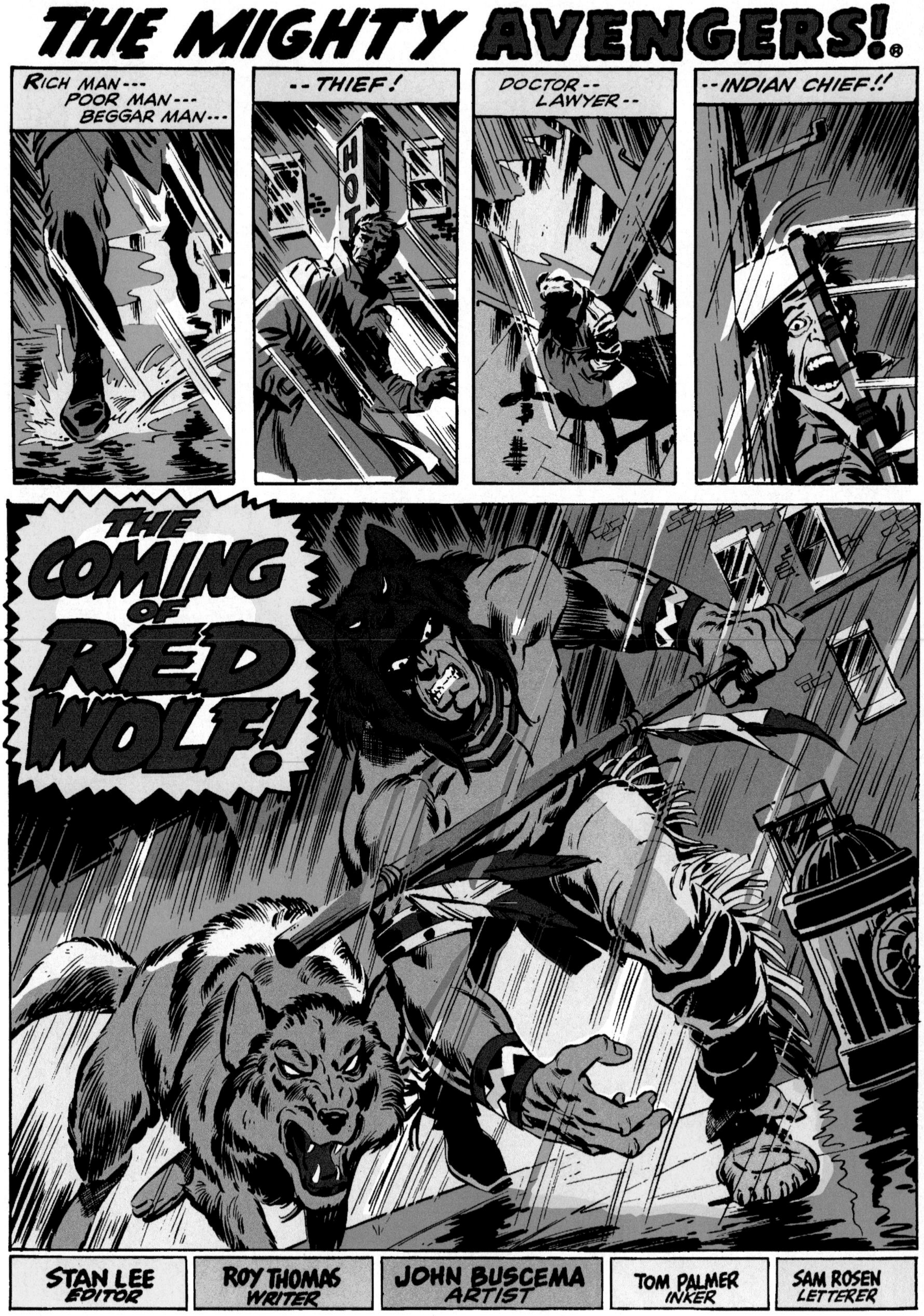
THE MIGHTY AVENGERS!
RICH MAN--- POOR MAN--- BEGGAR MAN---
--THIEF!
DOCTOR-- LAWYER--
--INDIAN CHIEF!!
THE COMING OF RED WOLF!
STAN LEE EDITOR
ROY THOMAS WRITER
JOHN BUSCEMA ARTIST
TOM PALMER INKER
SAM ROSEN LETTERER

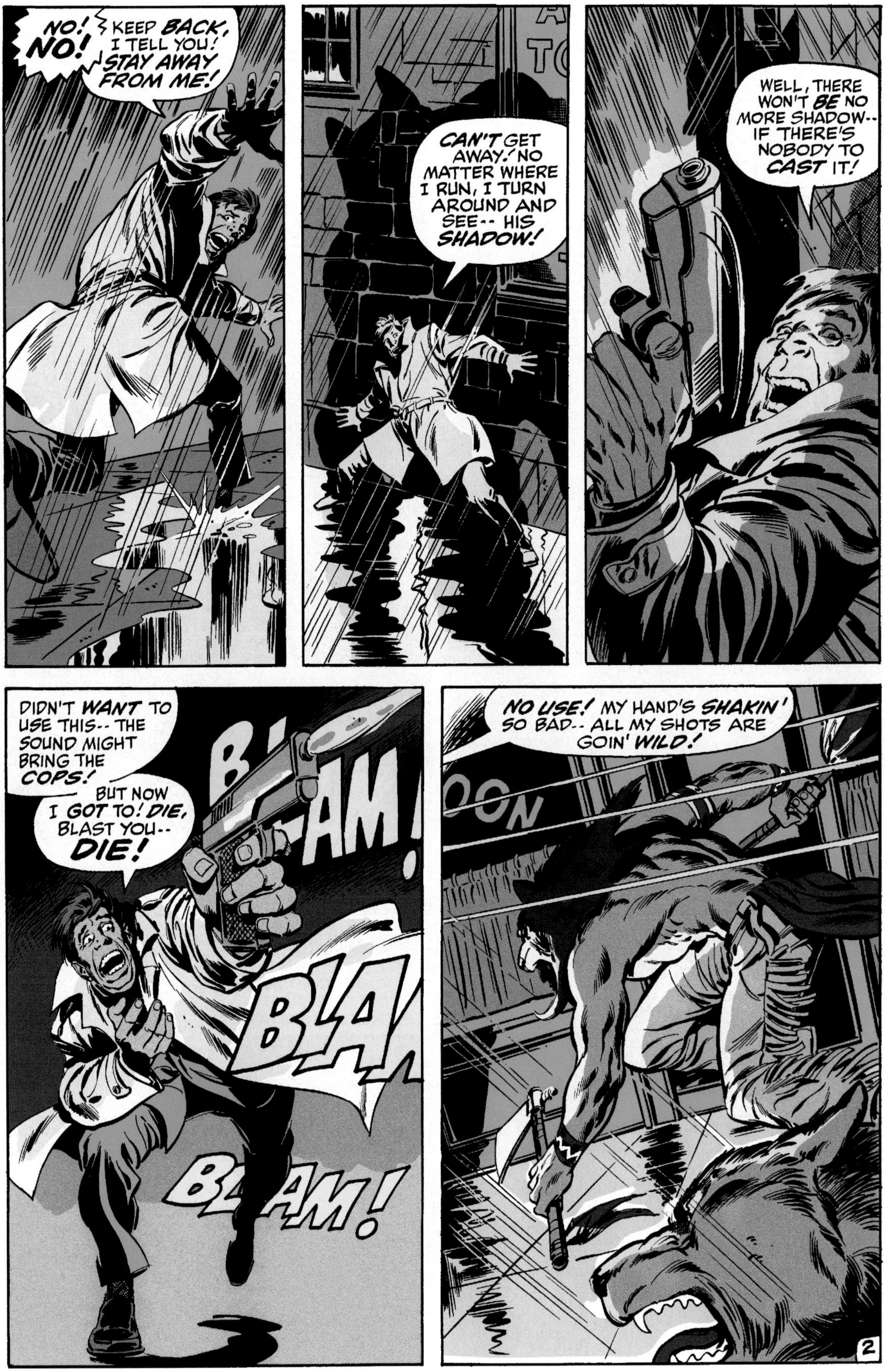
NO! NO!
KEEP BACK, I TELL YOU! STAY AWAY FROM ME!
CAN'T GET AWAY! NO MATTER WHERE I RUN, I TURN AROUND AND SEE-- HIS SHADOW!
WELL, THERE WON'T BE NO MORE SHADOW-- IF THERE'S NOBODY TO CAST IT!
DIDN'T WANT TO USE THIS-- THE SOUND MIGHT BRING THE COPS!
BUT NOW I GOT TO! DIE, BLAST YOU-- DIE!
BLAM!
BLA
BLAM!
NO USE! MY HAND'S SHAKIN' SO BAD-- ALL MY SHOTS ARE GOIN' WILD!
2

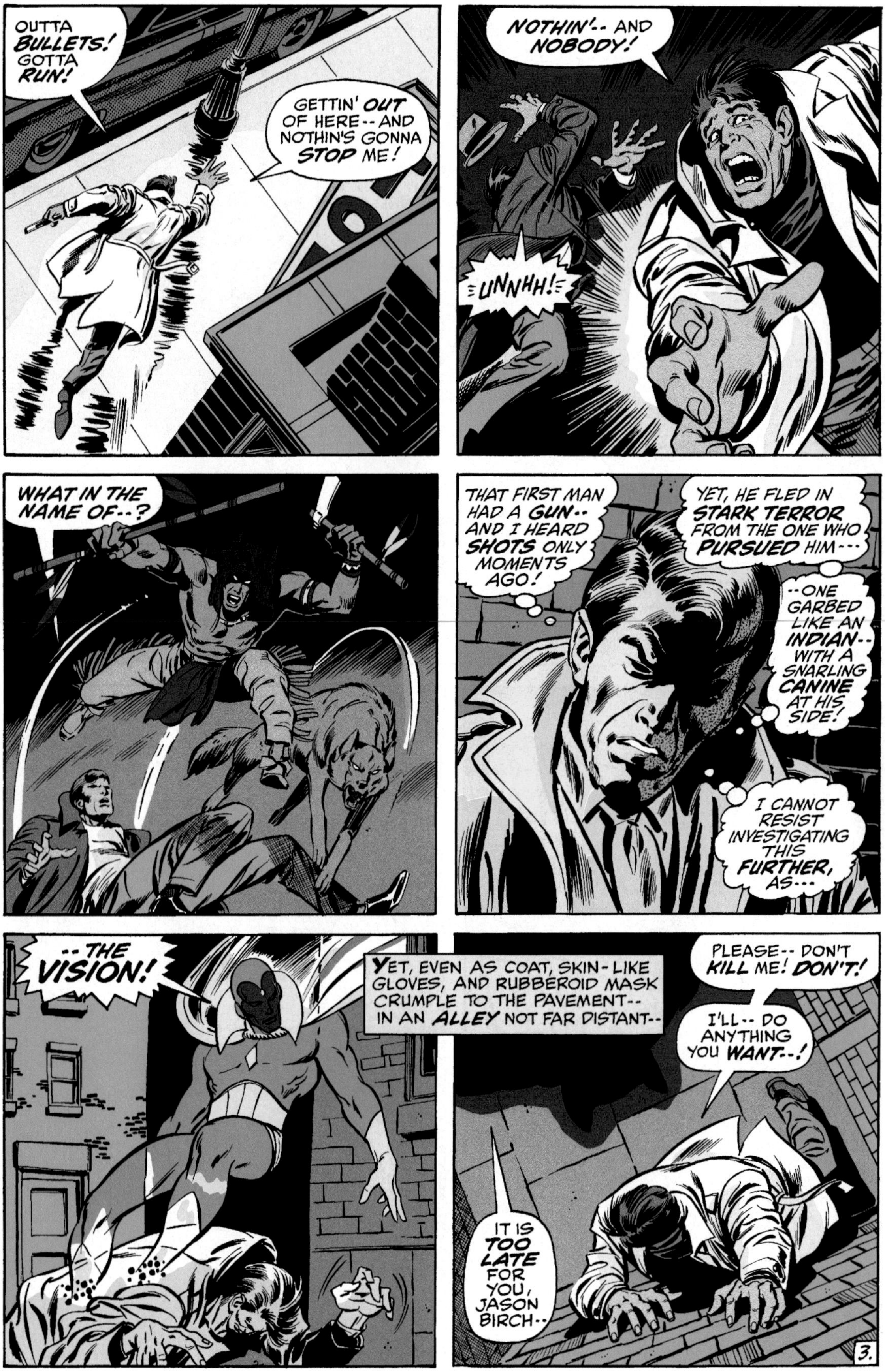
OUTTA BULLETS! GOTTA RUN!
GETTIN' OUT OF HERE-- AND NOTHIN'S GONNA STOP ME!
NOTHIN'-- AND NOBODY!
UNNHH!
WHAT IN THE NAME OF--?
THAT FIRST MAN HAD A GUN-- AND I HEARD SHOTS ONLY MOMENTS AGO!
YET, HE FLED IN STARK TERROR FROM THE ONE WHO PURSUED HIM---
--ONE GARBED LIKE AN INDIAN-- WITH A SNARLING CANINE AT HIS SIDE!
I CANNOT RESIST INVESTIGATING THIS FURTHER, AS---
--THE VISION!
YET, EVEN AS COAT, SKIN-LIKE GLOVES, AND RUBBEROID MASK CRUMPLE TO THE PAVEMENT-- IN AN ALLEY NOT FAR DISTANT--
PLEASE-- DON'T KILL ME! DON'T!
I'LL-- DO ANYTHING YOU WANT--!
IT IS TOO LATE FOR YOU, JASON BIRCH--
3.

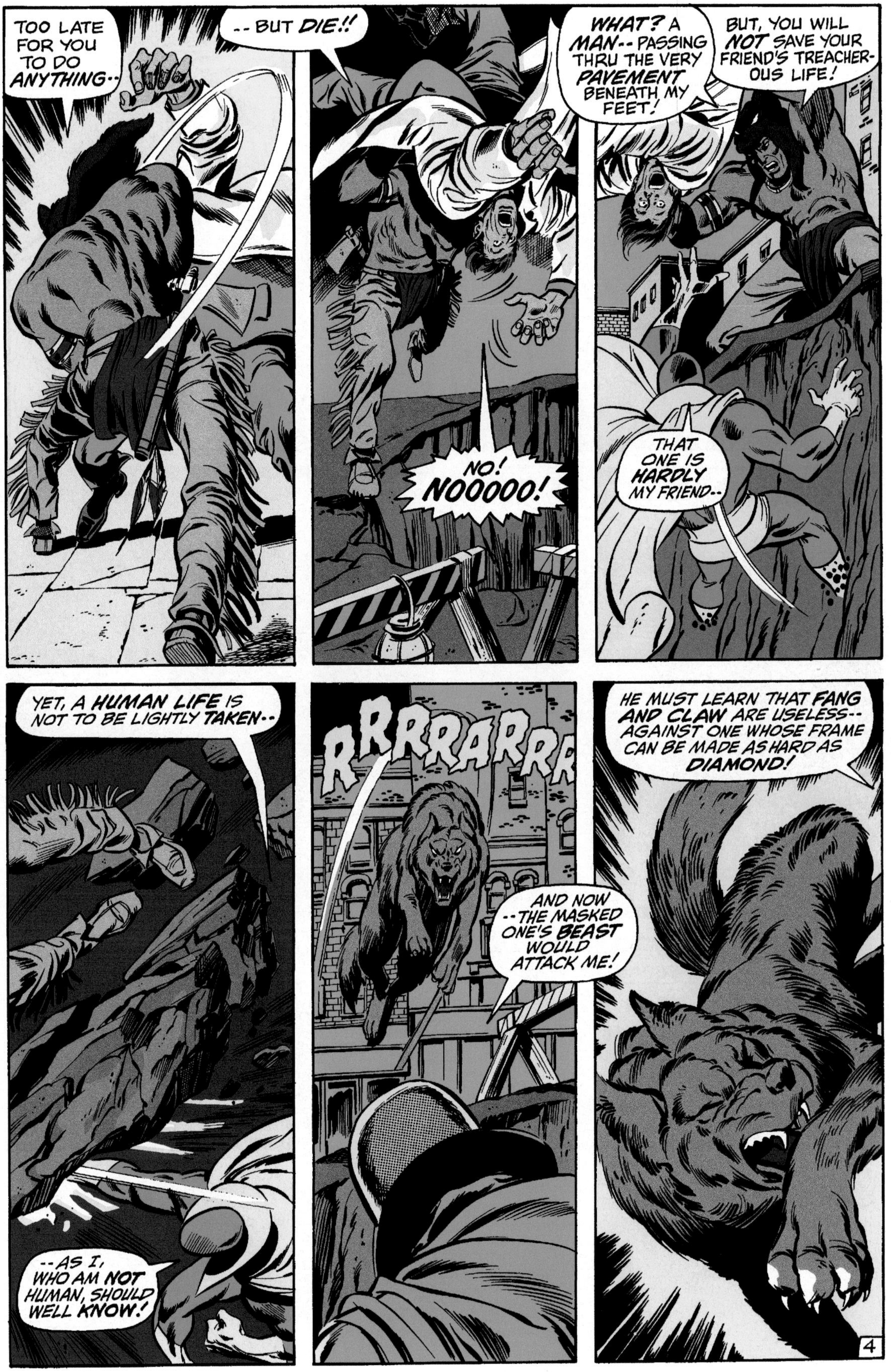
TOO LATE FOR YOU TO DO ANYTHING--
--BUT DIE!!
WHAT? A MAN--PASSING THRU THE VERY PAVEMENT BENEATH MY FEET!
NO! NOOOOO!
BUT, YOU WILL NOT SAVE YOUR FRIEND'S TREACHEROUS LIFE!
THAT ONE IS HARDLY MY FRIEND--
YET, A HUMAN LIFE IS NOT TO BE LIGHTLY TAKEN--
--AS I, WHO AM NOT HUMAN, SHOULD WELL KNOW!
RRRRARRRR
AND NOW--THE MASKED ONE'S BEAST WOULD ATTACK ME!
HE MUST LEARN THAT FANG AND CLAW ARE USELESS--AGAINST ONE WHOSE FRAME CAN BE MADE AS HARD AS DIAMOND!
4

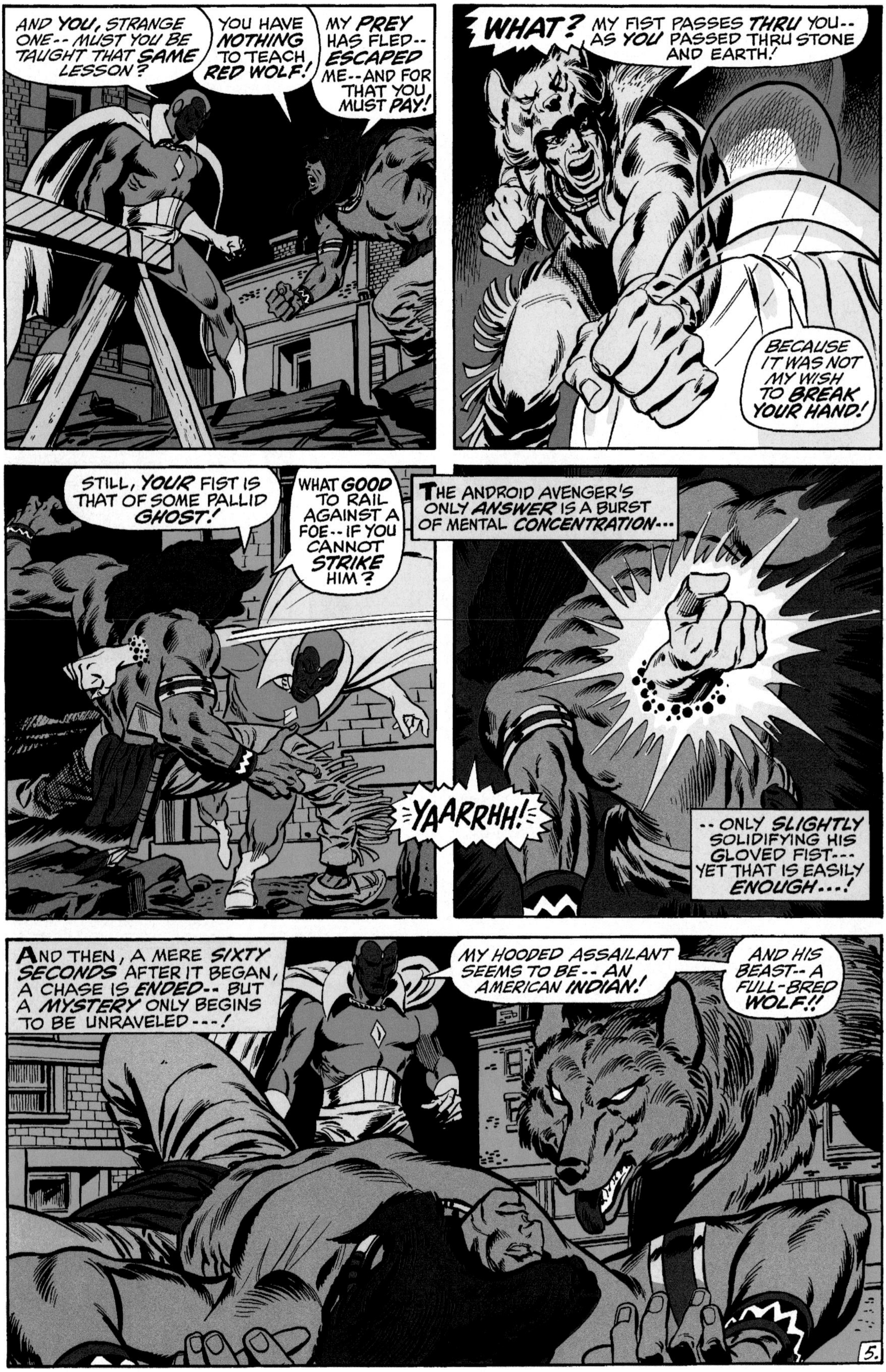
AND YOU, STRANGE ONE-- MUST YOU BE TAUGHT THAT SAME LESSON?
YOU HAVE NOTHING TO TEACH RED WOLF!
MY PREY HAS FLED-- ESCAPED ME--AND FOR THAT YOU MUST PAY!
WHAT? MY FIST PASSES THRU YOU-- AS YOU PASSED THRU STONE AND EARTH!
BECAUSE IT WAS NOT MY WISH TO BREAK YOUR HAND!
STILL, YOUR FIST IS THAT OF SOME PALLID GHOST!
WHAT GOOD TO RAIL AGAINST A FOE-- IF YOU CANNOT STRIKE HIM?
THE ANDROID AVENGER'S ONLY ANSWER IS A BURST OF MENTAL CONCENTRATION...
YAARRHH!
--ONLY SLIGHTLY SOLIDIFYING HIS GLOVED FIST--- YET THAT IS EASILY ENOUGH...!
AND THEN, A MERE SIXTY SECONDS AFTER IT BEGAN, A CHASE IS ENDED-- BUT A MYSTERY ONLY BEGINS TO BE UNRAVELED---!
MY HOODED ASSAILANT SEEMS TO BE-- AN AMERICAN INDIAN!
AND HIS BEAST-- A FULL-BRED WOLF!!
5.

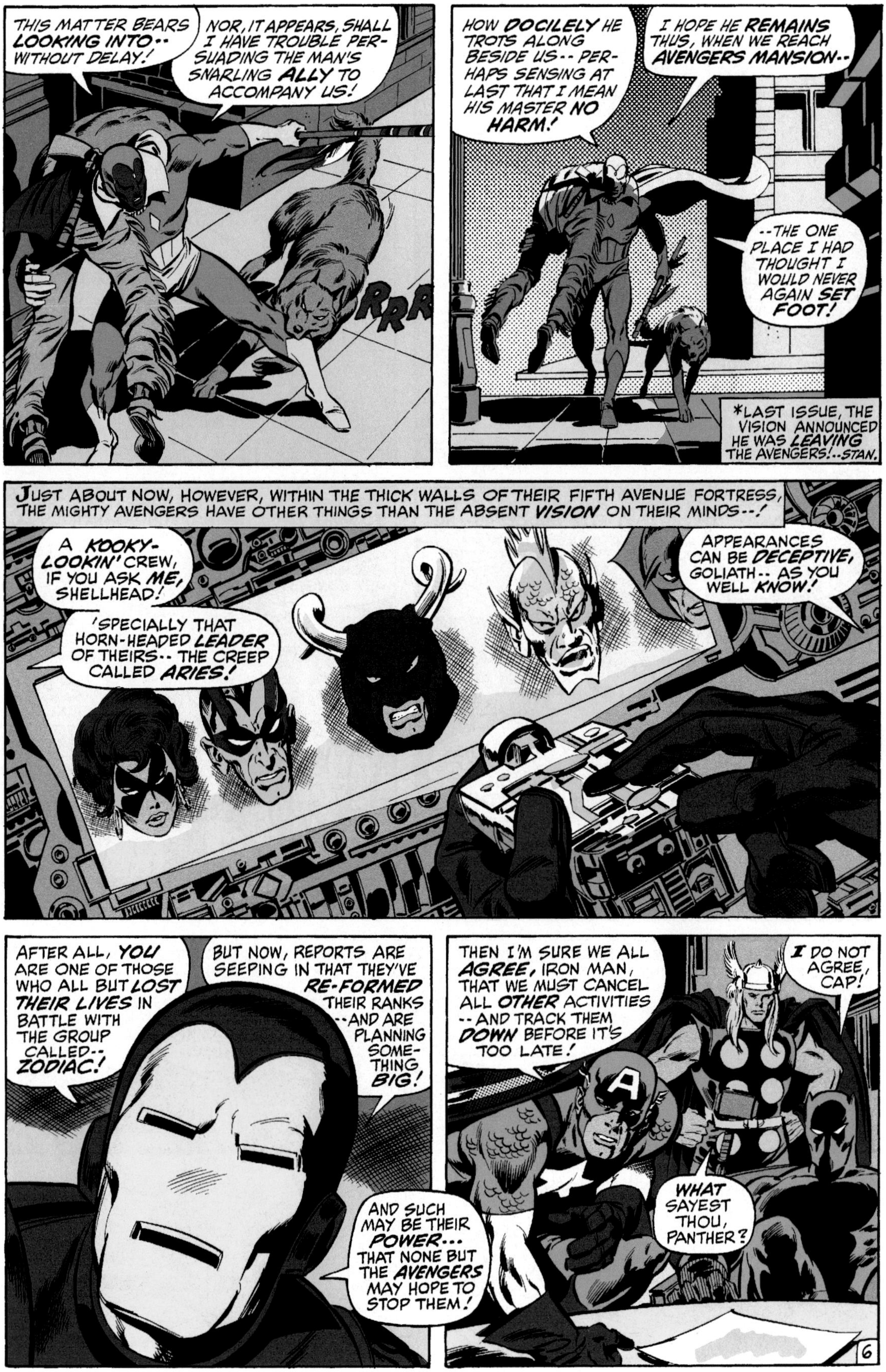
THIS MATTER BEARS LOOKING INTO-- WITHOUT DELAY!
NOR, IT APPEARS, SHALL I HAVE TROUBLE PERSUADING THE MAN'S SNARLING ALLY TO ACCOMPANY US!
RRRR
HOW DOCILELY HE TROTS ALONG BESIDE US-- PERHAPS SENSING AT LAST THAT I MEAN HIS MASTER NO HARM!
I HOPE HE REMAINS THUS, WHEN WE REACH AVENGERS MANSION--
--THE ONE PLACE I HAD THOUGHT I WOULD NEVER AGAIN SET FOOT!
*LAST ISSUE, THE VISION ANNOUNCED HE WAS LEAVING THE AVENGERS!--STAN.
JUST ABOUT NOW, HOWEVER, WITHIN THE THICK WALLS OF THEIR FIFTH AVENUE FORTRESS, THE MIGHTY AVENGERS HAVE OTHER THINGS THAN THE ABSENT VISION ON THEIR MINDS--!
A KOOKY-LOOKIN' CREW, IF YOU ASK ME, SHELLHEAD!
'SPECIALLY THAT HORN-HEADED LEADER OF THEIRS-- THE CREEP CALLED ARIES!
APPEARANCES CAN BE DECEPTIVE, GOLIATH-- AS YOU WELL KNOW!
AFTER ALL, YOU ARE ONE OF THOSE WHO ALL BUT LOST THEIR LIVES IN BATTLE WITH THE GROUP CALLED-- ZODIAC!
BUT NOW, REPORTS ARE SEEPING IN THAT THEY'VE RE-FORMED THEIR RANKS --AND ARE PLANNING SOMETHING BIG!
AND SUCH MAY BE THEIR POWER... THAT NONE BUT THE AVENGERS MAY HOPE TO STOP THEM!
THEN I'M SURE WE ALL AGREE, IRON MAN, THAT WE MUST CANCEL ALL OTHER ACTIVITIES --AND TRACK THEM DOWN BEFORE IT'S TOO LATE!
I DO NOT AGREE, CAP!
WHAT SAYEST THOU, PANTHER?
6

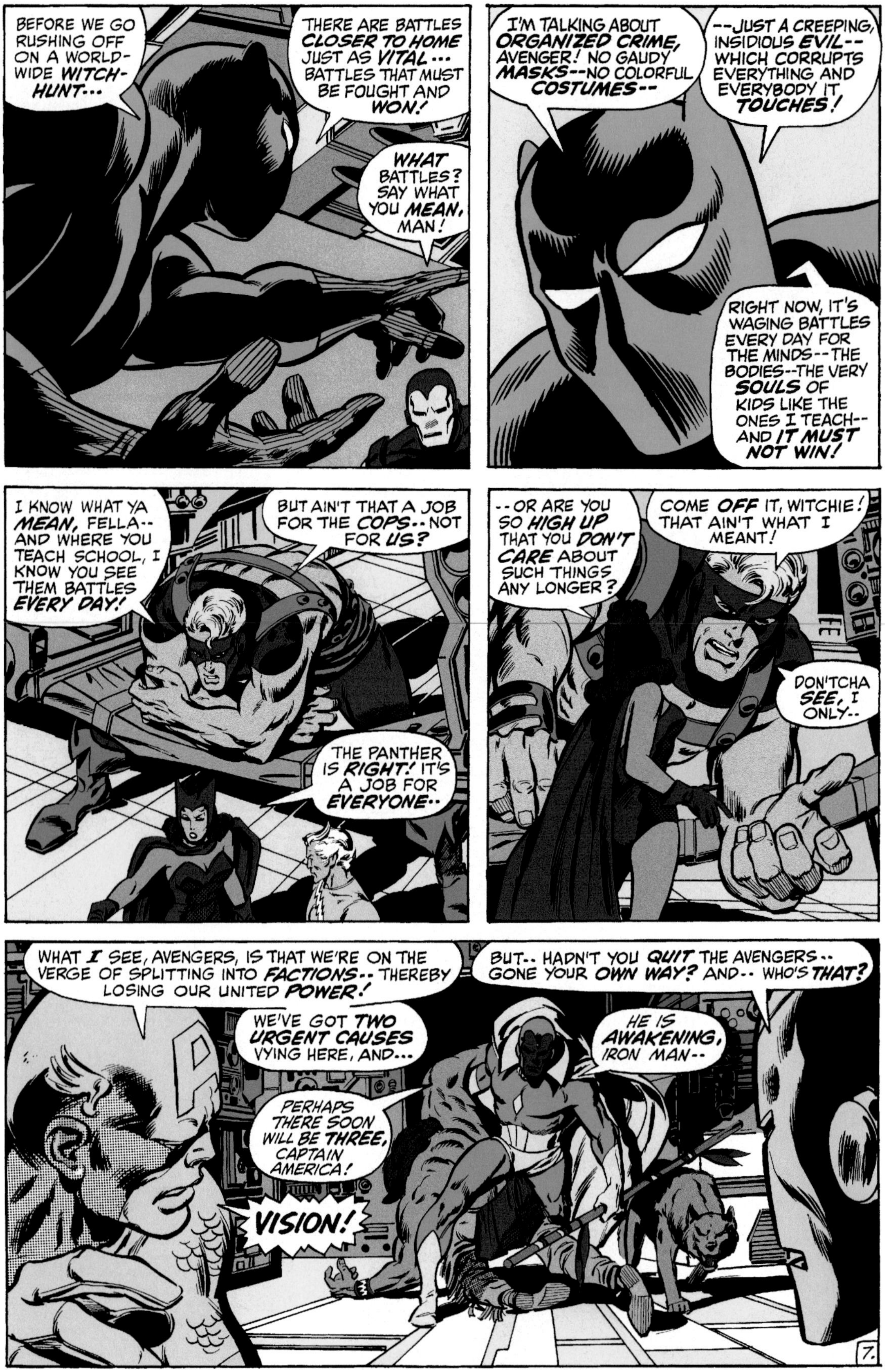
BEFORE WE GO RUSHING OFF ON A WORLD-WIDE WITCH-HUNT...
THERE ARE BATTLES CLOSER TO HOME JUST AS VITAL... BATTLES THAT MUST BE FOUGHT AND WON!
WHAT BATTLES? SAY WHAT YOU MEAN, MAN!
I'M TALKING ABOUT ORGANIZED CRIME, AVENGER! NO GAUDY MASKS--NO COLORFUL COSTUMES--
--JUST A CREEPING, INSIDIOUS EVIL--WHICH CORRUPTS EVERYTHING AND EVERYBODY IT TOUCHES!
RIGHT NOW, IT'S WAGING BATTLES EVERY DAY FOR THE MINDS--THE BODIES--THE VERY SOULS OF KIDS LIKE THE ONES I TEACH--AND IT MUST NOT WIN!
I KNOW WHAT YA MEAN, FELLA--AND WHERE YOU TEACH SCHOOL, I KNOW YOU SEE THEM BATTLES EVERY DAY!
BUT AIN'T THAT A JOB FOR THE COPS--NOT FOR US?
THE PANTHER IS RIGHT! IT'S A JOB FOR EVERYONE--
--OR ARE YOU SO HIGH UP THAT YOU DON'T CARE ABOUT SUCH THINGS ANY LONGER?
COME OFF IT, WITCHIE! THAT AIN'T WHAT I MEANT!
DON'TCHA SEE, I ONLY--
WHAT I SEE, AVENGERS, IS THAT WE'RE ON THE VERGE OF SPLITTING INTO FACTIONS--THEREBY LOSING OUR UNITED POWER!
WE'VE GOT TWO URGENT CAUSES VYING HERE, AND...
PERHAPS THERE SOON WILL BE THREE, CAPTAIN AMERICA!
VISION!
BUT--HADN'T YOU QUIT THE AVENGERS--GONE YOUR OWN WAY? AND--WHO'S THAT?
HE IS AWAKENING, IRON MAN--
7.

SOON, HE MAY ANSWER BOTH *YOUR* QUESTIONS-- AND *MINE!*

RED WOLF SHALL ANSWER -- *NOTHING,* INTERLOPER!

YOU HAVE KEPT ME FROM THE *MISSION* FOR WHICH I WAS BORN-- THE MISSION I CROSSED A *CONTINENT* TO FULFILL!

I HAD *BUSINESS* WITH THE MAN YOU TOOK FROM ME-- *DEADLY* BUSINESS!

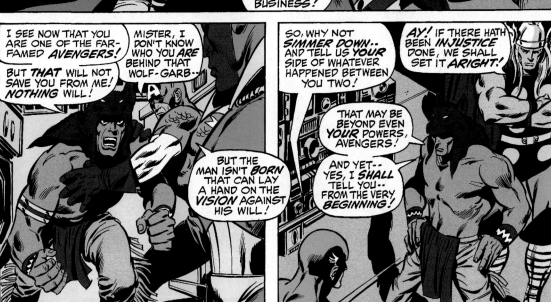

I SEE NOW THAT YOU ARE ONE OF THE FAR-FAMED *AVENGERS!*

MISTER, I DON'T KNOW WHO YOU *ARE* BEHIND THAT WOLF-GARB--

BUT *THAT* WILL NOT SAVE YOU FROM ME! *NOTHING* WILL!

BUT THE MAN ISN'T *BORN* THAT CAN LAY A HAND ON THE *VISION* AGAINST HIS WILL!

SO, WHY NOT *SIMMER DOWN..* AND TELL US *YOUR* SIDE OF WHATEVER HAPPENED BETWEEN YOU TWO!

AY! IF THERE HATH BEEN *INJUSTICE* DONE, WE SHALL SET IT *ARIGHT!*

THAT MAY BE BEYOND EVEN *YOUR* POWERS, AVENGERS!

AND YET-- YES, I *SHALL* TELL YOU-- FROM THE VERY *BEGINNING!*

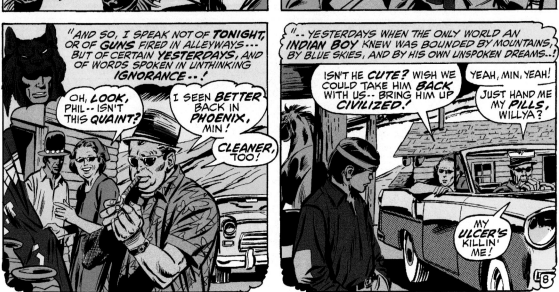

"AND SO, I SPEAK NOT OF *TONIGHT,* OR OF *GUNS* FIRED IN ALLEYWAYS--- BUT OF CERTAIN *YESTERDAYS,* AND OF WORDS SPOKEN IN UNTHINKING *IGNORANCE*--!

OH, *LOOK,* PHIL-- ISN'T THIS *QUAINT?*

I SEEN *BETTER* BACK IN *PHOENIX,* MIN!

CLEANER, TOO!

"-- *YESTERDAYS* WHEN THE ONLY WORLD AN *INDIAN BOY* KNEW WAS BOUNDED BY MOUNTAINS, BY BLUE SKIES, AND BY HIS OWN UNSPOKEN DREAMS..!

ISN'T HE *CUTE?* WISH WE COULD TAKE HIM *BACK* WITH US-- BRING HIM UP *CIVILIZED!*

YEAH, MIN, YEAH!

JUST HAND ME MY *PILLS,* WILLYA?

MY *ULCER'S* KILLIN' ME!

8

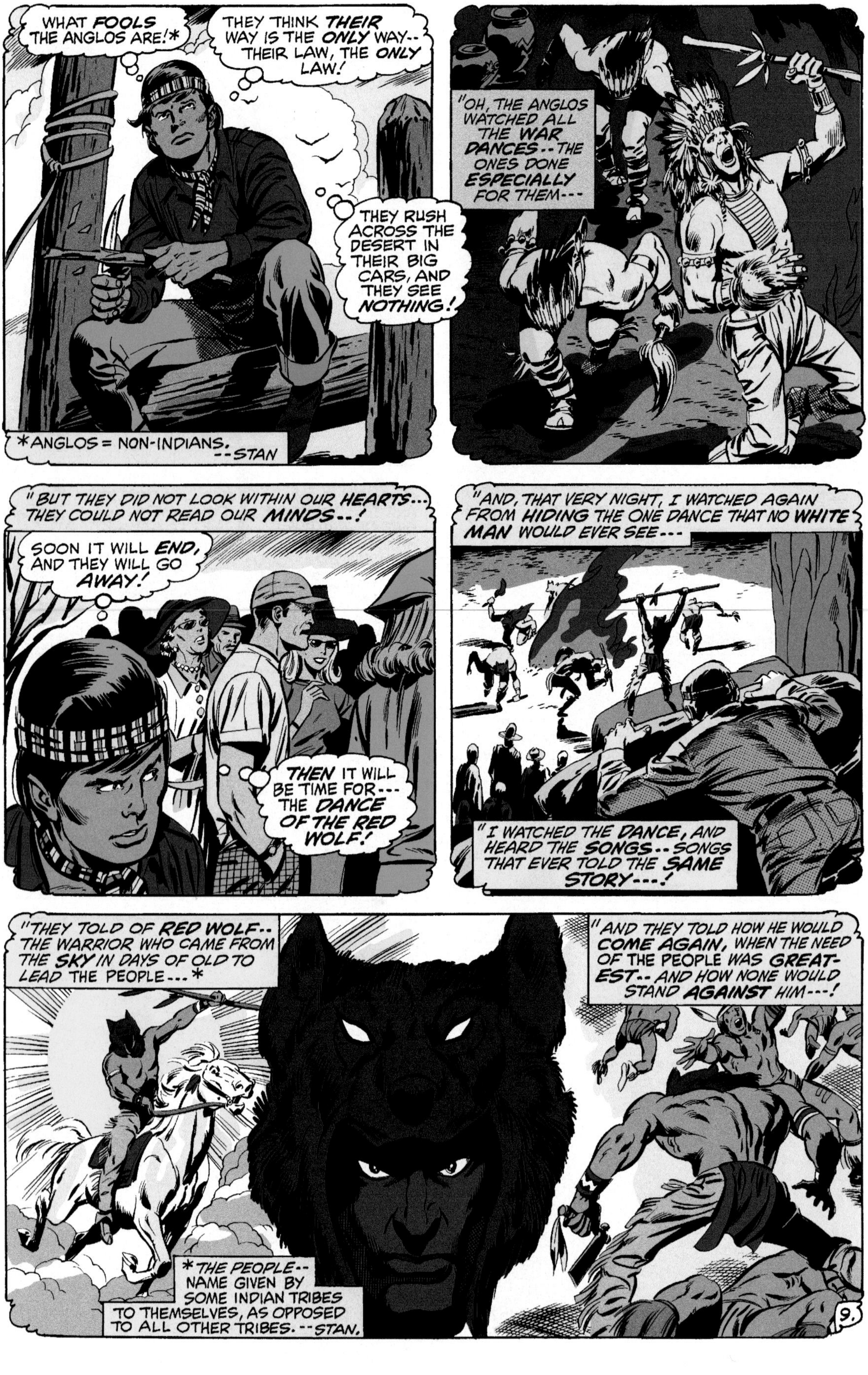

WHAT FOOLS THE ANGLOS ARE!*
THEY THINK THEIR WAY IS THE ONLY WAY-- THEIR LAW, THE ONLY LAW!
THEY RUSH ACROSS THE DESERT IN THEIR BIG CARS, AND THEY SEE NOTHING!
*ANGLOS = NON-INDIANS. --STAN
"OH, THE ANGLOS WATCHED ALL THE WAR DANCES--THE ONES DONE ESPECIALLY FOR THEM---
"BUT THEY DID NOT LOOK WITHIN OUR HEARTS... THEY COULD NOT READ OUR MINDS--!
SOON IT WILL END, AND THEY WILL GO AWAY!
THEN IT WILL BE TIME FOR--- THE DANCE OF THE RED WOLF!
"AND, THAT VERY NIGHT, I WATCHED AGAIN FROM HIDING THE ONE DANCE THAT NO WHITE MAN WOULD EVER SEE---
"I WATCHED THE DANCE, AND HEARD THE SONGS--SONGS THAT EVER TOLD THE SAME STORY---!
"THEY TOLD OF RED WOLF-- THE WARRIOR WHO CAME FROM THE SKY IN DAYS OF OLD TO LEAD THE PEOPLE---*
"AND THEY TOLD HOW HE WOULD COME AGAIN, WHEN THE NEED OF THE PEOPLE WAS GREAT-EST-- AND HOW NONE WOULD STAND AGAINST HIM---!
*THE PEOPLE-- NAME GIVEN BY SOME INDIAN TRIBES TO THEMSELVES, AS OPPOSED TO ALL OTHER TRIBES. --STAN.
9.

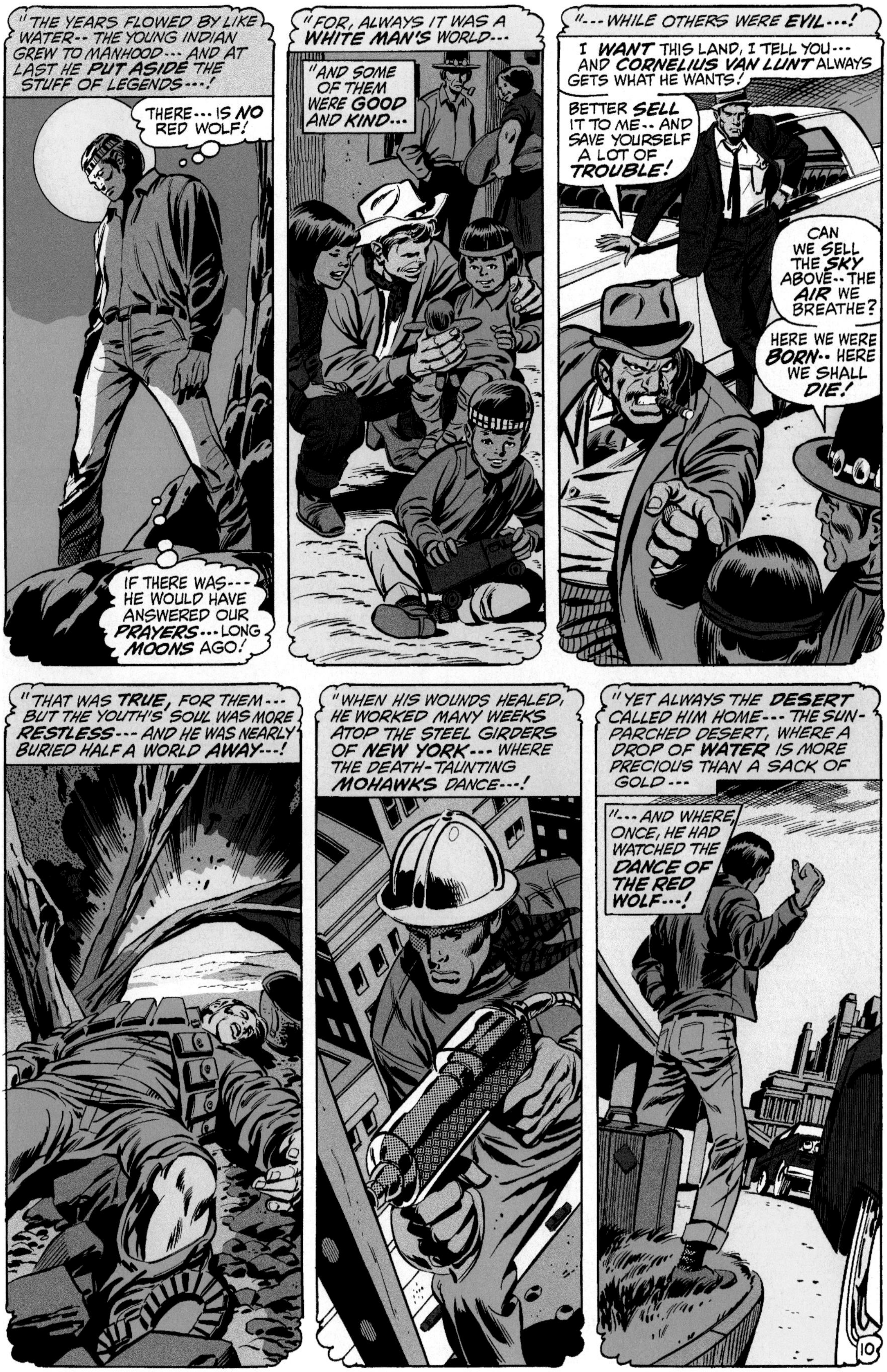
"THE YEARS FLOWED BY LIKE WATER-- THE YOUNG INDIAN GREW TO MANHOOD--- AND AT LAST HE PUT ASIDE THE STUFF OF LEGENDS---!
THERE--- IS NO RED WOLF!
IF THERE WAS--- HE WOULD HAVE ANSWERED OUR PRAYERS--- LONG MOONS AGO!
"FOR, ALWAYS IT WAS A WHITE MAN'S WORLD---
"AND SOME OF THEM WERE GOOD AND KIND---
"--- WHILE OTHERS WERE EVIL---!
I WANT THIS LAND, I TELL YOU--- AND CORNELIUS VAN LUNT ALWAYS GETS WHAT HE WANTS!
BETTER SELL IT TO ME-- AND SAVE YOURSELF A LOT OF TROUBLE!
CAN WE SELL THE SKY ABOVE-- THE AIR WE BREATHE?
HERE WE WERE BORN-- HERE WE SHALL DIE!
"THAT WAS TRUE, FOR THEM--- BUT THE YOUTH'S SOUL WAS MORE RESTLESS--- AND HE WAS NEARLY BURIED HALF A WORLD AWAY---!
"WHEN HIS WOUNDS HEALED, HE WORKED MANY WEEKS ATOP THE STEEL GIRDERS OF NEW YORK--- WHERE THE DEATH-TAUNTING MOHAWKS DANCE---!
"YET ALWAYS THE DESERT CALLED HIM HOME--- THE SUN-PARCHED DESERT, WHERE A DROP OF WATER IS MORE PRECIOUS THAN A SACK OF GOLD---
"--- AND WHERE, ONCE, HE HAD WATCHED THE DANCE OF THE RED WOLF---!
10

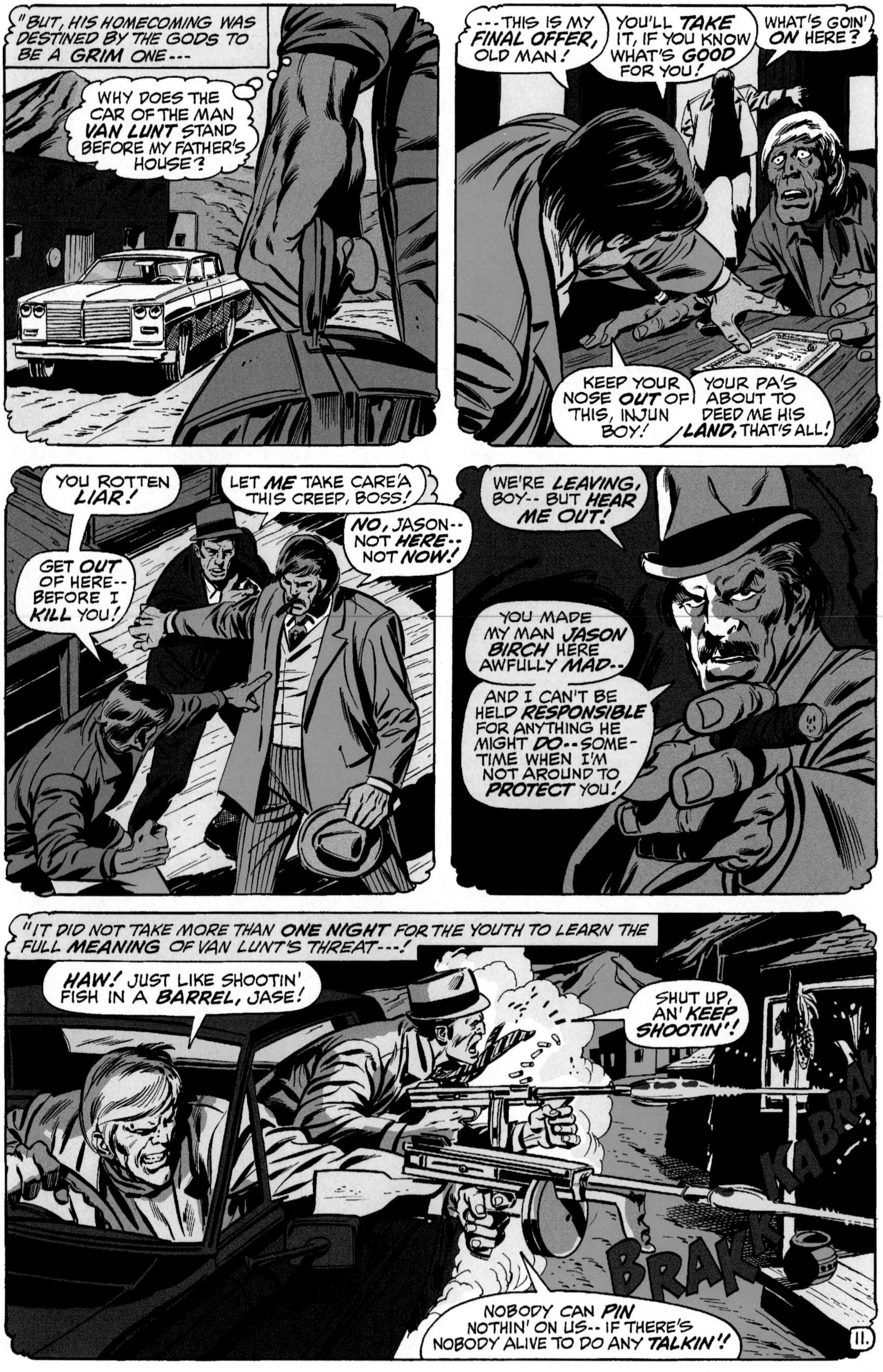
"BUT, HIS HOMECOMING WAS DESTINED BY THE GODS TO BE A GRIM ONE---
WHY DOES THE CAR OF THE MAN VAN LUNT STAND BEFORE MY FATHER'S HOUSE?
---THIS IS MY FINAL OFFER, OLD MAN!
YOU'LL TAKE IT, IF YOU KNOW WHAT'S GOOD FOR YOU!
WHAT'S GOIN' ON HERE?
KEEP YOUR NOSE OUT OF THIS, INJUN BOY!
YOUR PA'S ABOUT TO DEED ME HIS LAND, THAT'S ALL!
YOU ROTTEN LIAR!
GET OUT OF HERE-- BEFORE I KILL YOU!
LET ME TAKE CARE'A THIS CREEP, BOSS!
NO, JASON-- NOT HERE-- NOT NOW!
WE'RE LEAVING, BOY-- BUT HEAR ME OUT!
YOU MADE MY MAN JASON BIRCH HERE AWFULLY MAD--
AND I CAN'T BE HELD RESPONSIBLE FOR ANYTHING HE MIGHT DO-- SOME-TIME WHEN I'M NOT AROUND TO PROTECT YOU!
"IT DID NOT TAKE MORE THAN ONE NIGHT FOR THE YOUTH TO LEARN THE FULL MEANING OF VAN LUNT'S THREAT---!
HAW! JUST LIKE SHOOTIN' FISH IN A BARREL, JASE!
SHUT UP, AN' KEEP SHOOTIN'!
KABRAK
BRAKK
NOBODY CAN PIN NOTHIN' ON US-- IF THERE'S NOBODY ALIVE TO DO ANY TALKIN'!
11.

"BUT, THE DEADLY HAIL OF BULLETS HAD NOT DONE *ALL ITS WORK*-- FOR, WITHIN THE HOUSE, ONE FIGURE STILL *STIRRED,* IF ONLY TO CRY OUT IN *ANGUISH*--

MOTHER! FATHER--!

OH NO-- NNOOOO!

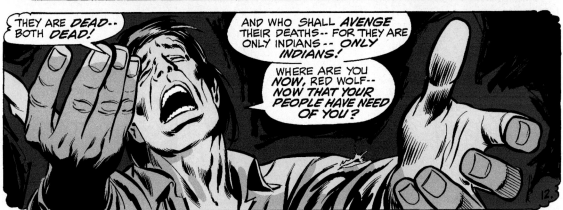

THEY ARE *DEAD*-- BOTH *DEAD!*

AND WHO SHALL *AVENGE* THEIR DEATHS-- FOR THEY ARE ONLY INDIANS-- *ONLY INDIANS!*

WHERE ARE YOU *NOW,* RED WOLF-- NOW THAT YOUR *PEOPLE HAVE NEED OF YOU?*

12.

"NEXT, HALF *FEVERISH* WITH A FLESH WOUND FROM A FLYING BULLET, THE YOUTH STAGGERED TO A CEREMONIAL *HOGAN* NEARBY---

"FOR, *THERE WERE KEPT* THE MASKS AND MEMORIES OF BYGONE *GLORIES*--!

"THEN, EVEN AS HIS *WOUND* THROBBED, HE STRUGGLED SILENTLY-- HALTINGLY-- UP THE PEOPLE'S *SACRED MOUNTAIN*---

"-- WHERE HE DANCED *ALONE,* AS IF IN A TRANCE-- THE *DANCE OF THE RED WOLF!!*

13.

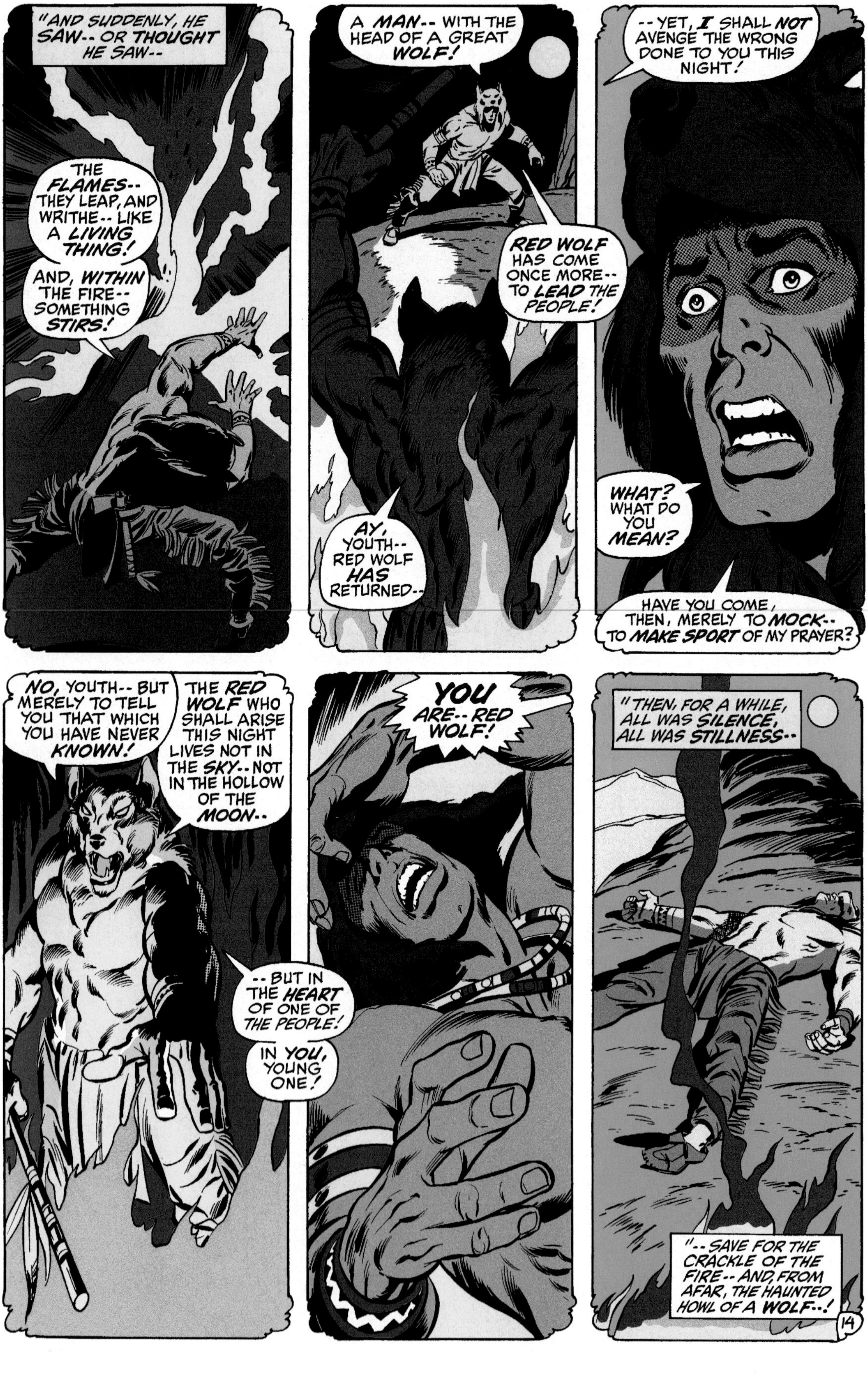
"AND SUDDENLY, HE SAW-- OR THOUGHT HE SAW--
THE FLAMES-- THEY LEAP, AND WRITHE-- LIKE A LIVING THING!
AND, WITHIN THE FIRE-- SOMETHING STIRS!
A MAN-- WITH THE HEAD OF A GREAT WOLF!
RED WOLF HAS COME ONCE MORE-- TO LEAD THE PEOPLE!
AY, YOUTH-- RED WOLF HAS RETURNED--
--YET, I SHALL NOT AVENGE THE WRONG DONE TO YOU THIS NIGHT!
WHAT? WHAT DO YOU MEAN?
HAVE YOU COME, THEN, MERELY TO MOCK-- TO MAKE SPORT OF MY PRAYER?
NO, YOUTH-- BUT MERELY TO TELL YOU THAT WHICH YOU HAVE NEVER KNOWN!
THE RED WOLF WHO SHALL ARISE THIS NIGHT LIVES NOT IN THE SKY-- NOT IN THE HOLLOW OF THE MOON--
--BUT IN THE HEART OF ONE OF THE PEOPLE!
IN YOU, YOUNG ONE!
YOU ARE-- RED WOLF!
"THEN, FOR A WHILE, ALL WAS SILENCE, ALL WAS STILLNESS--
"--SAVE FOR THE CRACKLE OF THE FIRE-- AND, FROM AFAR, THE HAUNTED HOWL OF A WOLF--!
14

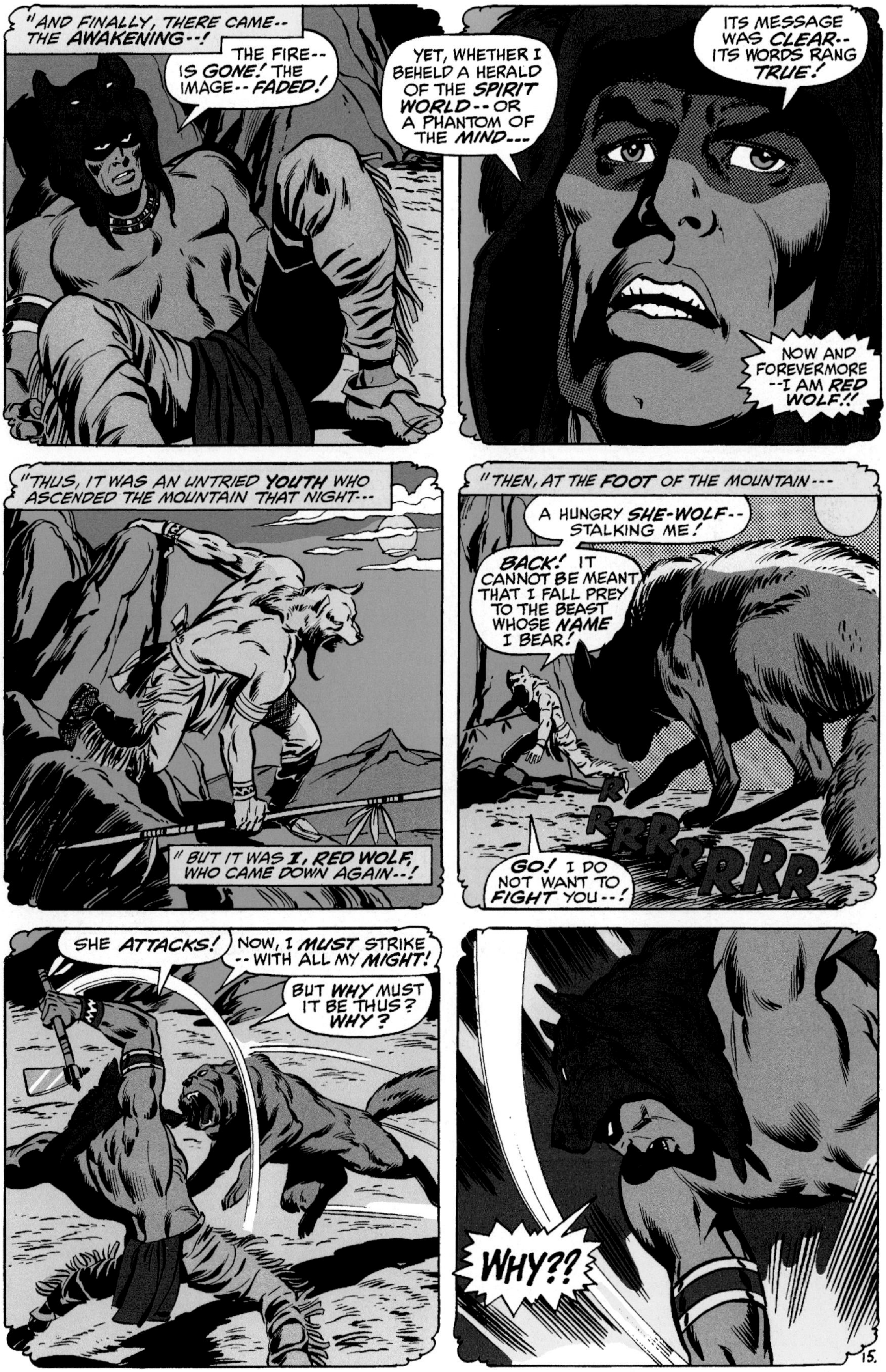

"AND FINALLY, THERE CAME-- THE AWAKENING--!
THE FIRE-- IS GONE! THE IMAGE-- FADED!
YET, WHETHER I BEHELD A HERALD OF THE SPIRIT WORLD-- OR A PHANTOM OF THE MIND---
ITS MESSAGE WAS CLEAR-- ITS WORDS RANG TRUE!
NOW AND FOREVERMORE --I AM RED WOLF!!
"THUS, IT WAS AN UNTRIED YOUTH WHO ASCENDED THE MOUNTAIN THAT NIGHT---
"BUT IT WAS I, RED WOLF, WHO CAME DOWN AGAIN--!
"THEN, AT THE FOOT OF THE MOUNTAIN---
A HUNGRY SHE-WOLF-- STALKING ME!
BACK! IT CANNOT BE MEANT THAT I FALL PREY TO THE BEAST WHOSE NAME I BEAR!
RRRRRRRRR
GO! I DO NOT WANT TO FIGHT YOU--!
SHE ATTACKS!
NOW, I MUST STRIKE --WITH ALL MY MIGHT!
BUT WHY MUST IT BE THUS? WHY?
WHY??

SHE IS *DEAD!* WEAK FROM HUNGER, SHE WAS *NO MATCH* FOR MY TOMAHAWK!

SURELY, THE *SPIRIT-WOLF* SENT HER AGAINST ME FOR A *REASON!* YET *WHAT--?*

WAIT! THAT *CRY* FROM WITHIN THE CAVE!

THERE IS THE *REASON--!*

SHE FOUGHT TO PROTECT-- HER *CUB!*

HE IS A *SIGN--* A LIVING OMEN OF THE *MISSION* I MUST FULFILL!

AND HE SHALL BE CALLED--- *LOBO!*

"*LONG* MONTHS I SPENT, IN *SECLUSION,* ON THE *SUN-SCORCHED* DESERT, PREPARING FOR WHAT WAS TO *COME--!*

"*THEN,* AT *LAST,* I CAME *AGAIN* TO THIS *CITY--!*

ROOM FOR RENT

"*ONCE MORE,* I LABORED AMONG *MAN-MADE* PEAKS--

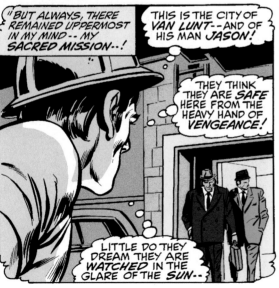

"BUT *ALWAYS,* THERE REMAINED UPPERMOST IN MY MIND-- MY *SACRED* MISSION--!"

THIS IS THE CITY OF *VAN LUNT*-- AND OF HIS MAN *JASON!*

THEY THINK THEY ARE *SAFE* HERE FROM THE *HEAVY HAND* OF *VENGEANCE!*

LITTLE DO THEY *DREAM* THEY ARE *WATCHED* IN THE *GLARE* OF THE *SUN--*

-- AND IN THE *GLOW* OF THE *MOON!*

16

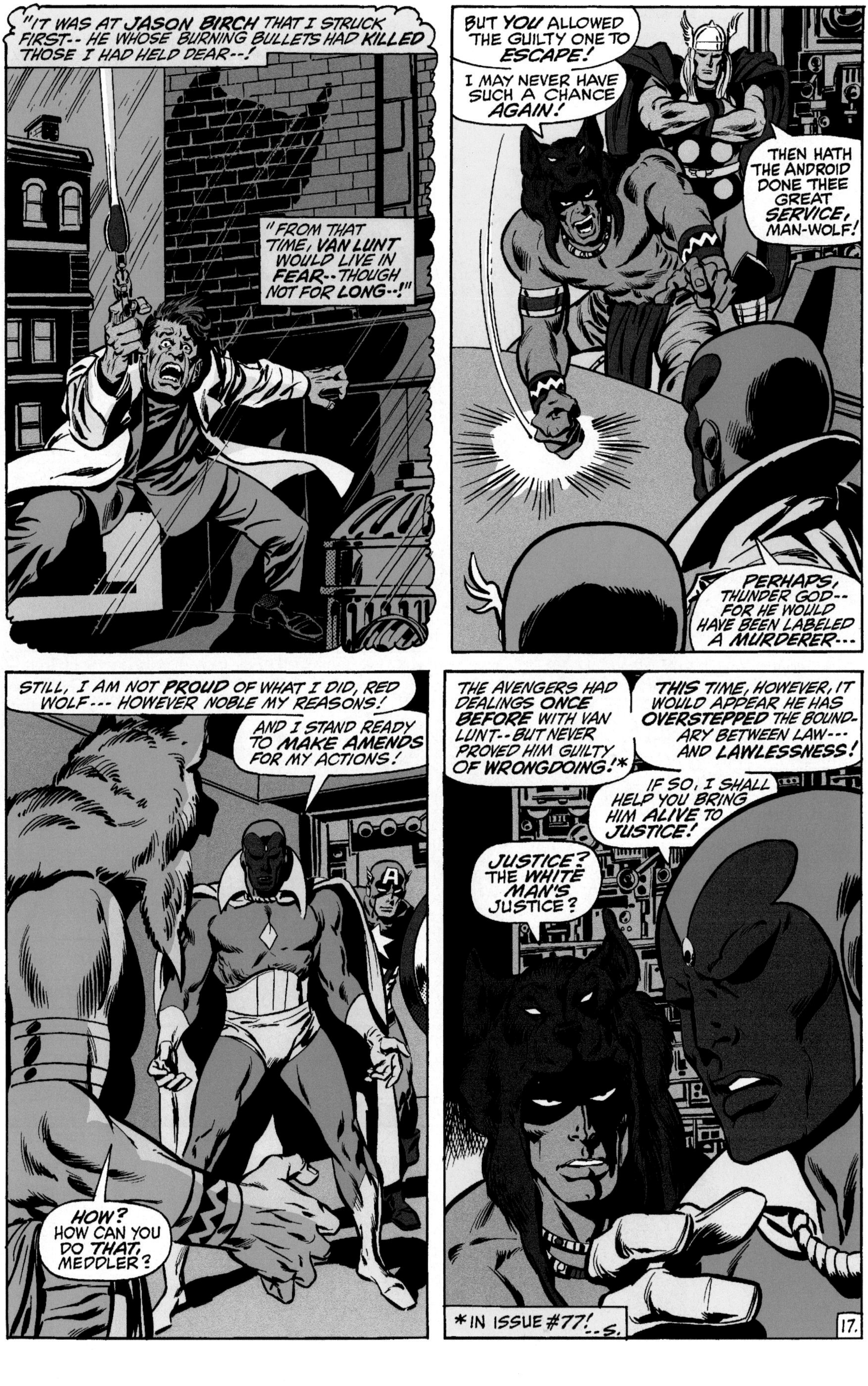
"IT WAS AT JASON BIRCH THAT I STRUCK FIRST-- HE WHOSE BURNING BULLETS HAD KILLED THOSE I HAD HELD DEAR--!
"FROM THAT TIME, VAN LUNT WOULD LIVE IN FEAR--THOUGH NOT FOR LONG--!"
BUT YOU ALLOWED THE GUILTY ONE TO ESCAPE!
I MAY NEVER HAVE SUCH A CHANCE AGAIN!
THEN HATH THE ANDROID DONE THEE GREAT SERVICE, MAN-WOLF!
PERHAPS, THUNDER GOD-- FOR HE WOULD HAVE BEEN LABELED A MURDERER---
STILL, I AM NOT PROUD OF WHAT I DID, RED WOLF--- HOWEVER NOBLE MY REASONS!
AND I STAND READY TO MAKE AMENDS FOR MY ACTIONS!
HOW? HOW CAN YOU DO THAT, MEDDLER?
THE AVENGERS HAD DEALINGS ONCE BEFORE WITH VAN LUNT--BUT NEVER PROVED HIM GUILTY OF WRONGDOING!*
THIS TIME, HOWEVER, IT WOULD APPEAR HE HAS OVERSTEPPED THE BOUNDARY BETWEEN LAW--- AND LAWLESSNESS!
IF SO, I SHALL HELP YOU BRING HIM ALIVE TO JUSTICE!
JUSTICE? THE WHITE MAN'S JUSTICE?
*IN ISSUE #77! --S.

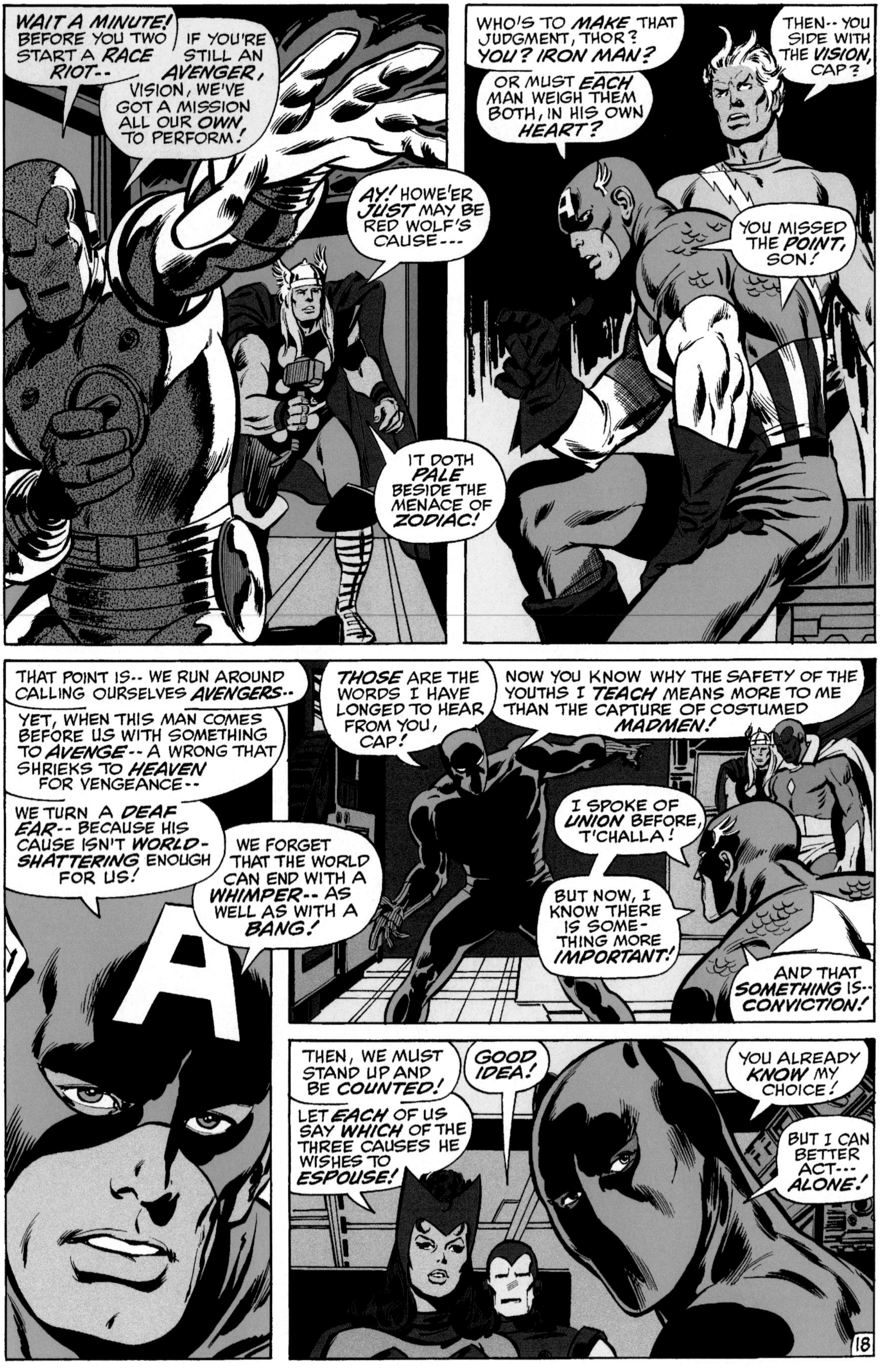
WAIT A MINUTE! BEFORE YOU TWO START A RACE RIOT--
IF YOU'RE STILL AN AVENGER, VISION, WE'VE GOT A MISSION ALL OUR OWN, TO PERFORM!
AY! HOWE'ER JUST MAY BE RED WOLF'S CAUSE---
IT DOTH PALE BESIDE THE MENACE OF ZODIAC!
WHO'S TO MAKE THAT JUDGMENT, THOR? YOU? IRON MAN?
OR MUST EACH MAN WEIGH THEM BOTH, IN HIS OWN HEART?
THEN-- YOU SIDE WITH THE VISION, CAP?
YOU MISSED THE POINT, SON!
THAT POINT IS-- WE RUN AROUND CALLING OURSELVES AVENGERS--
YET, WHEN THIS MAN COMES BEFORE US WITH SOMETHING TO AVENGE-- A WRONG THAT SHRIEKS TO HEAVEN FOR VENGEANCE--
WE TURN A DEAF EAR-- BECAUSE HIS CAUSE ISN'T WORLD-SHATTERING ENOUGH FOR US!
WE FORGET THAT THE WORLD CAN END WITH A WHIMPER-- AS WELL AS WITH A BANG!
THOSE ARE THE WORDS I HAVE LONGED TO HEAR FROM YOU, CAP!
NOW YOU KNOW WHY THE SAFETY OF THE YOUTHS I TEACH MEANS MORE TO ME THAN THE CAPTURE OF COSTUMED MADMEN!
I SPOKE OF UNION BEFORE, T'CHALLA!
BUT NOW, I KNOW THERE IS SOMETHING MORE IMPORTANT!
AND THAT SOMETHING IS-- CONVICTION!
THEN, WE MUST STAND UP AND BE COUNTED!
LET EACH OF US SAY WHICH OF THE THREE CAUSES HE WISHES TO ESPOUSE!
GOOD IDEA!
YOU ALREADY KNOW MY CHOICE!
BUT I CAN BETTER ACT--- ALONE!
18

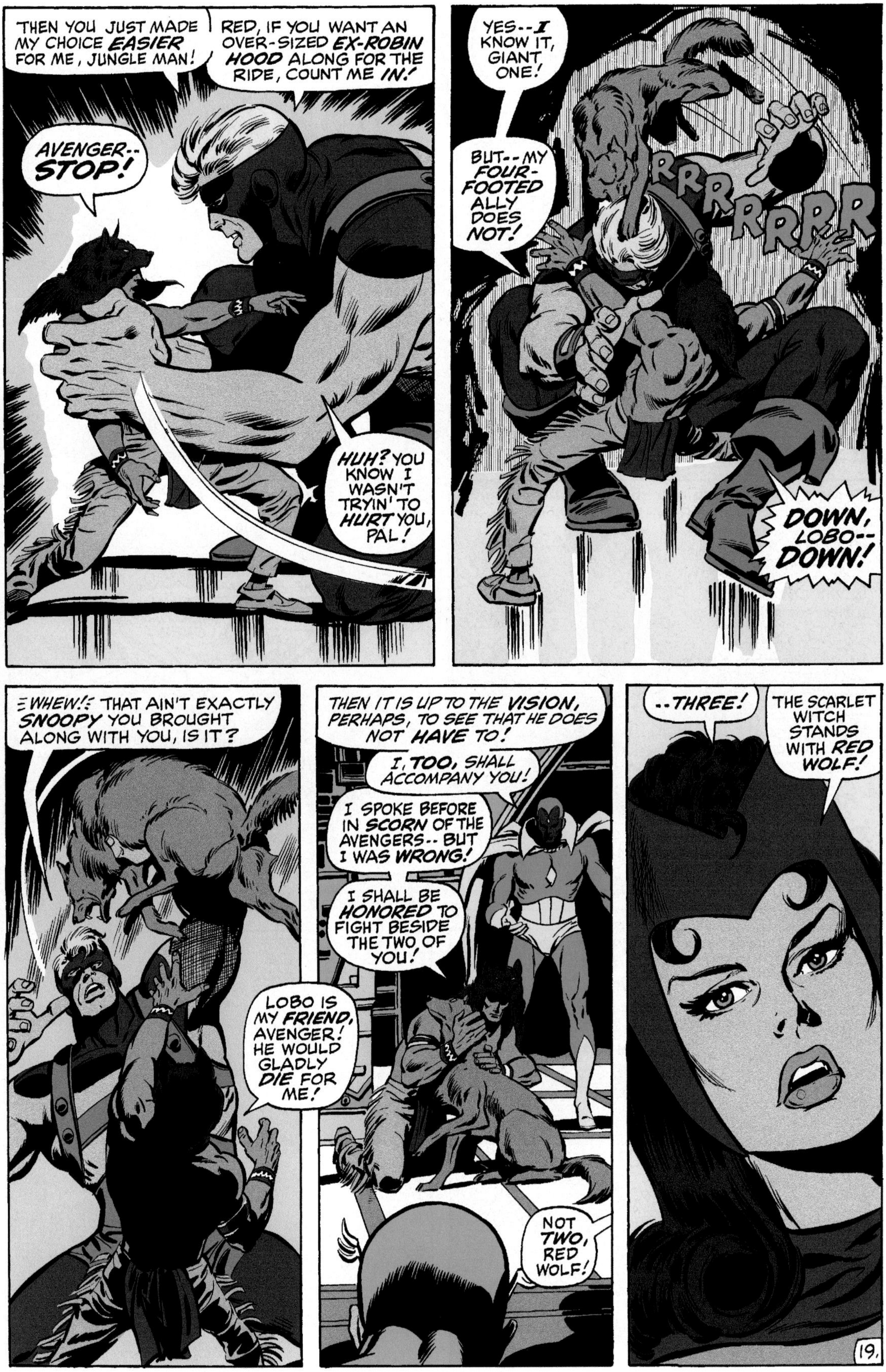
THEN YOU JUST MADE MY CHOICE EASIER FOR ME, JUNGLE MAN!
RED, IF YOU WANT AN OVER-SIZED EX-ROBIN HOOD ALONG FOR THE RIDE, COUNT ME IN!
AVENGER-- STOP!
HUH? YOU KNOW I WASN'T TRYIN' TO HURT YOU, PAL!
YES--I KNOW IT, GIANT ONE!
BUT--MY FOUR-FOOTED ALLY DOES NOT!
RRRRRRRRR
DOWN, LOBO-- DOWN!
WHEW! THAT AIN'T EXACTLY SNOOPY YOU BROUGHT ALONG WITH YOU, IS IT?
LOBO IS MY FRIEND, AVENGER! HE WOULD GLADLY DIE FOR ME!
THEN IT IS UP TO THE VISION, PERHAPS, TO SEE THAT HE DOES NOT HAVE TO!
I, TOO, SHALL ACCOMPANY YOU!
I SPOKE BEFORE IN SCORN OF THE AVENGERS-- BUT I WAS WRONG!
I SHALL BE HONORED TO FIGHT BESIDE THE TWO OF YOU!
NOT TWO, RED WOLF!
--THREE!
THE SCARLET WITCH STANDS WITH RED WOLF!

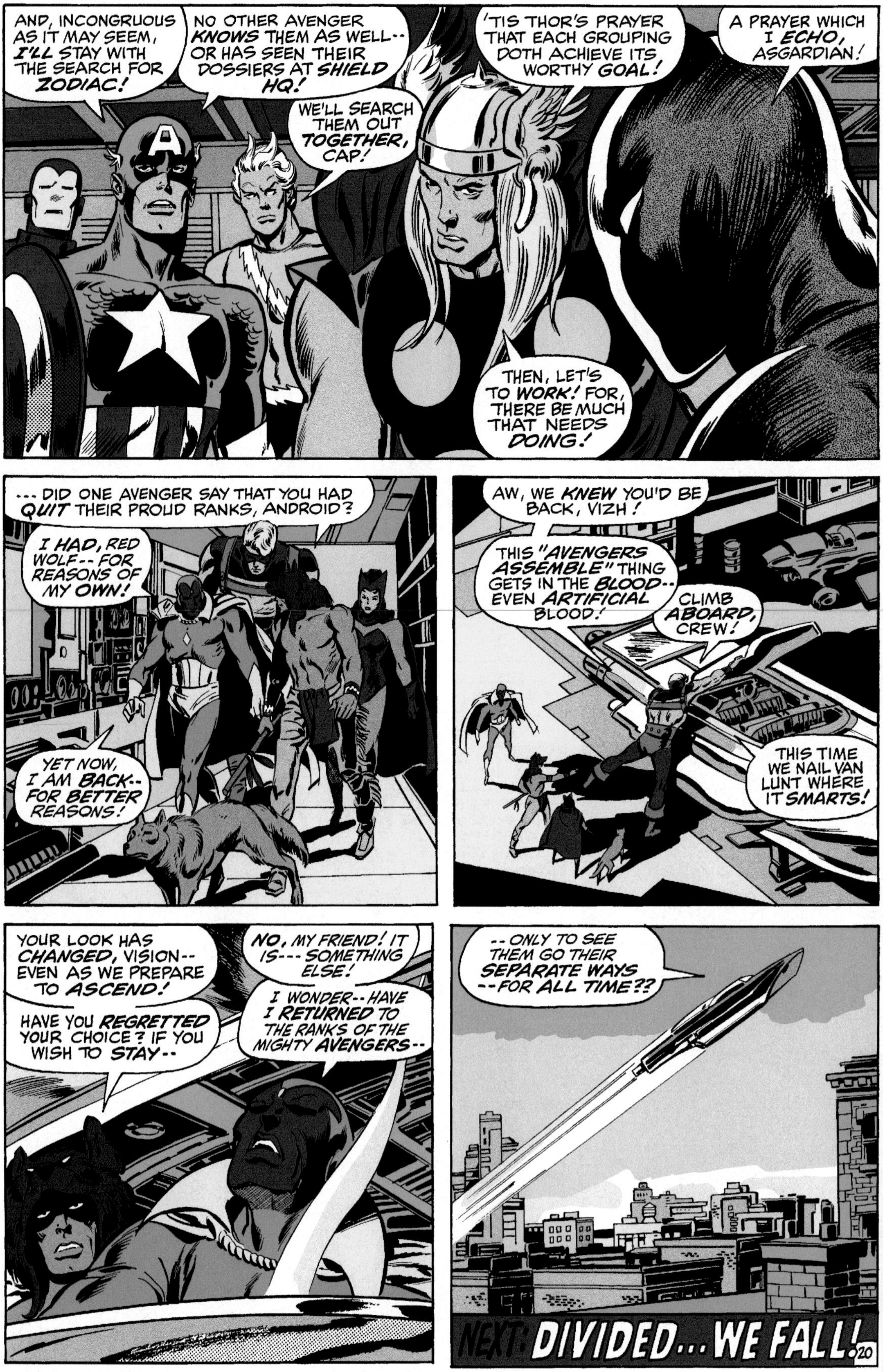

AND, INCONGRUOUS AS IT MAY SEEM, I'LL STAY WITH THE SEARCH FOR ZODIAC!
NO OTHER AVENGER KNOWS THEM AS WELL-- OR HAS SEEN THEIR DOSSIERS AT SHIELD HQ!
WE'LL SEARCH THEM OUT TOGETHER, CAP!
'TIS THOR'S PRAYER THAT EACH GROUPING DOTH ACHIEVE ITS WORTHY GOAL!
A PRAYER WHICH I ECHO, ASGARDIAN!
THEN, LET'S TO WORK! FOR, THERE BE MUCH THAT NEEDS DOING!
... DID ONE AVENGER SAY THAT YOU HAD QUIT THEIR PROUD RANKS, ANDROID?
I HAD, RED WOLF-- FOR REASONS OF MY OWN!
YET NOW, I AM BACK-- FOR BETTER REASONS!
AW, WE KNEW YOU'D BE BACK, VIZH!
THIS "AVENGERS ASSEMBLE" THING GETS IN THE BLOOD-- EVEN ARTIFICIAL BLOOD!
CLIMB ABOARD, CREW!
THIS TIME WE NAIL VAN LUNT WHERE IT SMARTS!
YOUR LOOK HAS CHANGED, VISION-- EVEN AS WE PREPARE TO ASCEND!
HAVE YOU REGRETTED YOUR CHOICE? IF YOU WISH TO STAY--
NO, MY FRIEND! IT IS--- SOMETHING ELSE!
I WONDER-- HAVE I RETURNED TO THE RANKS OF THE MIGHTY AVENGERS--
--ONLY TO SEE THEM GO THEIR SEPARATE WAYS --FOR ALL TIME??
NEXT: DIVIDED... WE FALL!
20

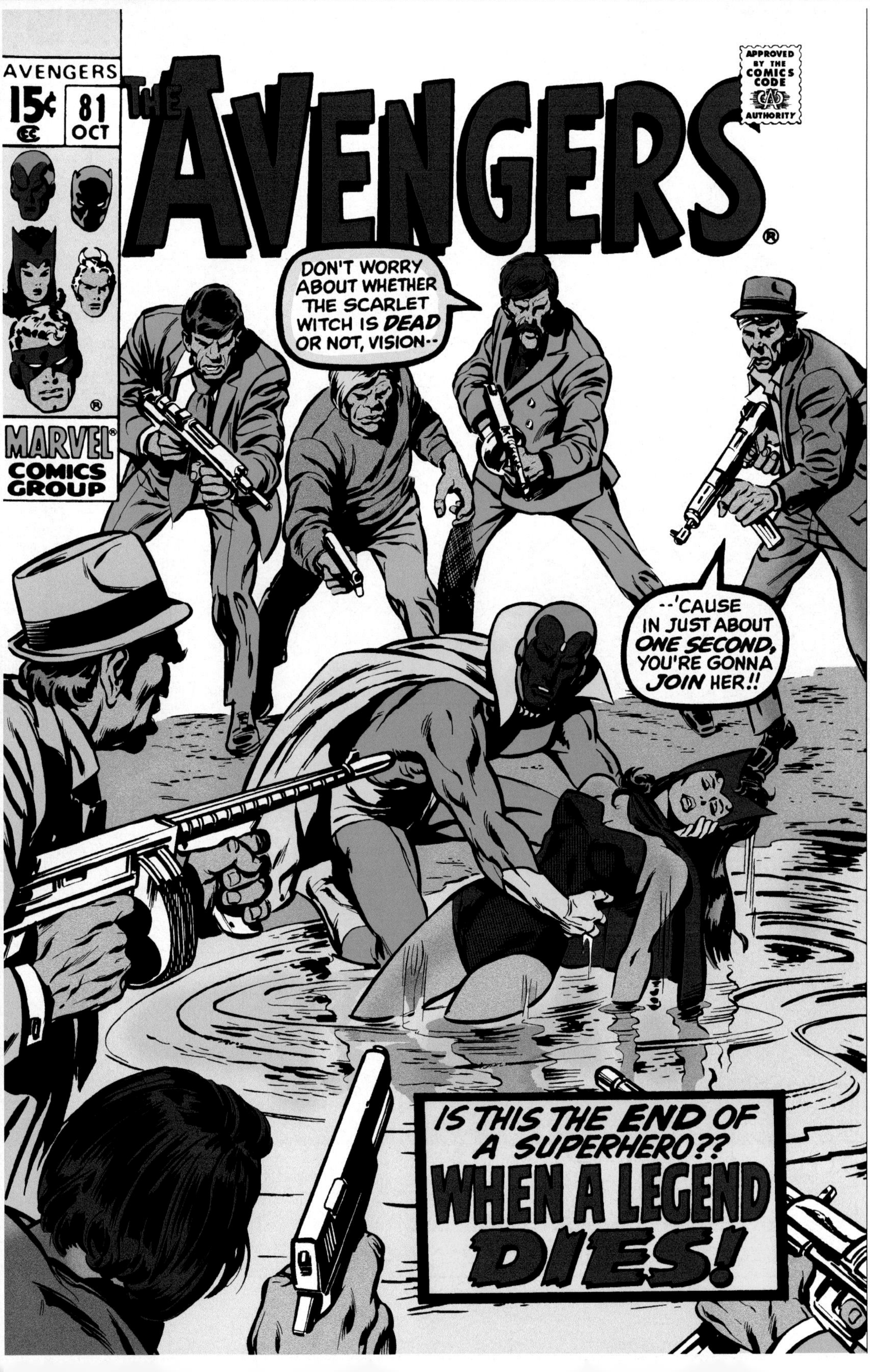
AVENGERS
15¢
81
OCT
MARVEL COMICS GROUP
APPROVED BY THE COMICS CODE AUTHORITY
THE AVENGERS
DON'T WORRY ABOUT WHETHER THE SCARLET WITCH IS DEAD OR NOT, VISION--
--'CAUSE IN JUST ABOUT ONE SECOND, YOU'RE GONNA JOIN HER!!
IS THIS THE END OF A SUPERHERO?? WHEN A LEGEND DIES!

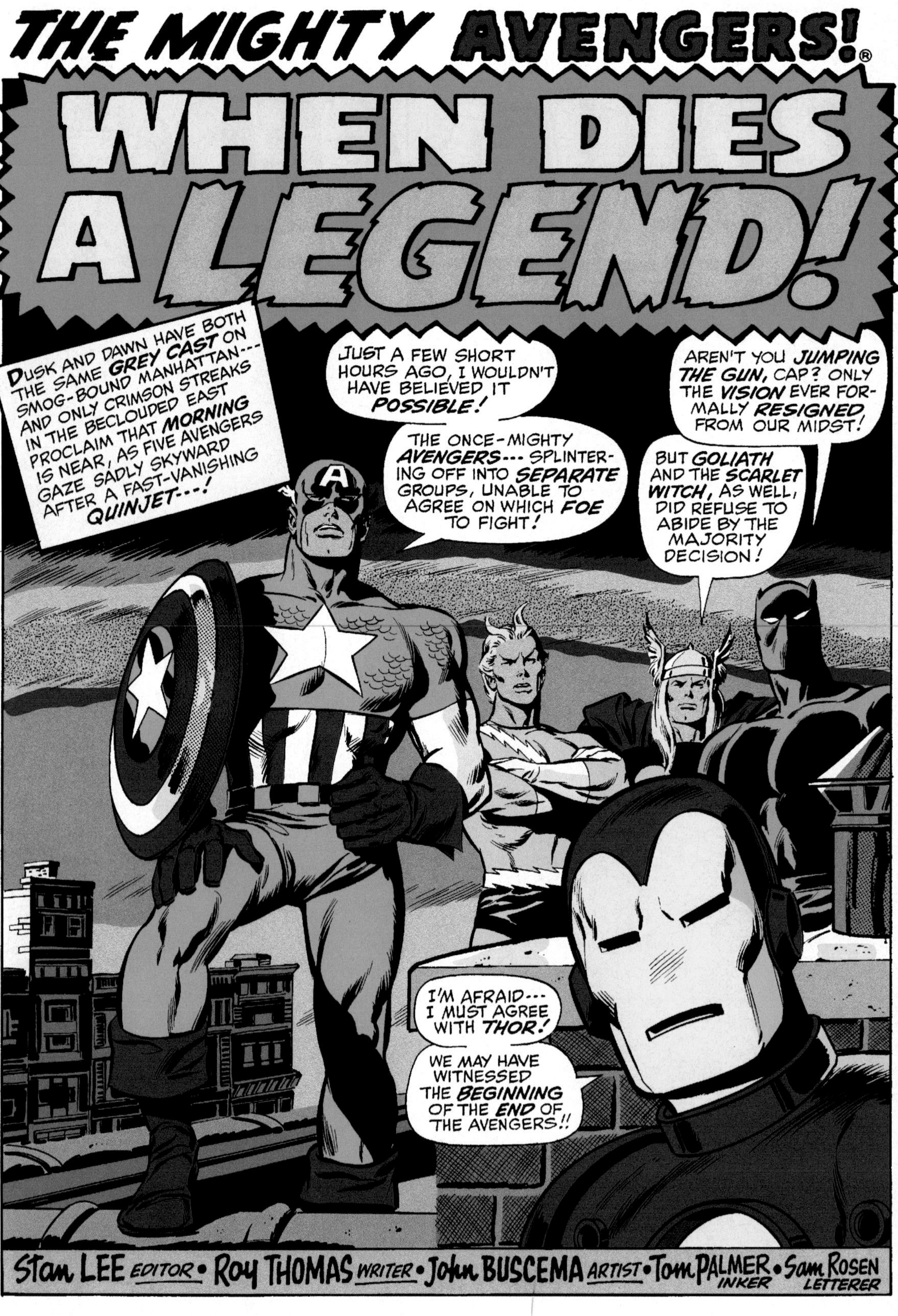
THE MIGHTY AVENGERS!®
WHEN DIES A LEGEND!
DUSK AND DAWN HAVE BOTH THE SAME GREY CAST ON SMOG-BOUND MANHATTAN--- AND ONLY CRIMSON STREAKS IN THE BECLOUDED EAST PROCLAIM THAT MORNING IS NEAR, AS FIVE AVENGERS GAZE SADLY SKYWARD AFTER A FAST-VANISHING QUINJET---!
JUST A FEW SHORT HOURS AGO, I WOULDN'T HAVE BELIEVED IT POSSIBLE!
THE ONCE-MIGHTY AVENGERS--- SPLINTERING OFF INTO SEPARATE GROUPS, UNABLE TO AGREE ON WHICH FOE TO FIGHT!
AREN'T YOU JUMPING THE GUN, CAP? ONLY THE VISION EVER FORMALLY RESIGNED FROM OUR MIDST!
BUT GOLIATH AND THE SCARLET WITCH, AS WELL, DID REFUSE TO ABIDE BY THE MAJORITY DECISION!
I'M AFRAID--- I MUST AGREE WITH THOR!
WE MAY HAVE WITNESSED THE BEGINNING OF THE END OF THE AVENGERS!!
Stan LEE EDITOR • Roy THOMAS WRITER • John BUSCEMA ARTIST • Tom PALMER INKER • Sam ROSEN LETTERER

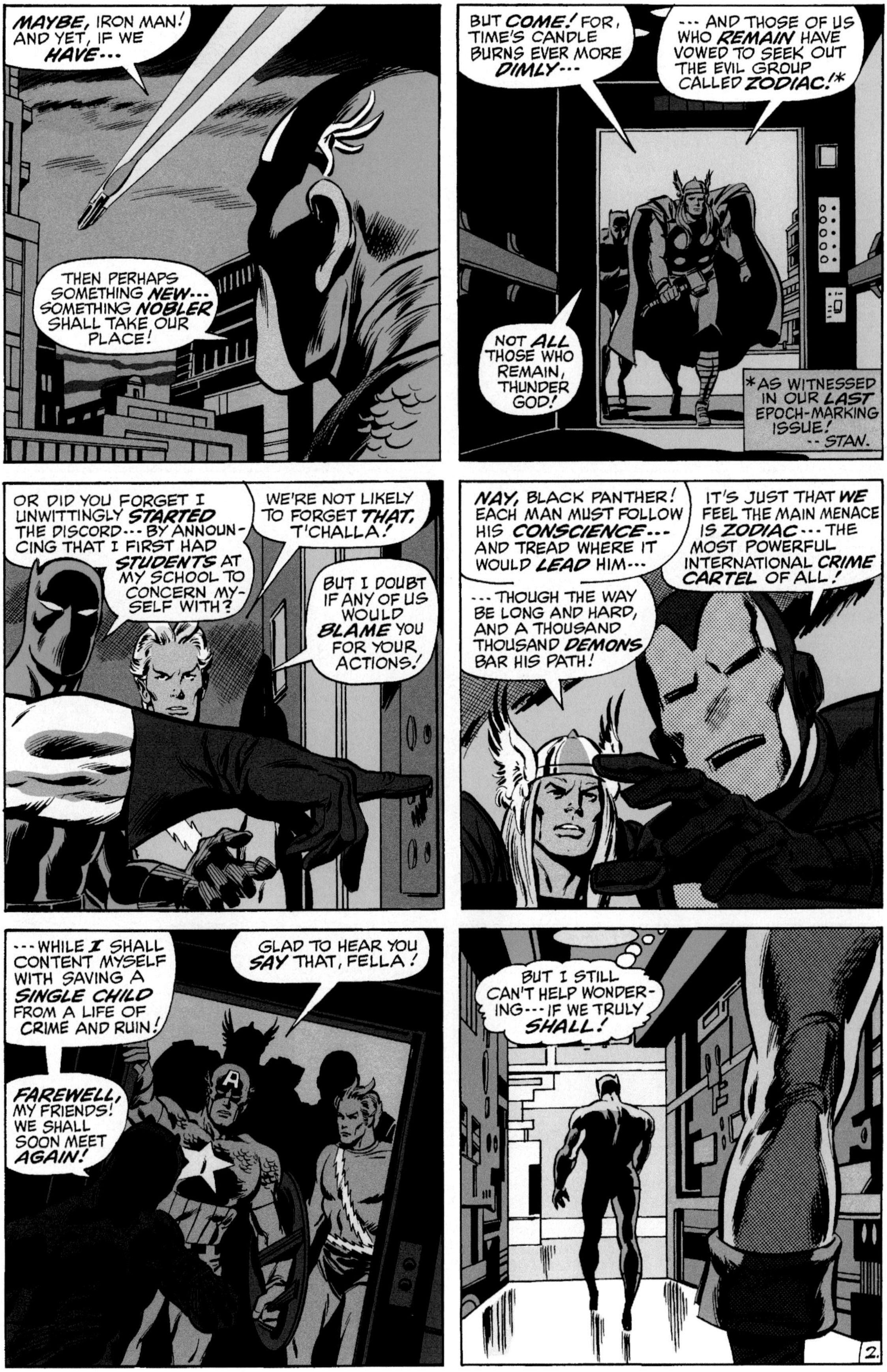
MAYBE, IRON MAN! AND YET, IF WE HAVE---
THEN PERHAPS SOMETHING NEW--- SOMETHING NOBLER SHALL TAKE OUR PLACE!
BUT COME! FOR, TIME'S CANDLE BURNS EVER MORE DIMLY---
--- AND THOSE OF US WHO REMAIN HAVE VOWED TO SEEK OUT THE EVIL GROUP CALLED ZODIAC!*
NOT ALL THOSE WHO REMAIN, THUNDER GOD!
*AS WITNESSED IN OUR LAST EPOCH-MARKING ISSUE! -- STAN.
OR DID YOU FORGET I UNWITTINGLY STARTED THE DISCORD--- BY ANNOUNCING THAT I FIRST HAD STUDENTS AT MY SCHOOL TO CONCERN MYSELF WITH?
WE'RE NOT LIKELY TO FORGET THAT, T'CHALLA!
BUT I DOUBT IF ANY OF US WOULD BLAME YOU FOR YOUR ACTIONS!
NAY, BLACK PANTHER! EACH MAN MUST FOLLOW HIS CONSCIENCE--- AND TREAD WHERE IT WOULD LEAD HIM---
--- THOUGH THE WAY BE LONG AND HARD, AND A THOUSAND THOUSAND DEMONS BAR HIS PATH!
IT'S JUST THAT WE FEEL THE MAIN MENACE IS ZODIAC--- THE MOST POWERFUL INTERNATIONAL CRIME CARTEL OF ALL!
--- WHILE I SHALL CONTENT MYSELF WITH SAVING A SINGLE CHILD FROM A LIFE OF CRIME AND RUIN!
GLAD TO HEAR YOU SAY THAT, FELLA!
FAREWELL, MY FRIENDS! WE SHALL SOON MEET AGAIN!
BUT I STILL CAN'T HELP WONDERING--- IF WE TRULY SHALL!
2.

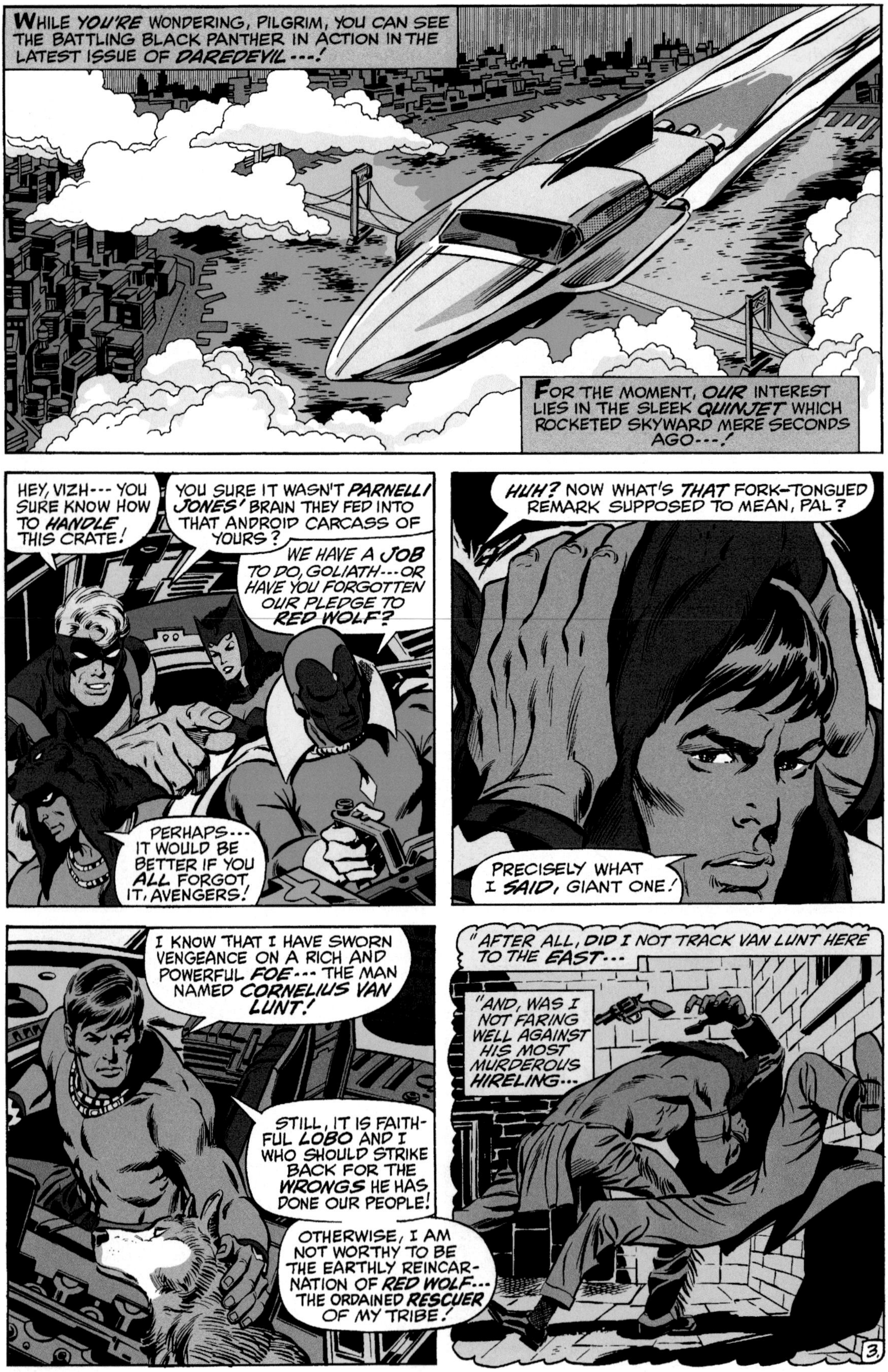

WHILE YOU'RE WONDERING, PILGRIM, YOU CAN SEE THE BATTLING BLACK PANTHER IN ACTION IN THE LATEST ISSUE OF DAREDEVIL---!
FOR THE MOMENT, OUR INTEREST LIES IN THE SLEEK QUINJET WHICH ROCKETED SKYWARD MERE SECONDS AGO---!
HEY, VIZH--- YOU SURE KNOW HOW TO HANDLE THIS CRATE!
YOU SURE IT WASN'T PARNELLI JONES' BRAIN THEY FED INTO THAT ANDROID CARCASS OF YOURS?
WE HAVE A JOB TO DO, GOLIATH---OR HAVE YOU FORGOTTEN OUR PLEDGE TO RED WOLF?
PERHAPS--- IT WOULD BE BETTER IF YOU ALL FORGOT IT, AVENGERS!
HUH? NOW WHAT'S THAT FORK-TONGUED REMARK SUPPOSED TO MEAN, PAL?
PRECISELY WHAT I SAID, GIANT ONE!
I KNOW THAT I HAVE SWORN VENGEANCE ON A RICH AND POWERFUL FOE--- THE MAN NAMED CORNELIUS VAN LUNT!
STILL, IT IS FAITHFUL LOBO AND I WHO SHOULD STRIKE BACK FOR THE WRONGS HE HAS DONE OUR PEOPLE!
OTHERWISE, I AM NOT WORTHY TO BE THE EARTHLY REINCARNATION OF RED WOLF... THE ORDAINED RESCUER OF MY TRIBE!
"AFTER ALL, DID I NOT TRACK VAN LUNT HERE TO THE EAST...
"AND, WAS I NOT FARING WELL AGAINST HIS MOST MURDEROUS HIRELING...
3

"--- WHEN *SUDDENLY,* LIKE A WRAITH FROM BEYOND THE GRAVE ---

HALT, MAN-WHO-WOULD-BE-WOLF!

WOULD *YOU* BECOME AS EVIL AS THE ONE YOU HAVE *PURSUED?*

"THEN, WHILE WE TWO FOUGHT OUR UNEVEN BATTLE, MY DESPERATE PREY ESCAPED...!"

AS THE YOUTHFUL INDIAN FINISHES, A PALL OF *SILENCE* DRAPES THE CRUISING VESSEL ---

I AM NOT *PROUD* OF MY WORDS --- OF THEIR SEEMING *INGRATITUDE!*

IS *THIS* WHY I ENDED MY BRIEF SELF-EXILE FROM THE AVENGERS --- TO HELP ONE WHO *SCORNS* OUR AID?

BUT IT IS *RED WOLF* WHO MUST SAVE HIS PEOPLE --- AND NONE MUST *INTRUDE* UPON THAT DESTINY!

RED WOLF MAY BE A *HOTHEAD* --- BUT HE'S GOT *GUTS!*

I KNOW WHAT IT'S *LIKE* TO HAVE A ROUGH ROW TO HOE --- *ALONE!*

WHY DID *I* JOIN THIS MISSION --- HEEDING A RASH *IMPULSE?*

WAS IT *REALLY* TO HELP *RED WOLF* --- OR FOR SOME DEEPER, *HIDDEN* REASON?

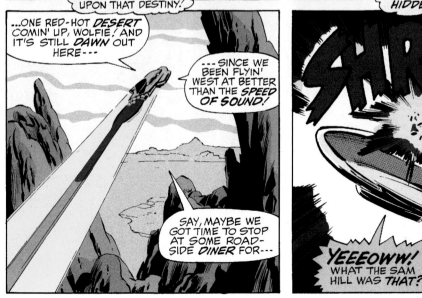

...ONE RED-HOT *DESERT* COMIN' UP, WOLFIE! AND IT'S STILL *DAWN* OUT HERE ---

--- SINCE WE BEEN FLYIN' WEST AT BETTER THAN THE *SPEED OF SOUND!*

SAY, MAYBE WE GOT TIME TO STOP AT SOME ROADSIDE *DINER* FOR ---

SHROOO

YEEEOWW! WHAT THE SAM HILL WAS *THAT??*

4

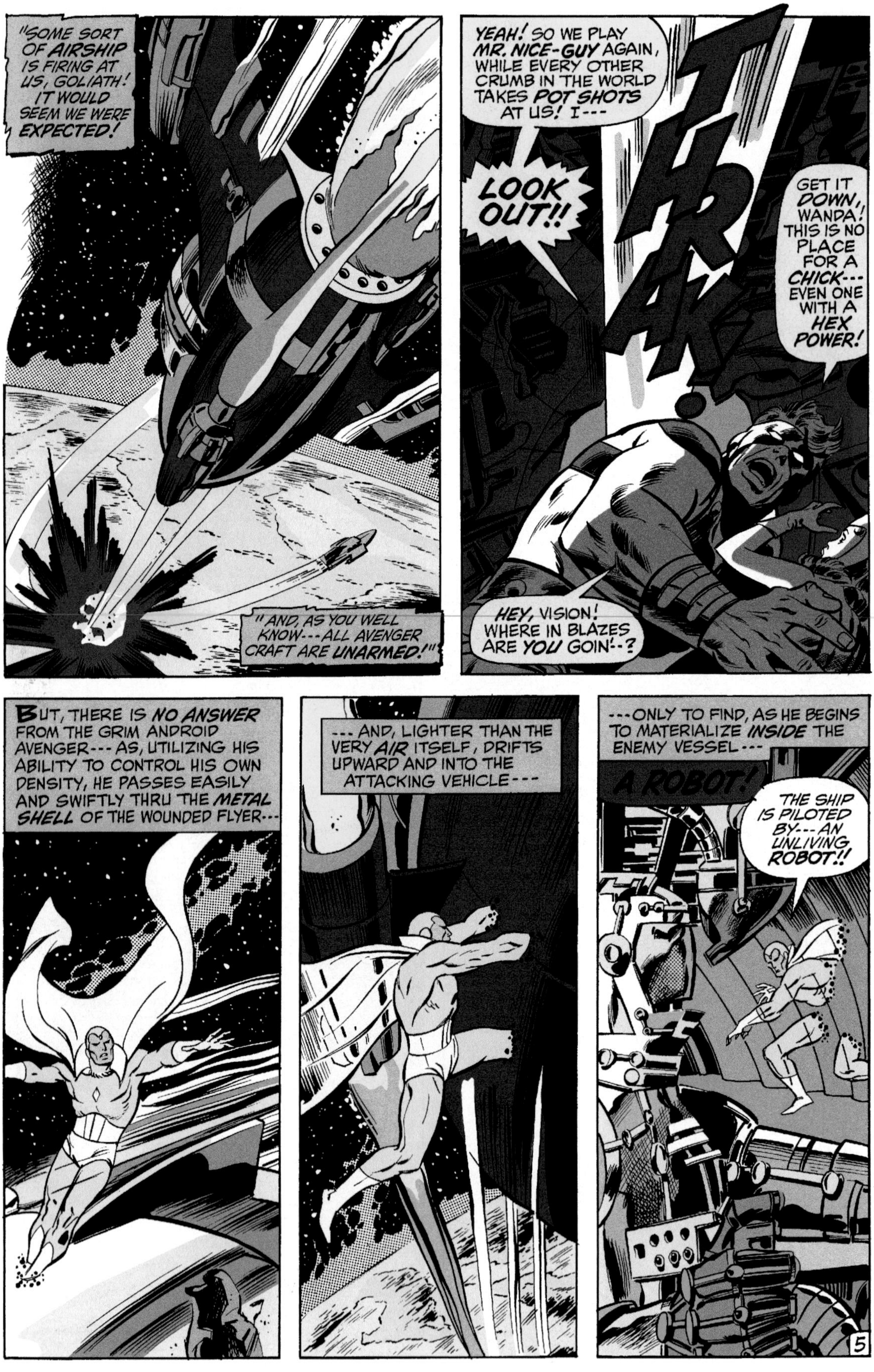
"SOME SORT OF AIRSHIP IS FIRING AT US, GOLIATH! IT WOULD SEEM WE WERE EXPECTED!
"AND, AS YOU WELL KNOW---ALL AVENGER CRAFT ARE UNARMED!"
YEAH! SO WE PLAY MR. NICE-GUY AGAIN, WHILE EVERY OTHER CRUMB IN THE WORLD TAKES POT SHOTS AT US! I---
LOOK OUT!!
THRAK!
GET IT DOWN, WANDA! THIS IS NO PLACE FOR A CHICK--- EVEN ONE WITH A HEX POWER!
HEY, VISION! WHERE IN BLAZES ARE YOU GOIN'--?
BUT, THERE IS NO ANSWER FROM THE GRIM ANDROID AVENGER---AS, UTILIZING HIS ABILITY TO CONTROL HIS OWN DENSITY, HE PASSES EASILY AND SWIFTLY THRU THE METAL SHELL OF THE WOUNDED FLYER---
---AND, LIGHTER THAN THE VERY AIR ITSELF, DRIFTS UPWARD AND INTO THE ATTACKING VEHICLE---
---ONLY TO FIND, AS HE BEGINS TO MATERIALIZE INSIDE THE ENEMY VESSEL---
A ROBOT!
THE SHIP IS PILOTED BY---AN UNLIVING ROBOT!!
5

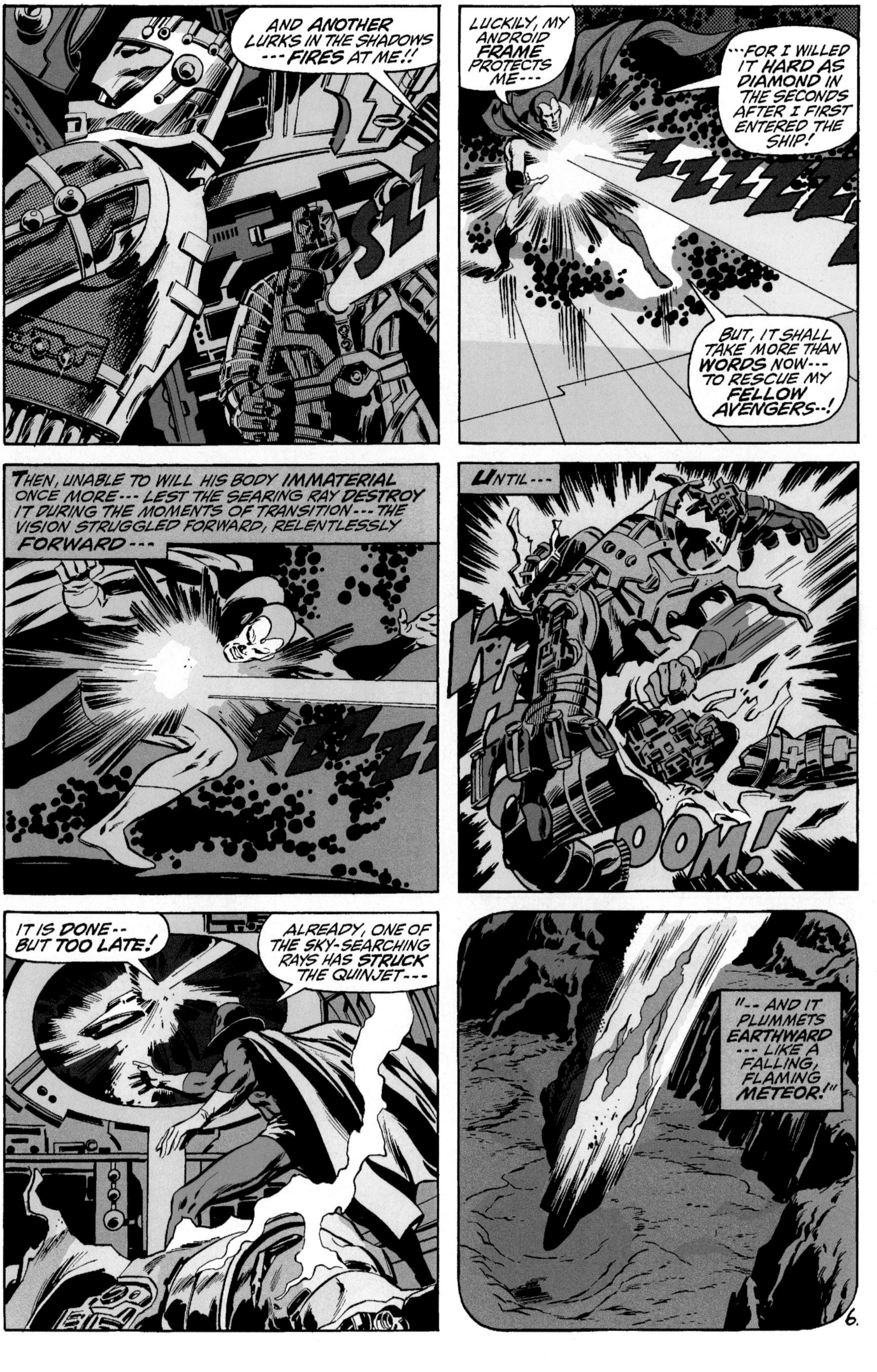

AND ANOTHER LURKS IN THE SHADOWS --- FIRES AT ME!!
LUCKILY, MY ANDROID FRAME PROTECTS ME---
...FOR I WILLED IT HARD AS DIAMOND IN THE SECONDS AFTER I FIRST ENTERED THE SHIP!
BUT, IT SHALL TAKE MORE THAN WORDS NOW--- TO RESCUE MY FELLOW AVENGERS--!
THEN, UNABLE TO WILL HIS BODY IMMATERIAL ONCE MORE--- LEST THE SEARING RAY DESTROY IT DURING THE MOMENTS OF TRANSITION--- THE VISION STRUGGLED FORWARD, RELENTLESSLY FORWARD---
UNTIL---
OOM!
IT IS DONE-- BUT TOO LATE!
ALREADY, ONE OF THE SKY-SEARCHING RAYS HAS STRUCK THE QUINJET---
"-- AND IT PLUMMETS EARTHWARD --- LIKE A FALLING, FLAMING METEOR!"

SEARCHER #1 TO VAN LUNT: UFO HAS BEEN DOWNED --- RETURNING TO BASE---

THEN VAN LUNT IS BEHIND THIS MURDER-MISSION ---AS I SUSPECTED!

WELL, NEVER AGAIN SHALL HE SEND FORTH LIFELESS ROBOTS IN LIFELESS MISSILES TO SNUFF OUT HUMAN LIVES!

SO SWEARS THE VISION!

DANCING---SWIRLING --- GLOWING--- THE VERY MOLECULES OF THE AIR ITSELF ARE DRUNK IN BY THE REVENGE-MAD ANDROID, AS IF BY SOME LIVING VACUUM---

...UNTIL SO GREAT BECOMES HIS MASS--- SO INCALCULABLE HIS WEIGHT--- THAT THE STRAINING ROCKET IS PULLED DOWN, DOWN-WARD BY THE MIGHTY FORCE CALLED GRAVITY---

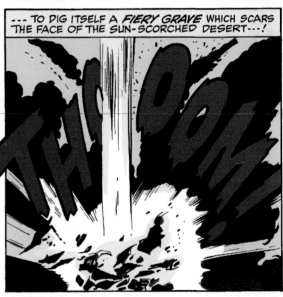

--- TO DIG ITSELF A FIERY GRAVE WHICH SCARS THE FACE OF THE SUN-SCORCHED DESERT---!

THOOM!

ROBOT AND ROCKET ARE GONE, BUT THE QUESTIONS REMAIN!

WHERE DID EVEN ONE OF VAN LUNT'S WEALTH OBTAIN WEAPONRY AND ROBOTS OF SUCH ADVANCED TYPE?

IS THERE PERHAPS MORE TO THIS DESERT MYSTERY THAN THE BLOOD-VENGEANCE OF A MASKED INDIAN?

MORE IMPORTANT--- DOES RED WOLF STILL LIVE? DO GOLIATH AND THE SCARLET WITCH?

IT SEEMS HOPELESS --- BUT I MUST SCAN THE DESERT FLOOR---PER-HAPS TO FIND SOME TRACE OF ---

WAIT! THERE... ALMOST DIRECTLY BELOW ME ---!

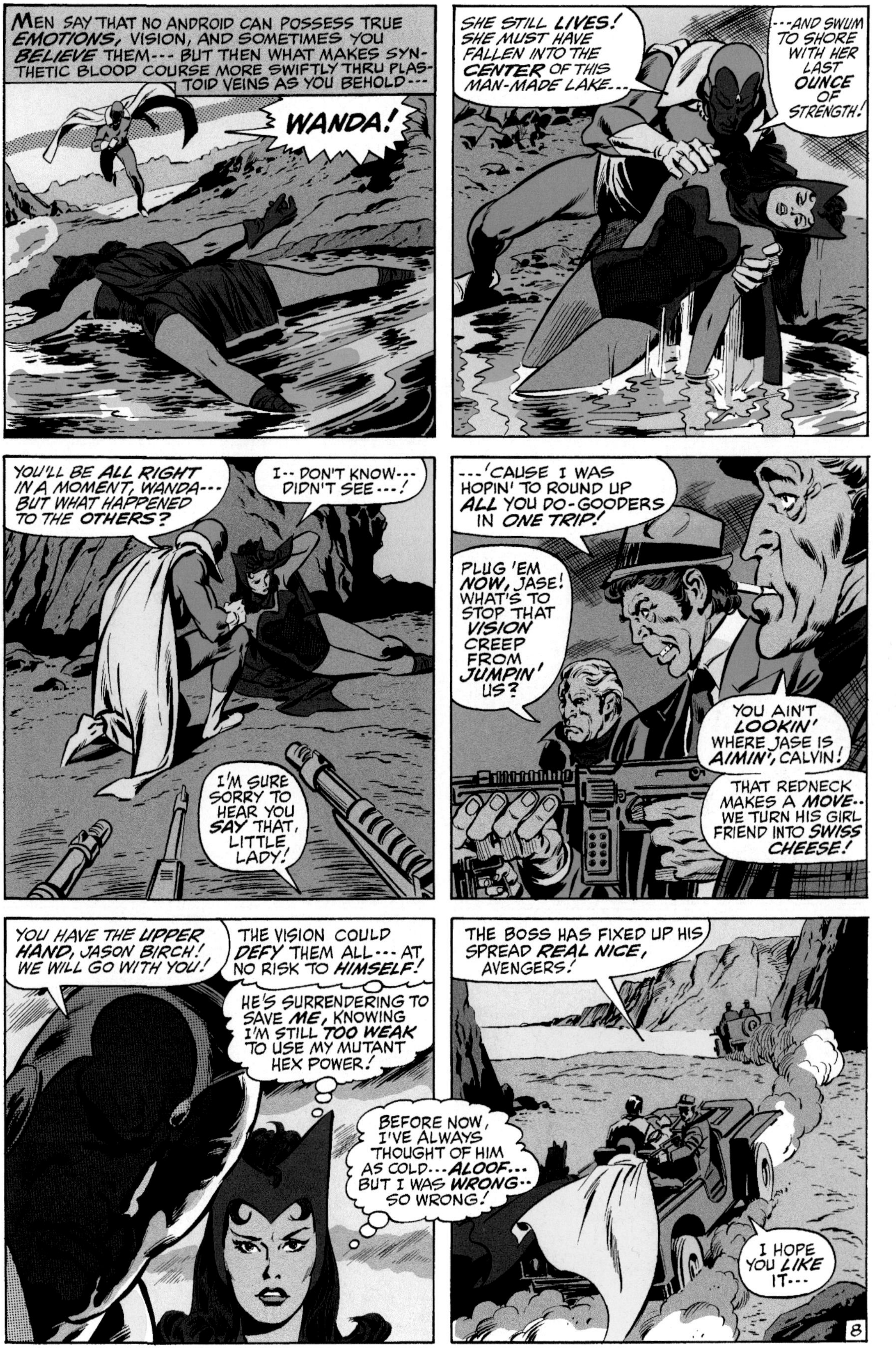
MEN SAY THAT NO ANDROID CAN POSSESS TRUE EMOTIONS, VISION, AND SOMETIMES YOU BELIEVE THEM--- BUT THEN WHAT MAKES SYNTHETIC BLOOD COURSE MORE SWIFTLY THRU PLASTOID VEINS AS YOU BEHOLD---
WANDA!
SHE STILL LIVES! SHE MUST HAVE FALLEN INTO THE CENTER OF THIS MAN-MADE LAKE...
---AND SWUM TO SHORE WITH HER LAST OUNCE OF STRENGTH!
YOU'LL BE ALL RIGHT IN A MOMENT, WANDA--- BUT WHAT HAPPENED TO THE OTHERS?
I-- DON'T KNOW--- DIDN'T SEE---!
I'M SURE SORRY TO HEAR YOU SAY THAT, LITTLE LADY!
---'CAUSE I WAS HOPIN' TO ROUND UP ALL YOU DO-GOODERS IN ONE TRIP!
PLUG 'EM NOW, JASE! WHAT'S TO STOP THAT VISION CREEP FROM JUMPIN' US?
YOU AIN'T LOOKIN' WHERE JASE IS AIMIN', CALVIN!
THAT REDNECK MAKES A MOVE.. WE TURN HIS GIRL FRIEND INTO SWISS CHEESE!
YOU HAVE THE UPPER HAND, JASON BIRCH! WE WILL GO WITH YOU!
THE VISION COULD DEFY THEM ALL--- AT NO RISK TO HIMSELF!
HE'S SURRENDERING TO SAVE ME, KNOWING I'M STILL TOO WEAK TO USE MY MUTANT HEX POWER!
BEFORE NOW, I'VE ALWAYS THOUGHT OF HIM AS COLD--- ALOOF... BUT I WAS WRONG.. SO WRONG!
THE BOSS HAS FIXED UP HIS SPREAD REAL NICE, AVENGERS!
I HOPE YOU LIKE IT---
8

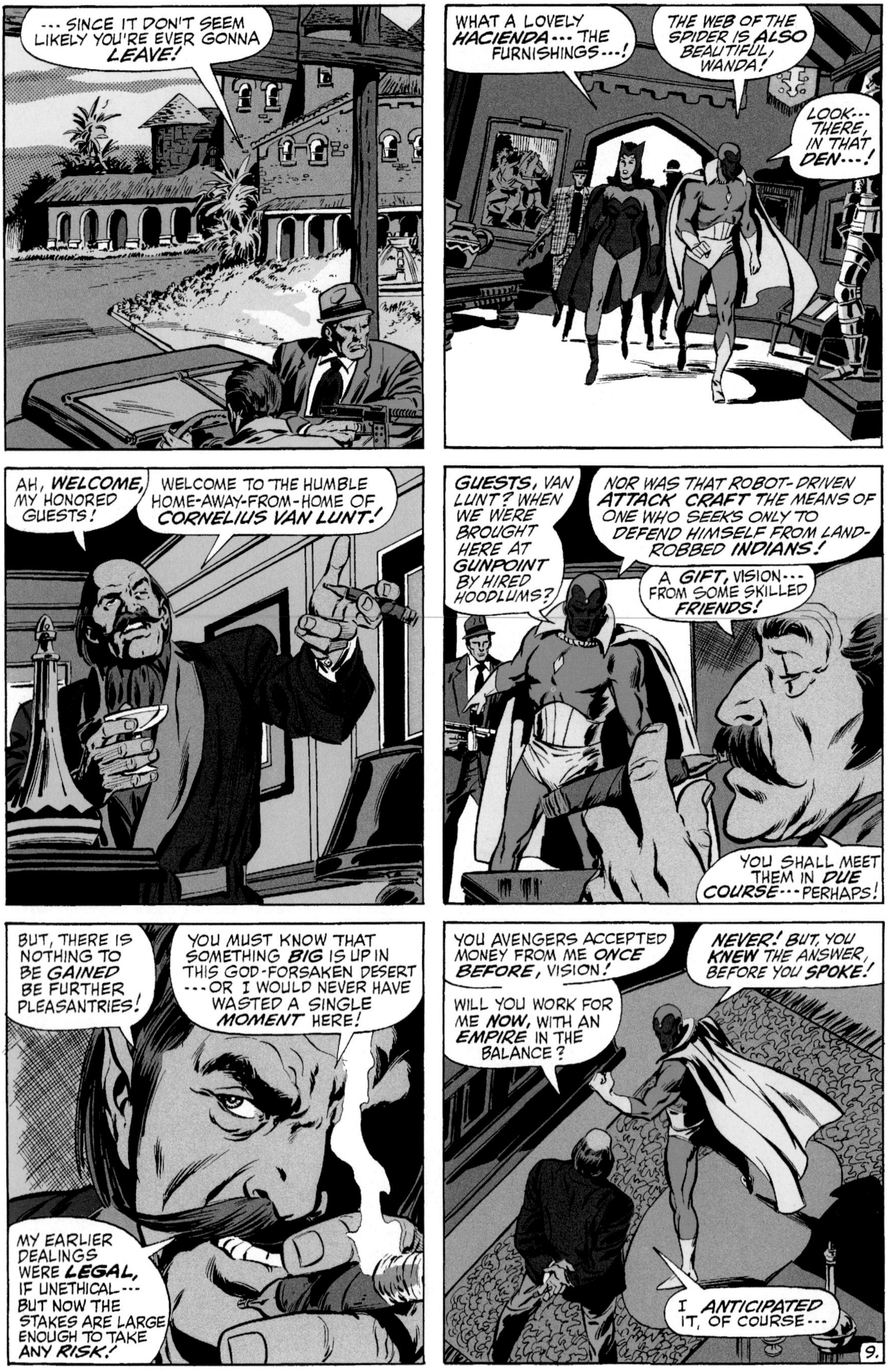

--- SINCE IT DON'T SEEM LIKELY YOU'RE EVER GONNA LEAVE!
WHAT A LOVELY HACIENDA --- THE FURNISHINGS ---!
THE WEB OF THE SPIDER IS ALSO BEAUTIFUL, WANDA!
LOOK --- THERE, IN THAT DEN ---!
AH, WELCOME, MY HONORED GUESTS!
WELCOME TO THE HUMBLE HOME-AWAY-FROM-HOME OF CORNELIUS VAN LUNT!
GUESTS, VAN LUNT? WHEN WE WERE BROUGHT HERE AT GUNPOINT BY HIRED HOODLUMS?
NOR WAS THAT ROBOT-DRIVEN ATTACK CRAFT THE MEANS OF ONE WHO SEEKS ONLY TO DEFEND HIMSELF FROM LAND-ROBBED INDIANS!
A GIFT, VISION --- FROM SOME SKILLED FRIENDS!
YOU SHALL MEET THEM IN DUE COURSE --- PERHAPS!
BUT, THERE IS NOTHING TO BE GAINED BE FURTHER PLEASANTRIES!
YOU MUST KNOW THAT SOMETHING BIG IS UP IN THIS GOD-FORSAKEN DESERT --- OR I WOULD NEVER HAVE WASTED A SINGLE MOMENT HERE!
MY EARLIER DEALINGS WERE LEGAL, IF UNETHICAL --- BUT NOW THE STAKES ARE LARGE ENOUGH TO TAKE ANY RISK!
YOU AVENGERS ACCEPTED MONEY FROM ME ONCE BEFORE, VISION!
WILL YOU WORK FOR ME NOW, WITH AN EMPIRE IN THE BALANCE?
NEVER! BUT, YOU KNEW THE ANSWER, BEFORE YOU SPOKE!
I ANTICIPATED IT, OF COURSE ---
9.

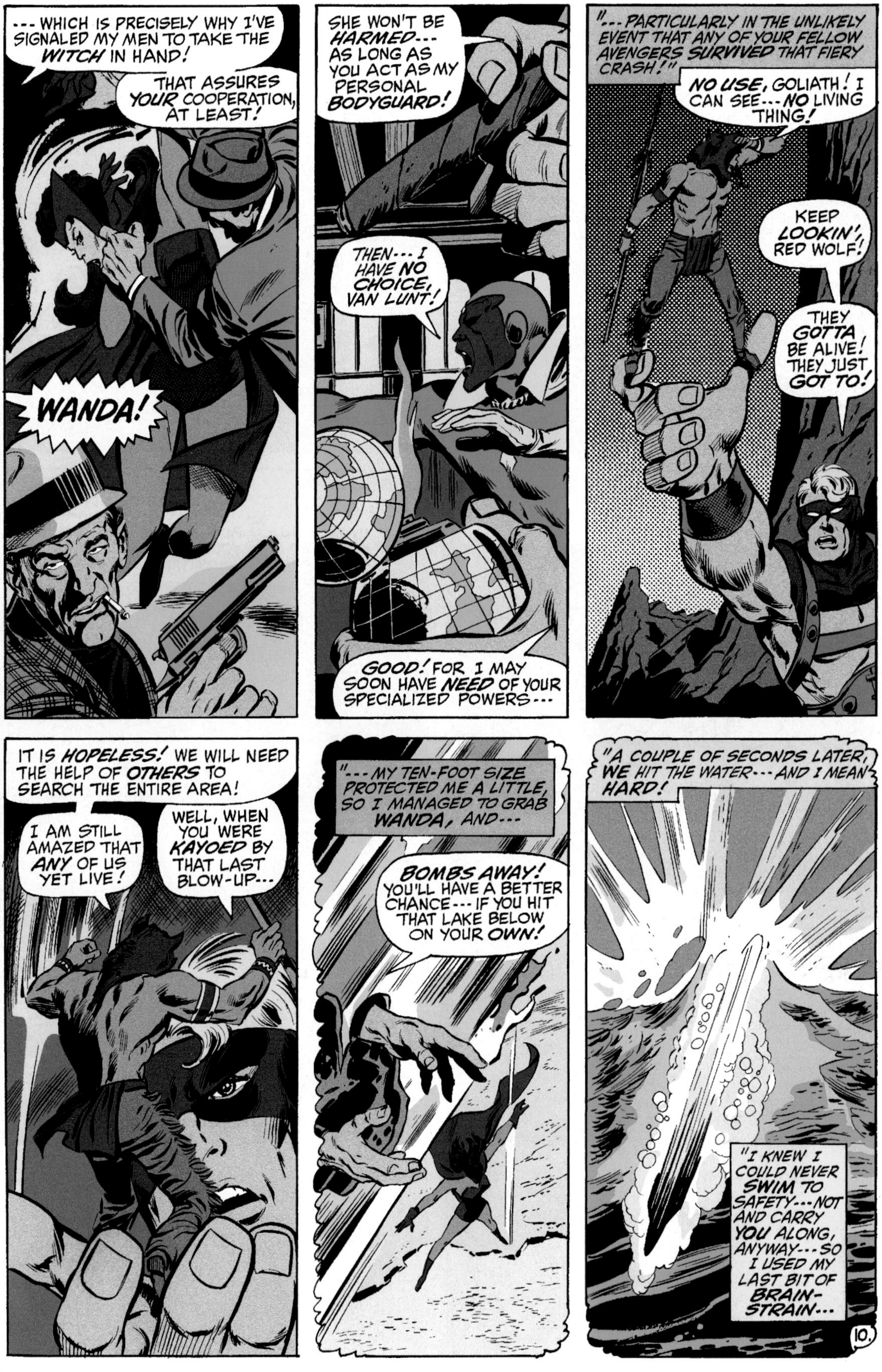

--- WHICH IS PRECISELY WHY I'VE SIGNALED MY MEN TO TAKE THE WITCH IN HAND!
THAT ASSURES YOUR COOPERATION, AT LEAST!
WANDA!
SHE WON'T BE HARMED--- AS LONG AS YOU ACT AS MY PERSONAL BODYGUARD!
THEN--- I HAVE NO CHOICE, VAN LUNT!
GOOD! FOR I MAY SOON HAVE NEED OF YOUR SPECIALIZED POWERS---
"--- PARTICULARLY IN THE UNLIKELY EVENT THAT ANY OF YOUR FELLOW AVENGERS SURVIVED THAT FIERY CRASH!"
NO USE, GOLIATH! I CAN SEE--- NO LIVING THING!
KEEP LOOKIN', RED WOLF!
THEY GOTTA BE ALIVE! THEY JUST GOT TO!
IT IS HOPELESS! WE WILL NEED THE HELP OF OTHERS TO SEARCH THE ENTIRE AREA!
I AM STILL AMAZED THAT ANY OF US YET LIVE!
WELL, WHEN YOU WERE KAYOED BY THAT LAST BLOW-UP---
"--- MY TEN-FOOT SIZE PROTECTED ME A LITTLE, SO I MANAGED TO GRAB WANDA, AND---
BOMBS AWAY! YOU'LL HAVE A BETTER CHANCE--- IF YOU HIT THAT LAKE BELOW ON YOUR OWN!
"A COUPLE OF SECONDS LATER, WE HIT THE WATER--- AND I MEAN HARD!
"I KNEW I COULD NEVER SWIM TO SAFETY--- NOT AND CARRY YOU ALONG, ANYWAY--- SO I USED MY LAST BIT OF BRAIN-STRAIN---
10.

"...TO SHOOT UP TO *THIRTY FEET*... WHICH WAS MORE THAN OUR LITTLE GO-BUGGY COULD TAKE---!"

"THEN, AS I WAS TAKIN' A COUPLE OF SEVEN-LEAGUE STRIDES TOWARD *SHORE*---"

THAT *DAM*--- AND THE *LAKE* IT MAKES--- SURE SAVED OUR *HIDES!*

BUT IT'S GOTTA BE THE ONE *VAN LUNT* BUILT---

AND IF I FIND OUT HE SENT UP THAT *ROCKET* AFTER US--- I'LL HAMMER IT DOWN WITH MY *BARE KNUCKS!*

THERE ARE THOSE WHO SAY YOU DID NOT *EARN* YOUR GROWING POWERS, *GOLIATH*--- BECAUSE ANOTHER MAN CREATED THE *FORMULA!*

YET, THIS DAY, I KNOW THEY ARE WHOLLY *WRONG!*

ALL *I* KNOW, MAN, IS THAT TWO *AVENGERS* ARE MISSING!

THAT MEANS THIS IS *MY* SHOW NOW--- AS WELL AS *YOURS!*

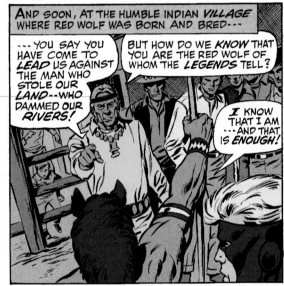

AND SOON, AT THE HUMBLE INDIAN *VILLAGE* WHERE RED WOLF WAS BORN AND BRED---

--- YOU SAY YOU HAVE COME TO *LEAD* US AGAINST THE MAN WHO STOLE OUR *LAND*--WHO DAMMED OUR *RIVERS!*

BUT HOW DO WE *KNOW* THAT YOU ARE THE RED WOLF OF WHOM THE *LEGENDS* TELL?

I KNOW THAT I AM ---AND THAT IS *ENOUGH!*

IT IS NOT ENOUGH FOR *US!* THERE WAS ANOTHER OF *THE PEOPLE* WHO SPOKE OUT AGAINST THE EVIL *VAN LUNT!*

HE WAS *TOMMY TALLTREES*, MY BROTHER---AND WE *BURIED* HIM MONTHS AGO, ALONG WITH OUR *HOPE!*

EVEN HIS SON *WILL* HAS VANISHED!

WHERE TOMMY TALLTREES *FAILED*--- RED WOLF WILL *SUCCEED*, WITH YOUR HELP!

WE *WANT* TO BELIEVE YOU, WAYFARER!

I DO NOT *RELISH* THE THOUGHT THAT I AM--- AN *UNCLE TOMAHAWK!*

AND YOU *DO* COME TO US STRIDING BESIDE A SNARLING *WOLF*---!

11.

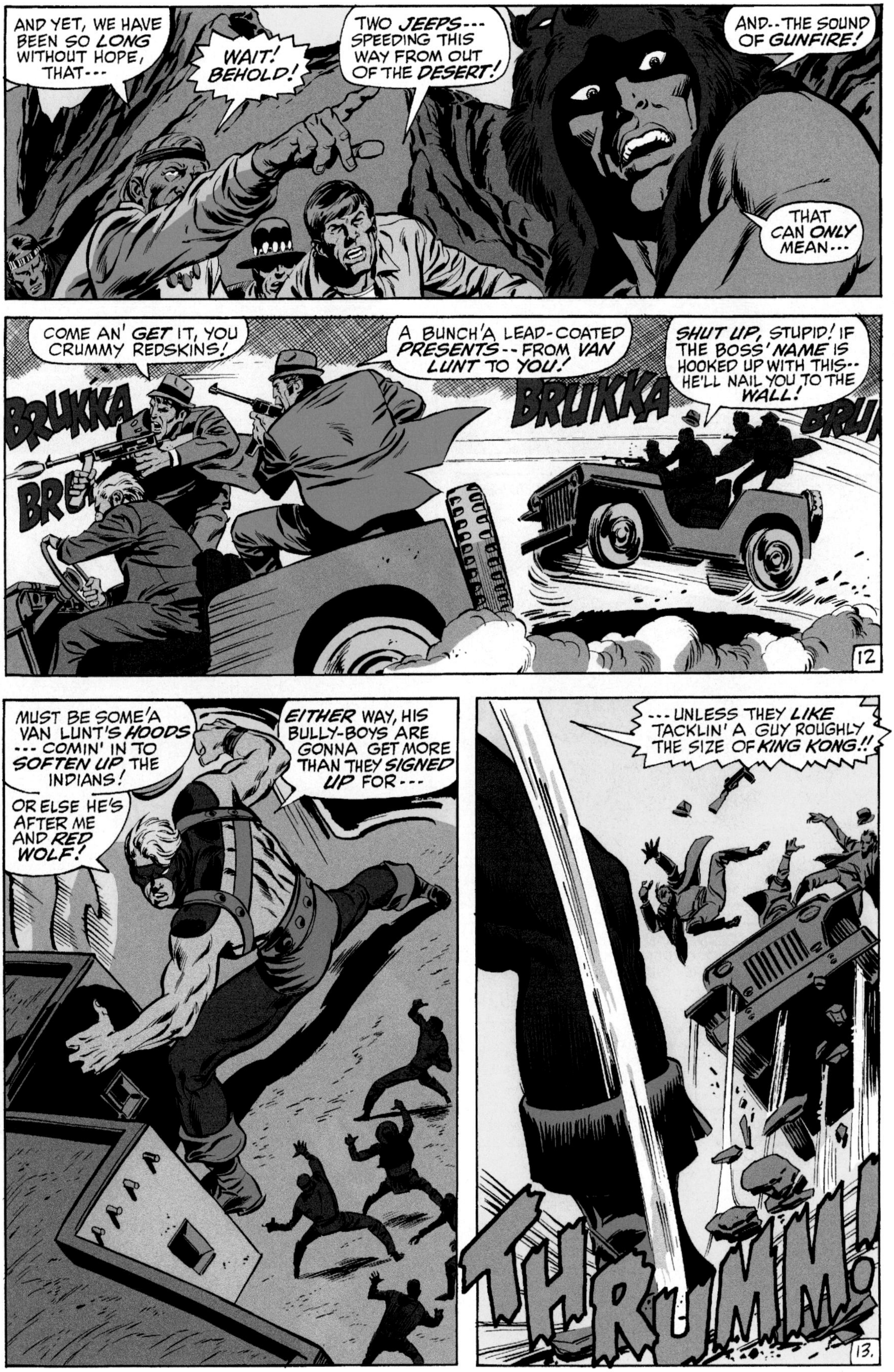
AND YET, WE HAVE BEEN SO LONG WITHOUT HOPE, THAT---
WAIT! BEHOLD!
TWO JEEPS--- SPEEDING THIS WAY FROM OUT OF THE DESERT!
AND--THE SOUND OF GUNFIRE!
THAT CAN ONLY MEAN---
COME AN' GET IT, YOU CRUMMY REDSKINS!
BRUKKA
BRU
A BUNCH'A LEAD-COATED PRESENTS--FROM VAN LUNT TO YOU!
BRUKKA
SHUT UP, STUPID! IF THE BOSS' NAME IS HOOKED UP WITH THIS--HE'LL NAIL YOU TO THE WALL!
12
MUST BE SOME'A VAN LUNT'S HOODS --- COMIN' IN TO SOFTEN UP THE INDIANS!
OR ELSE HE'S AFTER ME AND RED WOLF!
EITHER WAY, HIS BULLY-BOYS ARE GONNA GET MORE THAN THEY SIGNED UP FOR---
---UNLESS THEY LIKE TACKLIN' A GUY ROUGHLY THE SIZE OF KING KONG!!
THRUMM!
13.

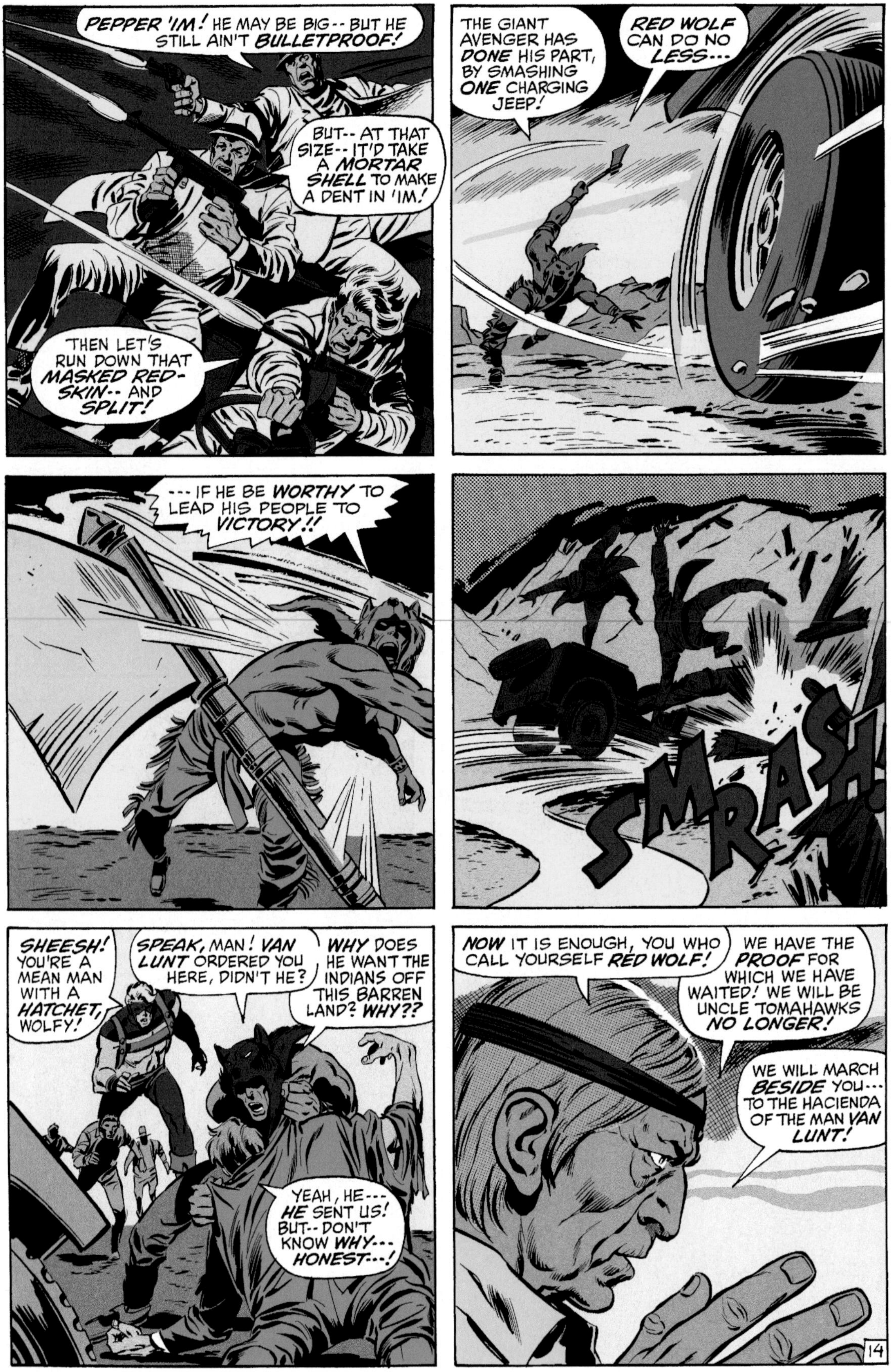
PEPPER 'IM! HE MAY BE BIG-- BUT HE STILL AIN'T BULLETPROOF!
BUT-- AT THAT SIZE-- IT'D TAKE A MORTAR SHELL TO MAKE A DENT IN 'IM!
THEN LET'S RUN DOWN THAT MASKED RED-SKIN-- AND SPLIT!
THE GIANT AVENGER HAS DONE HIS PART, BY SMASHING ONE CHARGING JEEP!
RED WOLF CAN DO NO LESS...
---IF HE BE WORTHY TO LEAD HIS PEOPLE TO VICTORY!!
SMRASH!
SHEESH! YOU'RE A MEAN MAN WITH A HATCHET, WOLFY!
SPEAK, MAN! VAN LUNT ORDERED YOU HERE, DIDN'T HE?
WHY DOES HE WANT THE INDIANS OFF THIS BARREN LAND? WHY??
YEAH, HE--- HE SENT US! BUT-- DON'T KNOW WHY... HONEST--!
NOW IT IS ENOUGH, YOU WHO CALL YOURSELF RED WOLF!
WE HAVE THE PROOF FOR WHICH WE HAVE WAITED! WE WILL BE UNCLE TOMAHAWKS NO LONGER!
WE WILL MARCH BESIDE YOU... TO THE HACIENDA OF THE MAN VAN LUNT!
14

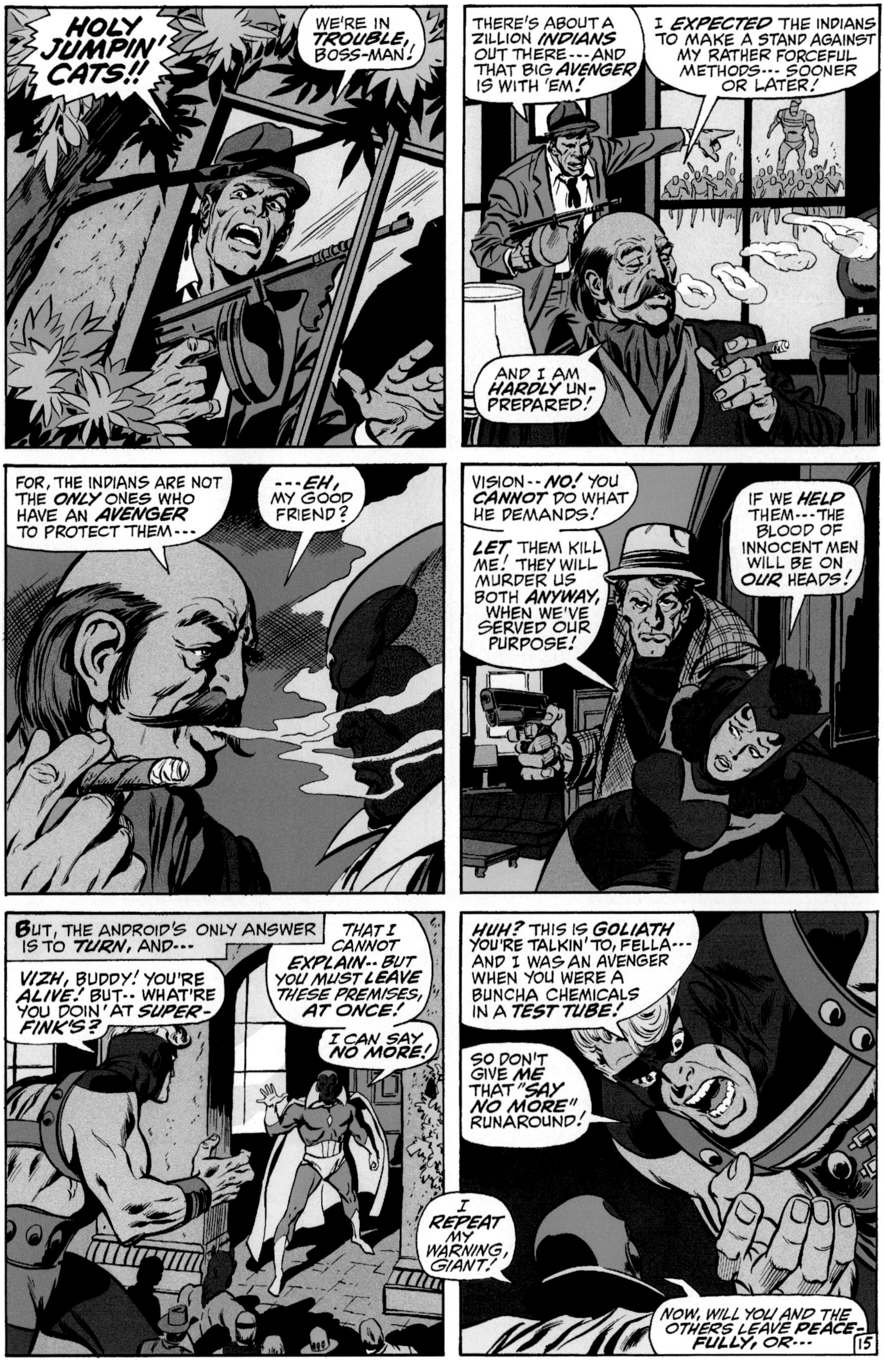

HOLY JUMPIN' CATS!!
WE'RE IN TROUBLE, BOSS-MAN!
THERE'S ABOUT A ZILLION INDIANS OUT THERE---AND THAT BIG AVENGER IS WITH 'EM!
I EXPECTED THE INDIANS TO MAKE A STAND AGAINST MY RATHER FORCEFUL METHODS--- SOONER OR LATER!
AND I AM HARDLY UN-PREPARED!
FOR, THE INDIANS ARE NOT THE ONLY ONES WHO HAVE AN AVENGER TO PROTECT THEM---
---EH, MY GOOD FRIEND?
VISION--NO! YOU CANNOT DO WHAT HE DEMANDS!
LET THEM KILL ME! THEY WILL MURDER US BOTH ANYWAY, WHEN WE'VE SERVED OUR PURPOSE!
IF WE HELP THEM---THE BLOOD OF INNOCENT MEN WILL BE ON OUR HEADS!
BUT, THE ANDROID'S ONLY ANSWER IS TO TURN, AND---
VIZH, BUDDY! YOU'RE ALIVE! BUT-- WHAT'RE YOU DOIN' AT SUPER-FINK'S?
THAT I CANNOT EXPLAIN-- BUT YOU MUST LEAVE THESE PREMISES, AT ONCE!
I CAN SAY NO MORE!
HUH? THIS IS GOLIATH YOU'RE TALKIN' TO, FELLA--- AND I WAS AN AVENGER WHEN YOU WERE A BUNCHA CHEMICALS IN A TEST TUBE!
SO DON'T GIVE ME THAT "SAY NO MORE" RUNAROUND!
I REPEAT MY WARNING, GIANT!
NOW, WILL YOU AND THE OTHERS LEAVE PEACE-FULLY, OR---
15

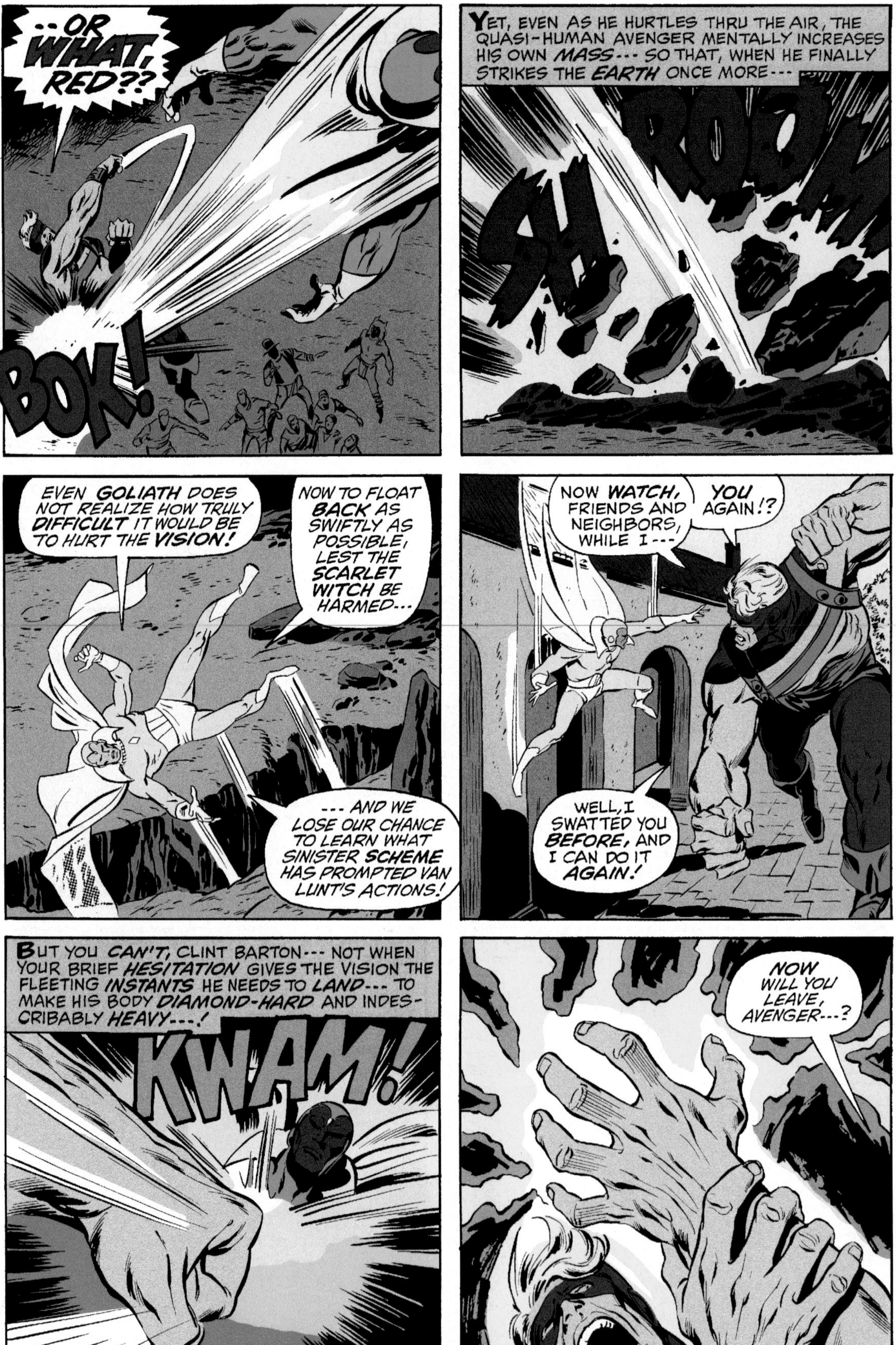

..OR WHAT, RED??
BOK!
YET, EVEN AS HE HURTLES THRU THE AIR, THE QUASI-HUMAN AVENGER MENTALLY INCREASES HIS OWN MASS--- SO THAT, WHEN HE FINALLY STRIKES THE EARTH ONCE MORE---
SHROOM
EVEN GOLIATH DOES NOT REALIZE HOW TRULY DIFFICULT IT WOULD BE TO HURT THE VISION!
NOW TO FLOAT BACK AS SWIFTLY AS POSSIBLE, LEST THE SCARLET WITCH BE HARMED...
--- AND WE LOSE OUR CHANCE TO LEARN WHAT SINISTER SCHEME HAS PROMPTED VAN LUNT'S ACTIONS!
NOW WATCH, FRIENDS AND NEIGHBORS, WHILE I ---
YOU AGAIN!?
WELL, I SWATTED YOU BEFORE, AND I CAN DO IT AGAIN!
BUT YOU CAN'T, CLINT BARTON--- NOT WHEN YOUR BRIEF HESITATION GIVES THE VISION THE FLEETING INSTANTS HE NEEDS TO LAND--- TO MAKE HIS BODY DIAMOND-HARD AND INDESCRIBABLY HEAVY---!
KWAM!
NOW WILL YOU LEAVE, AVENGER---?

---OR MUST I PROVE TO YOU THAT MY *FISTS* ARE AS *PAIN-FULLY SOLID* AS THE *REST* OF ME?

I *BELIEVE* YOU, ANDROID-MAN!

BUT YOU'LL *STILL* HAVE TO PROVE IT TO ME-- IF YOU DON'T *STEP ASIDE!*

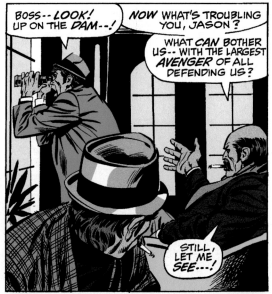

BOSS-- *LOOK!* UP ON THE *DAM*--!

NOW WHAT'S TROUBLING YOU, JASON?

WHAT *CAN* BOTHER US-- WITH THE LARGEST *AVENGER* OF ALL DEFENDING US?

STILL, LET ME *SEE*---!

GOOD GRIEF! WHY DIDN'T YOU *TELL* ME, YOU SNIVELING FOOL?

SOME OF THOSE *INFERNAL* SAVAGES ARE *ATOP* THE DAM!

THEY MUST BE PLANNING TO *BLOW IT UP!!*

THEY'VE ALWAYS *HATED* THE DAM--- BECAUSE IT DIVERTS *RIVERS* WHICH OTHERWISE WOULD WATER THEIR LANDS!

AND NOW-- THEY HOPE TO TAKE THINGS INTO THEIR *OWN HANDS!*

BRING THE *GIRL* ALONG-- JUST TO MAKE SURE NO *AVENGER* BOTHERS US!

AND *NOW,* BOYS... WE'RE GOING TO SHOOT US SOME *INDIANS!*

I'VE FELT SO *HELPLESS* THESE PAST HOURS--- AS WEAK AS A *KITTEN!*

BUT NOW--- I CAN FEEL MY *HEX POWER* RETURNING!

IF I CAN BUT *LOOSEN* THESE *BONDS..!*

ALL RIGHT, MEN---

17.

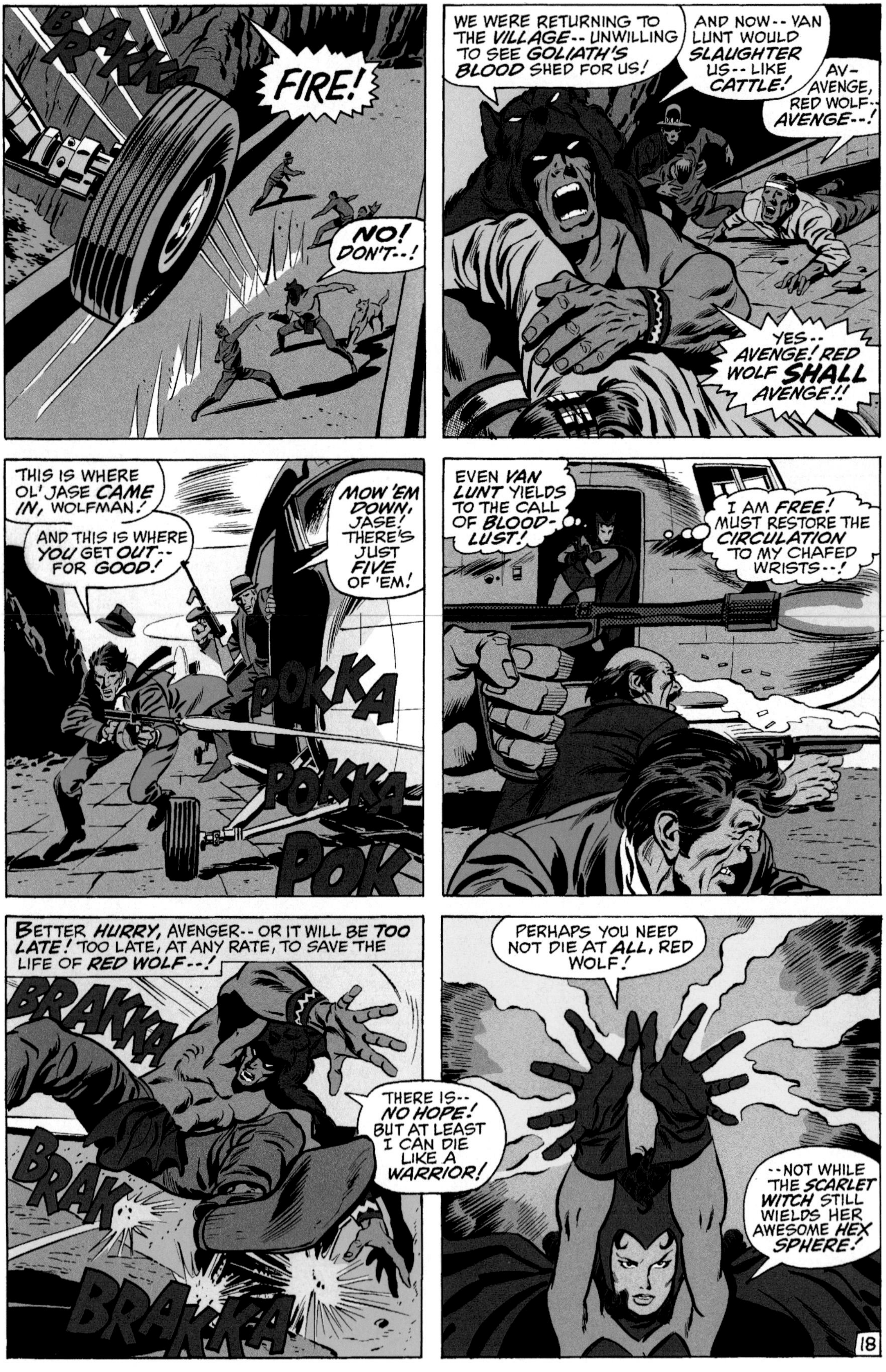
BRAKKA
FIRE!
NO! DON'T--!
WE WERE RETURNING TO THE VILLAGE-- UNWILLING TO SEE GOLIATH'S BLOOD SHED FOR US!
AND NOW-- VAN LUNT WOULD SLAUGHTER US-- LIKE CATTLE!
AV-AVENGE, RED WOLF-- AVENGE--!
YES-- AVENGE! RED WOLF SHALL AVENGE!!
THIS IS WHERE OL' JASE CAME IN, WOLFMAN!
AND THIS IS WHERE YOU GET OUT-- FOR GOOD!
MOW 'EM DOWN, JASE! THERE'S JUST FIVE OF 'EM!
POKKA
POKKA
POK
EVEN VAN LUNT YIELDS TO THE CALL OF BLOOD-LUST!
I AM FREE! MUST RESTORE THE CIRCULATION TO MY CHAFED WRISTS--!
BETTER HURRY, AVENGER-- OR IT WILL BE TOO LATE! TOO LATE, AT ANY RATE, TO SAVE THE LIFE OF RED WOLF--!
BRAKKA
THERE IS-- NO HOPE! BUT AT LEAST I CAN DIE LIKE A WARRIOR!
BRAK
BRAKKA
PERHAPS YOU NEED NOT DIE AT ALL, RED WOLF!
--NOT WHILE THE SCARLET WITCH STILL WIELDS HER AWESOME HEX SPHERE!
18

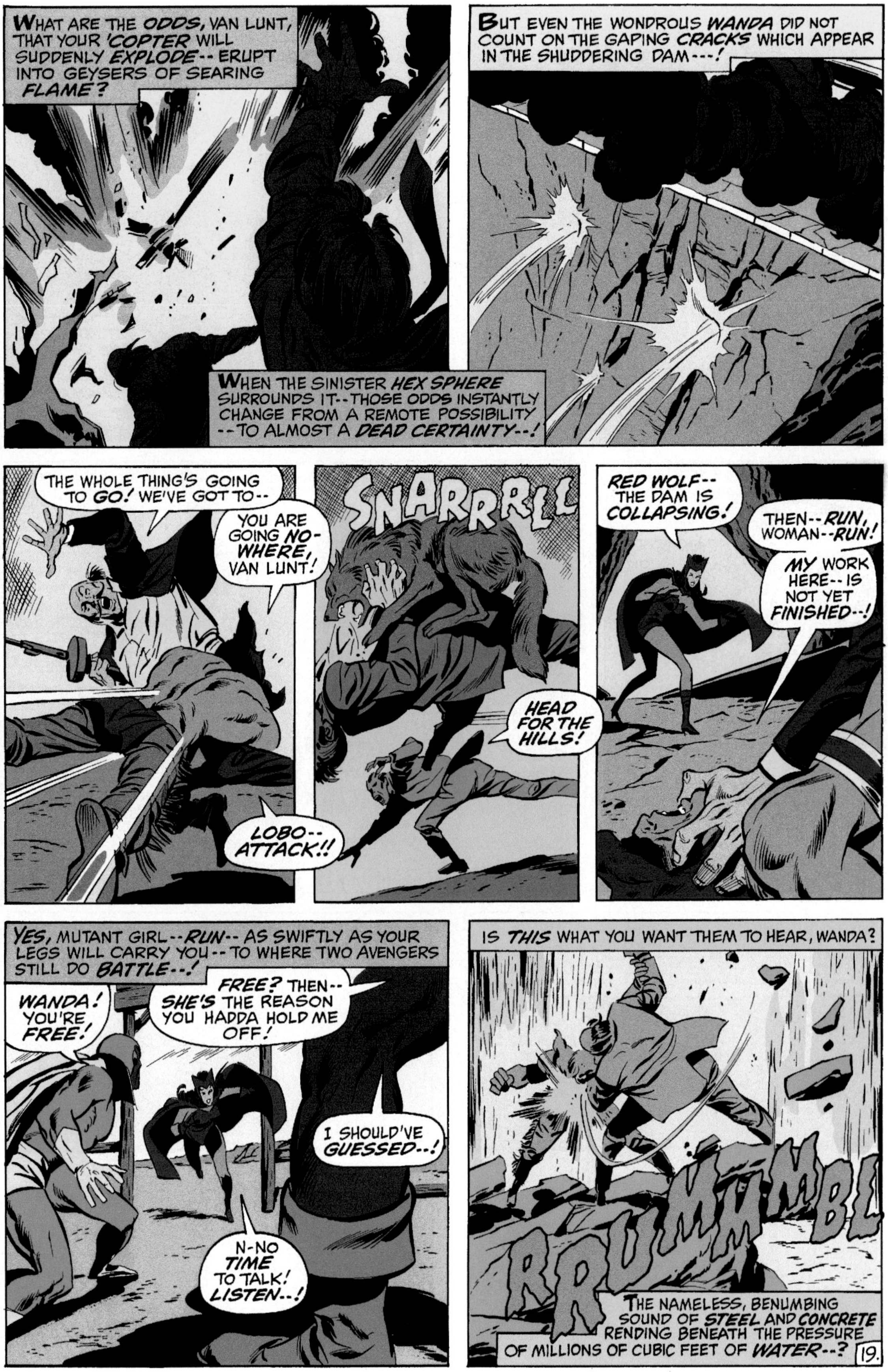
WHAT ARE THE ODDS, VAN LUNT, THAT YOUR 'COPTER WILL SUDDENLY EXPLODE-- ERUPT INTO GEYSERS OF SEARING FLAME?
WHEN THE SINISTER HEX SPHERE SURROUNDS IT--THOSE ODDS INSTANTLY CHANGE FROM A REMOTE POSSIBILITY --TO ALMOST A DEAD CERTAINTY--!
BUT EVEN THE WONDROUS WANDA DID NOT COUNT ON THE GAPING CRACKS WHICH APPEAR IN THE SHUDDERING DAM---!
THE WHOLE THING'S GOING TO GO! WE'VE GOT TO--
YOU ARE GOING NO-WHERE, VAN LUNT!
LOBO-- ATTACK!!
SNARRRLL
HEAD FOR THE HILLS!
RED WOLF-- THE DAM IS COLLAPSING!
THEN--RUN, WOMAN--RUN!
MY WORK HERE--IS NOT YET FINISHED--!
YES, MUTANT GIRL--RUN-- AS SWIFTLY AS YOUR LEGS WILL CARRY YOU-- TO WHERE TWO AVENGERS STILL DO BATTLE--!
WANDA! YOU'RE FREE!
FREE? THEN-- SHE'S THE REASON YOU HADDA HOLD ME OFF!
I SHOULD'VE GUESSED--!
N-NO TIME TO TALK! LISTEN--!
IS THIS WHAT YOU WANT THEM TO HEAR, WANDA?
RRUMMMBL
THE NAMELESS, BENUMBING SOUND OF STEEL AND CONCRETE RENDING BENEATH THE PRESSURE OF MILLIONS OF CUBIC FEET OF WATER--?
19.

-- OR THE EVEN MORE *TERRIFYING* THUNDER OF THE FINAL, FATAL *COLLAPSE*--?

THEY WERE *ALL* CAUGHT IN THE CATACLYSM---

RED WOLF--THE FAITHFUL *LOBO*... EVEN *VAN LUNT!*

YET PERHAPS *ONE* OF THEM STILL LIVES IN THE SWIRLING WATERS--!

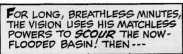

FOR LONG, BREATHLESS MINUTES, THE VISION USES HIS MATCHLESS POWERS TO *SCOUR* THE NOW-FLOODED BASIN! THEN---

THIS IS--- ALL I FOUND!

THE MASK OF---*RED WOLF!*

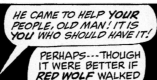
HE CAME TO HELP *YOUR* PEOPLE, OLD MAN! IT IS *YOU* WHO SHOULD HAVE IT!

PERHAPS---THOUGH IT WERE BETTER IF *RED WOLF* WALKED AMONG US ONCE MORE!

HE *DID* SAVE US--AND OUR LAND--- EVEN IN *DEATH!*

AND PERHAPS--- HE EVEN AVENGED THE MURDER OF *TOMMY TALL-TREES!*

DID I HEAR THE MENTION OF *MY FATHER'S* NAME?

THIS IS A *SORRY* HOMECOMING--- FOR I SEE THE BODIES OF *OLD FRIENDS* WAITING TO BE MOURNED OVER BY THEIR WOMEN!

WILL TALLTREES!

HUH? BUT THAT'S *RED WOLF*--- WITHOUT HIS MASK!

AND FROM THAT *TWINKLE* IN HIS UNCLE'S EYE-- I'M BETTING THE *OLD MAN* SEES RIGHT THRU HIM, *TOO!*

WELCOME *HOME*, MY CHILD! BUT-- THAT *BANDAGE* ABOUT YOUR BROW--!?

ONLY A REMINDER--- OF A RECENT *FALL*, UNCLE!

BUT COME, LET US TALK *NO MORE* OF THE PAST--- BUT ONLY OF THE *FUTURE!*

THERE IS *WORK* TO BE DONE, RECLAIMING OUR *LAND*---

---AND IT IS GOOD TO BE *HOME* AGAIN!

Finis

NEXT: THE SECRET OF CORNELIUS VAN LUNT!

20.

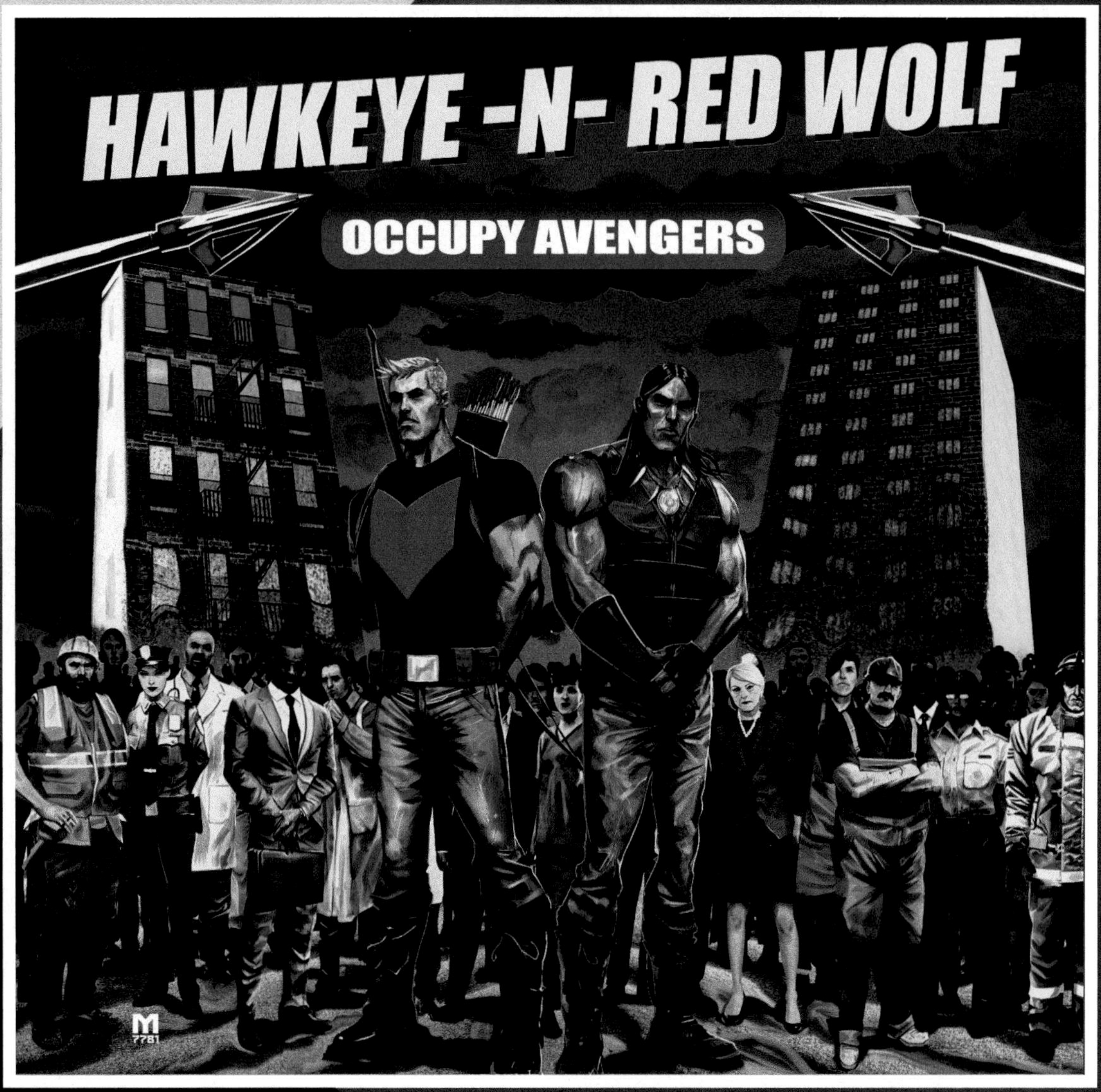
HAWKEYE -N- RED WOLF
OCCUPY AVENGERS

#1 hip-hop variant by Marco D'Alfonso

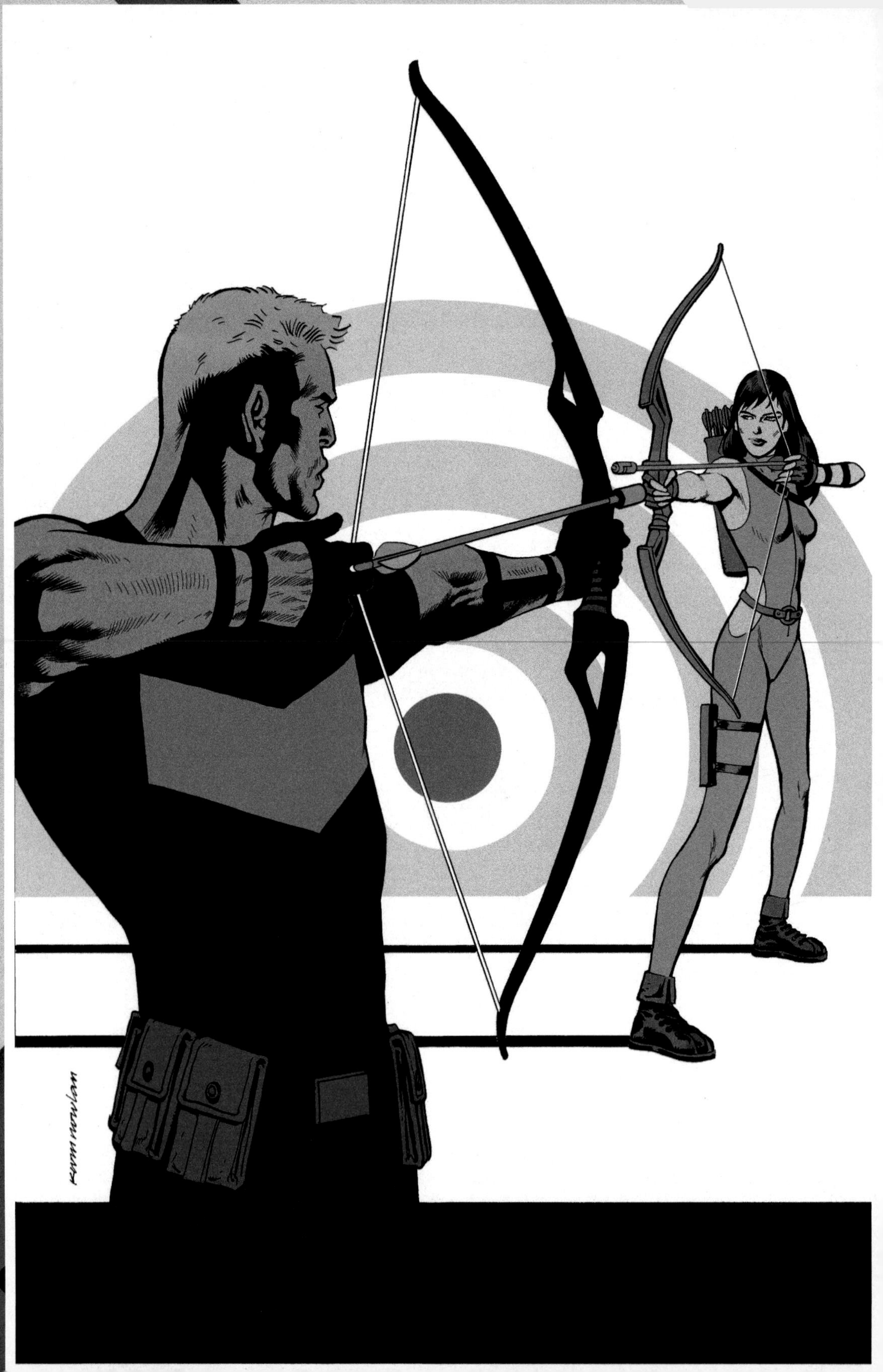
kevin nowlan

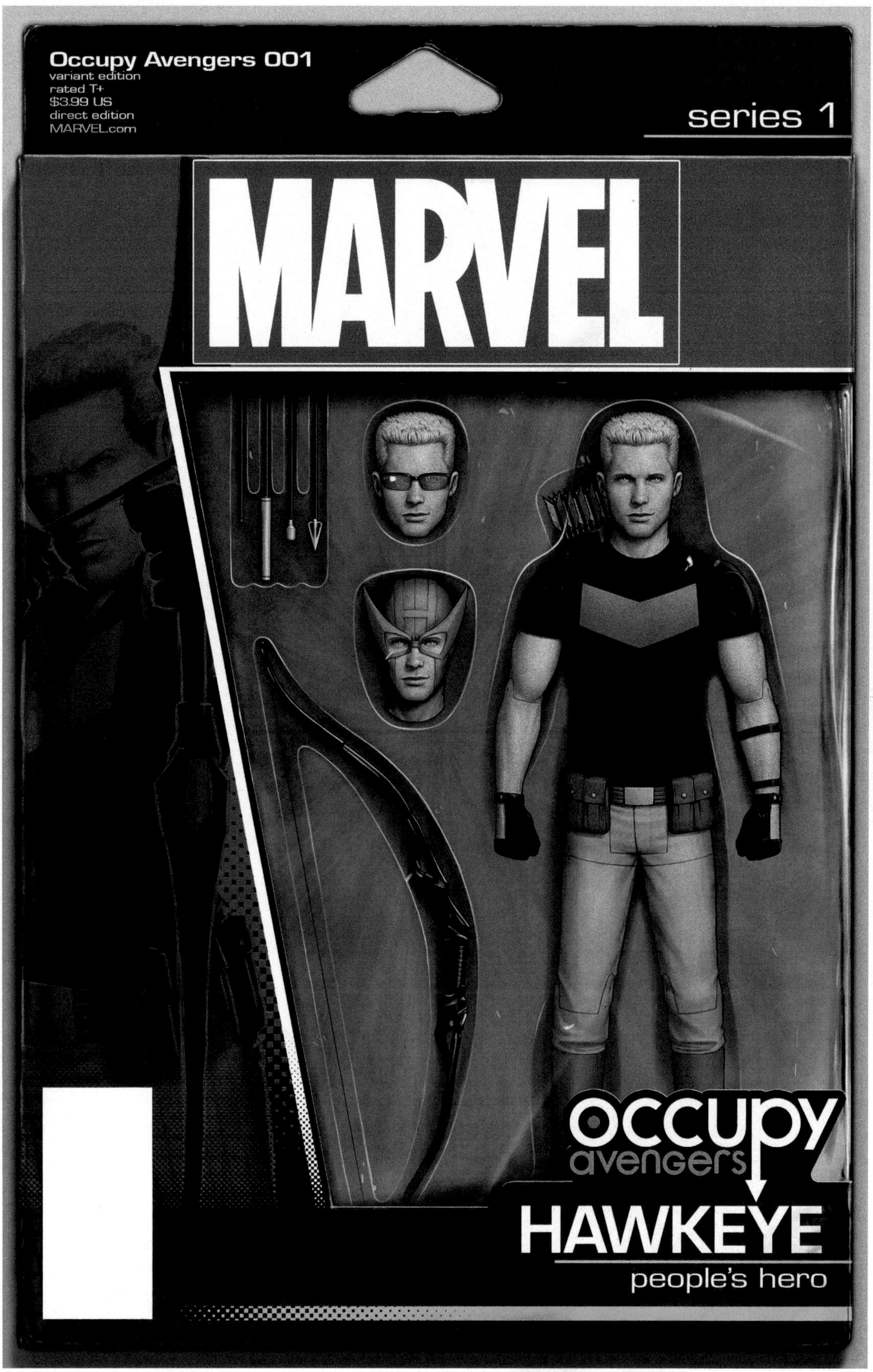
Occupy Avengers 001
variant edition
rated T+
$3.99 US
direct edition
MARVEL.com
series 1
MARVEL
occupy
avengers
HAWKEYE
people's hero

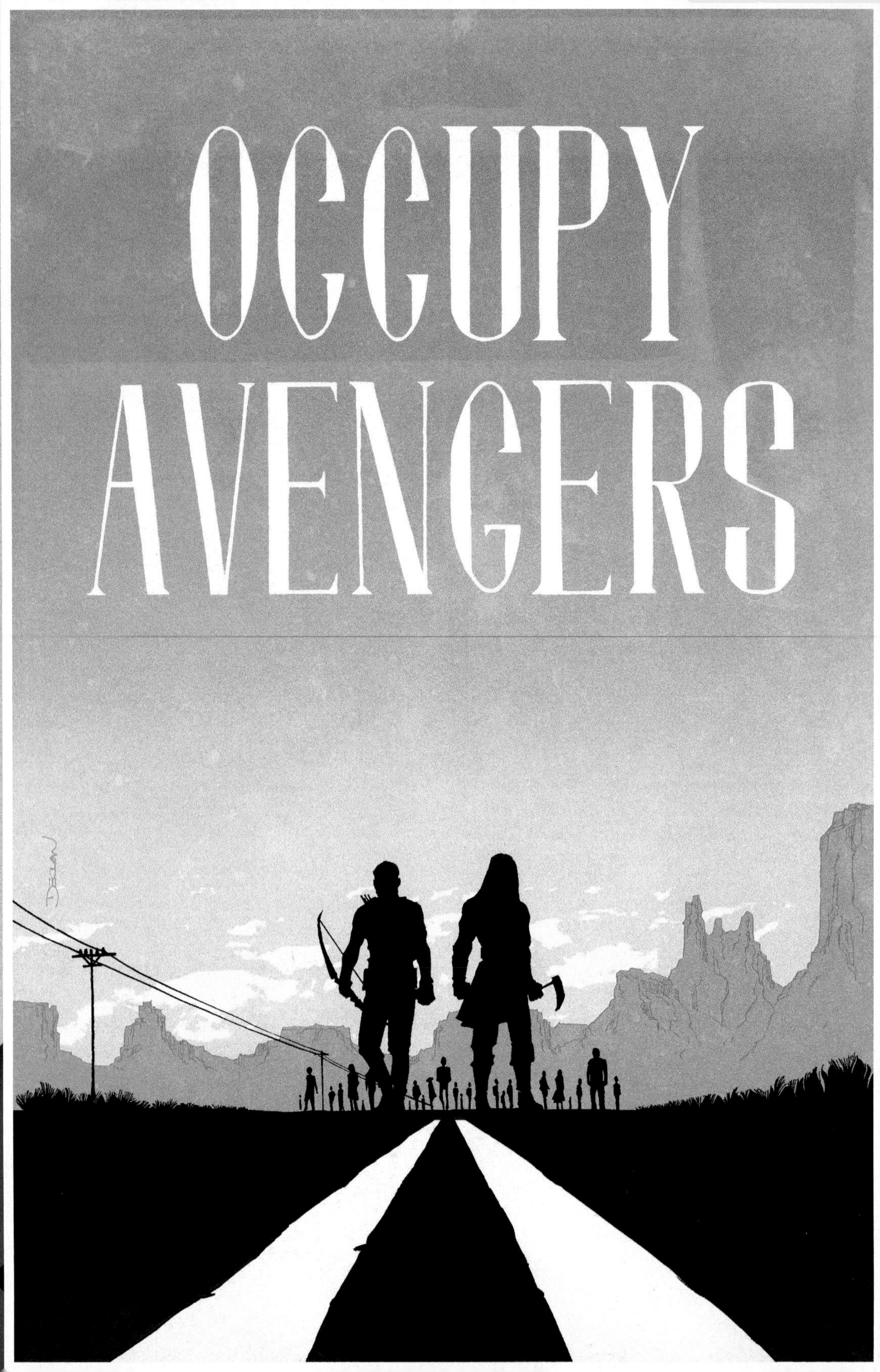
OCCUPY
AVENGERS

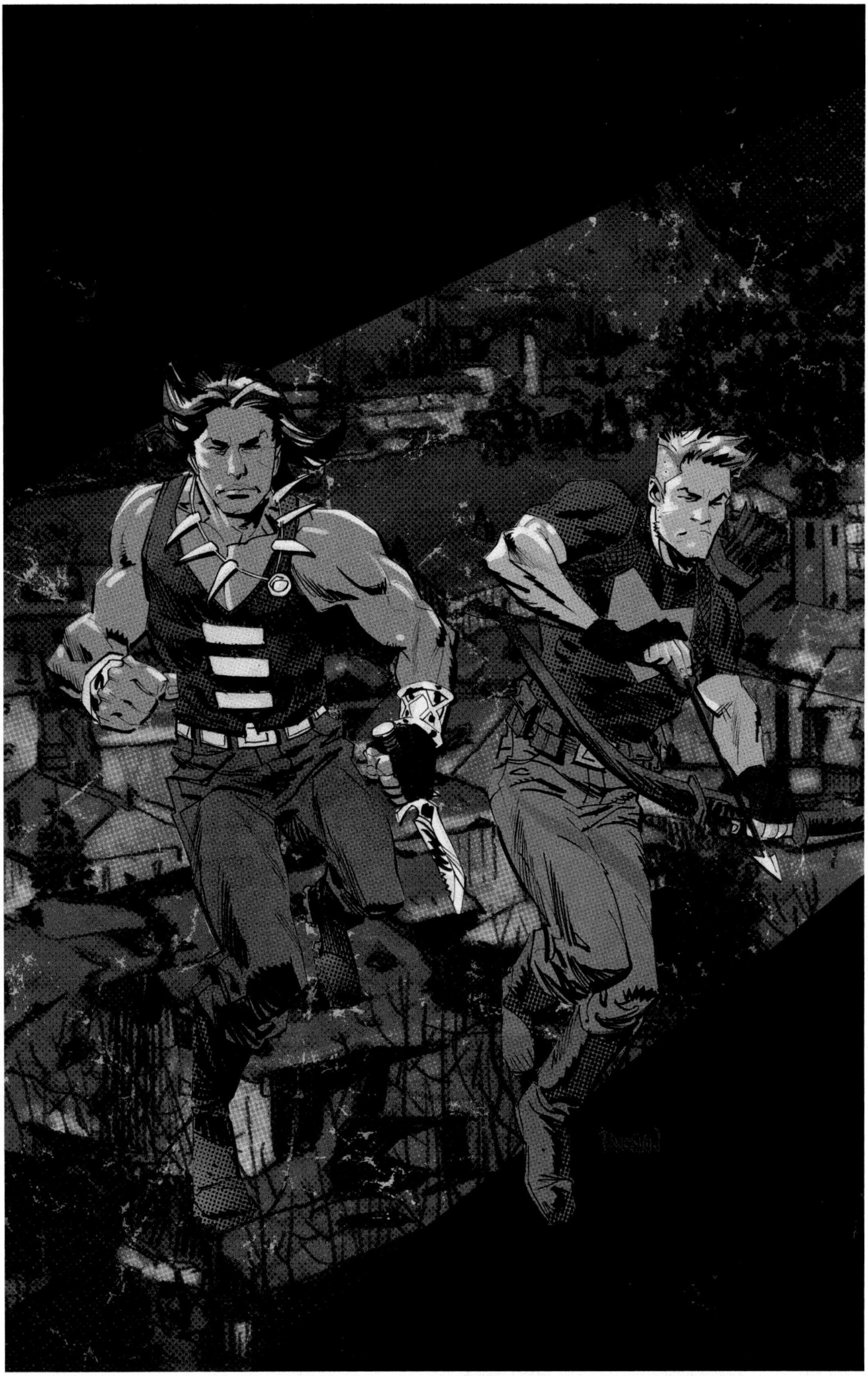

COMING THIS YEAR IN

OCCUPY avengers

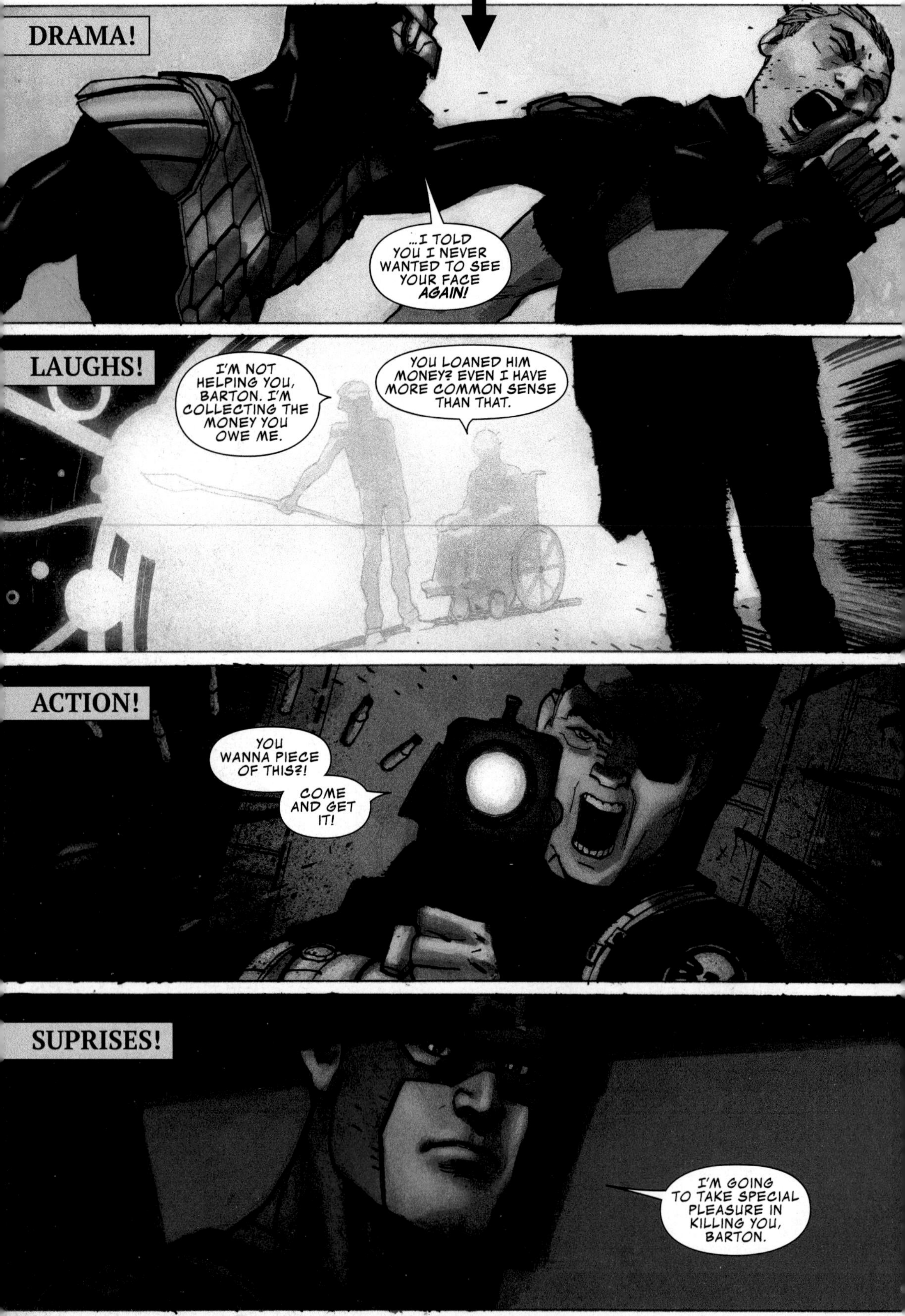
DRAMA!
...I TOLD YOU I NEVER WANTED TO SEE YOUR FACE AGAIN!
LAUGHS!
I'M NOT HELPING YOU, BARTON. I'M COLLECTING THE MONEY YOU OWE ME.
YOU LOANED HIM MONEY? EVEN I HAVE MORE COMMON SENSE THAN THAT.
ACTION!
YOU WANNA PIECE OF THIS?!
COME AND GET IT!
SUPRISES!
I'M GOING TO TAKE SPECIAL PLEASURE IN KILLING YOU, BARTON.

Art by Gabriel Hernandez Walta & Jordie Bellaire